MODERN COMMODITY
FUTURES TRADING

A Publication of

COMMODITY RESEARCH BUREAU, INC.

Established in 1934 for research in
price movements, production, distribution and consumption of commodities.

OTHER PUBLICATIONS AND SERVICES

- **Commodity Year Books (published annually)**

  Each annual volume contains new basic data on more than 110 different commodities, including price charts plus price records in
  tabular form; statistical tables of production, distribution and consumption; and original studies of factors that influence price movements and changes in supply and demand.

- **Economics of Futures Trading**

  This new book by an outstanding commodity market authority, is a
  "how to do it" book for commercial interests, a guide for speculators,
  and a college level textbook for a course in commodity futures
  markets and trading.

- **Guide To Commodity Price Forecasting**

  A comprehensive anthology of selected studies from the various
  editions of COMMODITY YEAR BOOK, designed to assist those
  who trade in commodity futures. Topics include utilization of charts
  in forecasting; factors influencing price trends in specific markets,
  etc.

- **Futures Market Service**

  A weekly analysis and forecast of price trends in the individual
  futures markets and the general commodity price level. Included
  are up-to-date charts and statistical data portraying price movements.

- **Commodity Chart Service**

  A comprehensive commodity chart service published weekly which
  consists of over 160 different daily charts plus additional chart studies
  provided at periodic intervals. The charts show the daily price movements of active futures deliveries traded on the United States and
  Canadian futures markets, plus "volume" and "open interest" data
  in chart form. A weekly "technical comment" section discusses significant chart formations and probable forthcoming price trends.

- **Special Chart Collections**

  From its extensive library of charts and statistics, the Bureau publishes numerous collections of price records in chart form for
  commodities traded on the futures markets.

MODERN COMMODITY FUTURES TRADING

By

GERALD GOLD

publishers

Commodity Research Bureau, Inc.
ONE LIBERTY PLAZA   NEW YORK, N. Y. 10006

Printed in the United States of America

TO

MY WIFE

BEATRICE

FOREWORD

A knowledge of commodity futures trading opens one of the few remaining fields in which vast profits can still be made by those who are speculatively inclined. It also offers unique profit protection facilities to "trade accounts" (producers, dealers, processors and manufacturing end-users) who are astute enough to use futures markets as part of their regular business operations.

For the speculator, futures trading offers the highly attractive combination of low margin requirements and price fluctuations which are both wide and rapid. Year after year, there have been opportunities in one or more of the commodities traded on organized exchanges for returns of several hundred percent on invested capital. Granting that these were exceptional, it must be underscored that these opportunities continue to occur. Needless to say, the chance to make profits of such magnitude is usually linked with large risks. A knowledge of trading fundamentals and methods is the key to reducing those risks.

Knowledgeable use of commodity exchanges by "trade accounts" can substantially reduce the hazards of many types of business operations. In this area, futures trading answers important and special economic needs which cannot be adequately met by banks, stock exchanges and other financial institutions. Just how this can be done is detailed in the chapters on Hedging in Theory, Hedging In Practice, and Advanced Hedging Procedures. This section of the book should be most carefully studied by those interested in the business (inventory price protection) aspects of commodity trading. Once absorbed and properly applied, they can be the source of considerably improved profits.

The chapters on chart trading and suggested trading techniques will appeal most generally to speculators, but will also be of major use to trade accounts. The latter may find themselves in the role of speculator more than once, either by choice or through the force of circumstances. The sections on the fundamentals of trading, individual commodity background data, the sources of information, and the factors which cause changes in commodity prices are all necessary to an understanding of market action. The detailed description of the federal government commodity support programs will undoubtedly prove to be a frequently consulted reference guide.

Throughout the book, length has been rigidly controlled. Sufficient details have been given to afford full coverage of all major facets of the subject. Excessive refinements of minor points, which might tend more to confuse than to clarify, have been scrupulously avoided.

A study on how to make money is always fascinating. Given adequate time and attention, it could also prove to be profitable.

While the author bears full responsibility for the contents of this book, grateful acknowledgement should be made to those who gave their valuable time to reading parts or all of the manuscript, who made suggestions which have improved the readability and accuracy of the text, and who have encouraged the author during the years of its formulation.

GERALD GOLD

TABLE OF CONTENTS

CHAPTER 1.

ORIGIN AND DEVELOPMENT OF
COMMODITY EXCHANGES

Commodity exchanges, like stock exchanges and the national banking system, came into being as a result of the tremendous growth of our national economy during the nineteenth century. They were created to meet specific needs of the business community which other institutions could not satisfy. An understanding of this historical background will make clear why commodity futures exchanges still flourish today, and the profit opportunities they afford.

The opening up of our country, and the development of new agricultural and industrial techniques and equipment, tremendously increased our productive capacity. Rapid population growth and continuing improvement of both internal and international communications opened vast new markets to absorb this production and encourage further expansion.

To produce economically for this national and foreign market, enormous amounts of capital funds were needed. Factories had to be built, and raw materials bought and processed on a large scale. Payment, however, would be deferred until the products could be sold. This process consumed many months. Meanwhile, inventories of raw material, goods in work, and finished products in transit, all had to be maintained. The fact that the market area was no longer local, and that a much greater period of time had to elapse between the production of commodities and their final utilization, also meant substantially increased risks for the person who owned those commodities. Prices were no longer the result of merely local conditions, but were subject to erratic swings based on world events. In addition, the risks of financial loss due to adverse price movements increased with the possibility of competitive products pouring into the same market—at the same time—from widely scattered producing points.

To summarize, the expansion of the market area and industrialization meant:

1) greater capital and credit requirements;
2) increased price risks due to:
   a) larger time period between production and final sale,
   b) greater competition between producers for markets.

As these new problems were recognized, new solutions were sought. The need for working capital was met by the organization of national and international banking systems. The stock exchange solved the need for the huge quantities of capital accumulation made necessary by the new type of production. But neither of these solutions met the second problem, that of increased price risk.

The Need For Protection Against Inventory Price Losses

Merchants, dealers, processors, warehousemen, etc. are interested in receiving a normal business profit (or a little more) for their services. However, they must avoid dangerous speculation. Were they to hold their necessarily large inventories of commodities while the price level declined, they could lose heavily . . . even go into bankruptcy. There are today, for example, grain elevators which hold several million bushels. It can readily be seen that a price decline of 10¢ or 20¢ per bushel could have serious financial repercussions for the owners of that grain. The same is true for any individual or company which holds unsold commodities. The gravity of this financial risk becomes even more apparent when it is realized that most firms operate primarily with capital borrowed from banks. In some cases as much as 90% of working capital is borrowed. It would therefore take a relatively small price decline to wipe out the firm's own capital, or lead to serious financial difficulties. Some means had to be found to limit or reduce this price risk.

The "To-Arrive" Contract — Why It Was Inadequate

The initial attempts at avoiding the price risks involved in owning commodities were made through selling grain before it had arrived at its destination. The owners of commodities, fearing that prices might decline while they were being transported to market, began to sell on a "to-arrive" basis. This passed the price risk on to the new buyer. Grain, for example, would be sold for arrival in Chicago in—let us say —two weeks.

For the price risks to be passed on, someone had to be willing to assume them. One such group would be dealers and processors of the raw commodity, who had to purchase in any event. However, this group soon faced the fact that they could not afford to absorb all the risks. Other risk takers had to be found.

Few individuals outside the trade were willing to speculate on grain prices as long as they had to do so through the medium of the "to-arrive" contract. It presented too many difficulties and presumed too extensive a knowledge of the grain market. Speculation there had to be—since someone had to own the commodity between the time it was produced and the time (perhaps a year later) when it was finally consumed. The question was whether this speculation was going to be voluntary or forced upon some segment of the trade.

There were many individuals throughout the world who were willing to assume these risks. But to induce this risk capital to enter the field, certain difficulties presented by the "to-arrive" contract had to be overcome.

These difficulties included:

1) *Varying grades and sizes of shipments*—Grains would be shipped to the terminal in varying quantities and grades, depending on what the shipper had. A proper offer for each lot would presuppose an extensive knowledge of the trade, and the premiums and discounts on the various grades. Individuals outside the grain trade could hardly be expected to have this knowledge.

2 *Varying terms of payment*—Although there were generally standard procedures for payment, variations were not uncommon. Whether the terms would be cash on arrival, payment in 10 or 30 days or something else with discounts or premiums involved was subject to individual bargaining.

3) *Prices, in many cases, were secret*—It was therefore difficult for those who were not directly involved in the day to day affairs of the specific industry to obtain equal treatment in terms of price. There was also the probability of price concessions to larger operators, at the expense of the smaller operators.

4) *Reliability of buyers and sellers*—The seller could not be sure that the buyer would always fulfill his end of the contract. Suppose the price did break before the grain arrived. Was the buyer sufficiently responsible financially to accept the grain and absorb the loss? Would he seek some way of getting out of the contract or renegotiating it? Conversely, the buyer could not be certain the seller would fulfill his obligation if prices advanced sharply.

5) *Damaged goods (or wrong quality) on arrival*—This proved to be a fairly common problem, and would at times involve extensive litigation to determine responsibility and the extent of damage. The trouble and delays involved were not conducive to attracting outside capital.

6) *Difficulty in finding new buyers*—Because of the limited numbers of individuals willing to accept the risks involved in trading in "to-arrive" contracts, it was difficult to dispose of the contract at will.

When the number of offers increased sharply (at the peak of the harvest movement) this difficulty became even more pronounced. Naturally, outside speculators were not interested in taking delivery of the actual grain. They wanted to sell out before the grain arrived. The difference between their buying and selling price would represent their speculative profit or loss.

Development of Futures Trading Solved A Vital Problem

With the expansion of production and trade accompanying our nation's growth, the search for a solution was intensified. The development of the futures exchange solved these problems and increased the flow of risk capital into this sphere of industry.

A futures exchange is nothing more than a central meeting place for buyers and sellers (or their representatives) to transact business. They enter into bona fide contracts for future delivery of actual commodities. (Such contracts are commonly known as "futures".) These commitments can, however, be fulfilled without having to deliver or receive delivery of the physical commodity. (How and why this is done will be explained later in the text.)

By attracting large quantities of risk capital to one location the futures exchange made possible "hedging"—an economic device which enables dealers, manufacturers, etc. to safeguard themselves against commodity price fluctuations. Basically, hedging is nothing more than the taking of an opposite position in the futures market from that held in the actual physical market. Thus, an individual or company that buys or owns actual commodities would sell an equivalent amount of futures. If prices decline, the loss on inventories of the actual commodity are expected to be recouped or offset by a profit in the futures market. Conversely, should the price level rise, the loss on futures is expected to be offset by the increased value of the actual commodities owned. In either event, a loss on one side of the transaction would normally be offset by a profit on the other. The dealer or manufacturer, freed from worry about price fluctuations, can concentrate on his particular service and merchandising his service at a normal profit. (We will delve much more fully into the theory and practice of hedging in subsequent chapters, but the primary purpose of future exchanges is explained above.)

The Advantage To The General Economy
Provided By Commodity Exchanges

An appreciation of why futures exchanges succeeded where the "to-arrive" contract failed, may be gained from examining the present organized futures exchange procedures which follow:

1) The grades that are deliverable and the size of the contract are fixed.

2) Payment must be made at time of delivery.

3) Prices are established openly, by open outcry of bids and offers, so that all receive equal opportunity to buy and sell at the best possible price at the moment.

4) The Clearing Association connected with the exchange will guarantee the fulfillment of the contract performance under the rules between clearing members even if one party to the contract goes into bankruptcy. Contract performance is thus assured.

(All trading in futures contracts of a commodity is done between members of an exchange. At the end of each day all trades that were executed on that day must be turned over to the Clearing Association by a *clearing* member. Thus, if the member of the exchange who handles futures transactions is not also a member of the Clearing Association, he must turn his trades over to a clearing member. The Clearing Association recognizes only its own members as parties to the transaction. Thus a brokerage firm may be a clearing member, and it will be named as a buyer or seller in the contract. Despite the fact that the brokerage firm is buying or selling for a customer, the name of that customer does not appear on the books of the Clearing Association or on the contract. The functions of the Clearing Association are discussed in detail later in the text.)

5) Commodities are inspected by government and/or exchange inspectors, with grades and qualities certified for delivery.

6) Because of the strict enforcement of rules of trading, and because all trading is concentrated at one point, there is no difficulty in liquidating contracts previously entered into (except temporarily, in extreme cases, where the exchange has been closed because of an emergency, or where the market has advanced or declined the daily permissible limit and trading has ceased. This is discussed more fully in a later section.) The market for a specific commodity is therefore much broader than it would be without the exchange.

In addition to inducing and concentrating a greater supply of risk capital and facilitating hedging, the futures exchanges act as a focal point for the dissemination of statistics and other information vital to the industries they serve. They also act as an alternate market for the commodity, increasing the liquidity of inventories, and thereby further reducing price risks. Finally, they reduce the price of the finished product to the public. Since the use of futures reduces the risks of doing business, the necessary profit margin can be, and in fact is, reduced . . . thus lowering product prices.

The Early Exchanges

The first futures exchange was the Chicago Board of Trade organized in 1848, with futures trading commencing in 1859*. The development of the railroad and canal system made Chicago the center of the major internal commerce of the country. The grains, hides and meat of the Western territories were funneled into that city for transshipment East and South while the manufactured products and raw materials of the latter areas in turn moved into Chicago for distribution to the surrounding territory. For much the same reasons New York developed as the center for cotton futures trading. New York was the focal point from which cotton would be shipped north to the New England mills or financed for overseas movement.

We have traced the development of commodity exchanges and outlined some of their advantages. We will now turn more specifically to the nature and mechanics of futures trading.

---

* The Japanese Grain Dealers Association, however, claims futures trading began in their country a century earlier.

CHAPTER 2.

THE MECHANICS OF FUTURES TRADING

Commodity trading is a simple affair. Commodity exchanges are organized markets—like the stock markets. The exchanges are "public" in the sense that anyone can trade who makes the necessary arrangements with member brokerage firms. Thus, you don't have to be in the cotton business to buy and sell cotton, or in the grain business in order to trade in wheat, soybeans, etc.

Who Trades In Commodities and Why

There are two broad classification of traders in commodity futures:

1. Business men who produce, market and process the various commodities. They use the markets primarily for hedging of inventories and other forms of hedging, as described in later chapters.

2. The other classification of commodity trader is the speculator, who voluntarily risks his capital with the expectation of making profits. He buys when he thinks prices are too low and sells when he thinks prices are too high. There are many reasons why commodity futures markets have a special appeal for those who are interested in taking capital risks:

a. Generally speaking, the profit potentialities from a given capital outlay are larger and can accrue more rapidly in commodity trading than in securities or real estate trading—if the trader's judgment is good. As is usually the case when profit opportunities are higher, the risk of loss in commodities also is greater when trading judgment is wrong. (However, potential losses in commodities can be reduced through the use of trading techniques described in the last chapter on speculation.)

b. The important statistics are "public" and the market judgment of the speculator in a given commodity futures market is often better than that of the business man who handles the physical commodity.

c. Margin requirements are relatively small.

d. Commission rates are small.

e. Many commodity futures markets are broad and active throughout the trading session. This condition provides a liquidity which is important to those who risk their capital.

Opening A Trading Account

Opening a commodity trading account is relatively easy. Most of the larger stock brokerage firms are also members of the various commodity exchanges. To open a commodity account, one merely signs the necessary margin agreement forms, deposits the amount of funds required for a particular transaction and gives the broker his order to buy or sell. If one has an account with a stock brokerage firm that also deals in commodities, the same account number can probably be used for both. (However, the brokerage firm will separate the two accounts to conform with various government and exchange requirements.)

Exchange Members

Commodity Exchanges are located throughout the United States and in important cities in other countries. Like the stock exchange, they are membership organizations. Most members are business men engaged in producing, marketing or processing commodities, and brokerage firms whose principal activity is to execute orders for others. Non-members trade through brokerage firms, which hold memberships through partners or officers. The exchanges are supported by dues and assessments on members.

Each exchange, like the stock exchange, has its own governing board, which sees to it that business is carried on fairly and efficiently under the rules. These rules are designed for equal fairness to large and small business interests and speculators, whether members or non-members. *The exchanges do not buy or sell, or set prices.*

Trading Units

Commodities are bought and sold through the medium of futures contracts. These contracts are standardized. They list, among other things, the quantity of the commodity to be traded. Thus, the contract of cotton on the New York Cotton Exchange involves 100 bales (50,000 lbs.). Everyone who buys and sells cotton on this Exchange does so in units of 100 bales. Each commodity exchange has its specific unit of trading—the quantity of the commodity covered by the futures contract. Thus, in most cases when giving a broker an order, you do not have to specify the number of pounds. For example, if you place an order to buy "one cotton contract" on the New York Cotton Exchange, it is understood that it is for the regular contract unit of 50,000 lbs.

Commissions

In its code of rules, every commodity exchange gives a prominent place to the matter of commissions. For most of the active members, commissions constitute the means of livelihood. All the exchanges have established fixed minimum commission rates that the members must charge to non-members. Commissions are charged only after the entire commodity transaction has been completed; for example, after a purchase of futures is subsequently liquidated. This procedure differs from that of the securities markets. When shares of stock are bought through a broker, the commission for the purchase is charged to the buyer immediately. An additional charge is incurred when the stock is eventually resold. A list of commission charges can be obtained from individual brokers.

Margins

One of the most striking differences between stock and commodity trading is the margin requirement. Whereas the margin deposit necessary for trading in stocks during the post-World War II period has ranged from 50% to 100% of their value, the margin needed for commodity trading normally averages between 5% and 10% of the value of the contract. Each commodity exchange establishes its own minimum margin requirement, which varies from time to time. A brokerage firm may ask for larger deposits, but cannot request less than the exchange minimum. Commodity futures trading has the additional advantage that a customer does not pay interest on the difference in value of the futures contract and the amount of margin he deposits.

A "margin deposit" is simply the placing of required funds with the clearing broker as performance security. This margin must be restored when the total current market values of all futures contracts in an account have declined by an amount specified in the particular rules for each Exchange. The additional margin required to keep an account liquid because of variation in the value of the contracts held is called the "VARIATION MARGIN" as contrasted to the "ORIGINAL MARGIN" which is put up when the transaction is initiated. Since the oringinal deposits are small in proportion to the value of the contract, often insufficient to cover two days' (and in some cases, one day's) possible fluctuation of the market, it is necessary for the broker to obtain the replacement funds quickly, or he may find himself without protection.

The size of the initial margin requirement will vary in accordance with two governing factors. These are: the value of the contract, and the extent of the normal daily price fluctuation. If prices for a particular commodity tend to move over a relatively narrow range, and the price level is relatively low, the margin requirement is usually small. Oats are a case in point. On the other hand, if prices are somewhat high and price fluctuations tend to be wide (as with soybeans), the margin requirement will be larger. Since conditions vary considerably not only among commodities, but even for the same commodity in different years or at various times during the year, margin requirements are not static.

On most exchanges, a somewhat larger margin is required for a speculative account than for a trade account. This is natural since the risk is presumed to be less in dealing with someone in the trade whose intimate knowledge of the field would enable him to meet situations that might arise with greater efficiency than a speculator. He is hedging inventory or forward sales or raw material needs or other features of his business, and uses the market as a form of price insurance. One in the trade would be in a better position to make or accept delivery of the actual commodity should it become necessary. Finally, the financial responsibility of a trade firm is usually more easily discerned and verified. At the present time, a broker is permitted to extend credit for the original margin to trade accounts in a few commodities. This means that trade accounts only need furnish funds to cover deficits in their account when a prescribed limit is reached, in the case of those commodities where this is allowed.

The Time Factor

Trading in most commodities is for delivery in specified months. These trading months may cover a period up to one year or to eighteen months in the future as indicated for each commodity:

UP TO ONE YEAR		THIRTEEN TO EIGHTEEN MONTHS
Wheat	Bellies	Cocoa
Flaxseed	Eggs	Cotton
Oats	Copper	Wool and Wooltops
Potatoes	Cattle	Hides
Corn	Silver	Coffee
Rye	Orange Concentrate	Sugar
Soybean Oil	Propane	Platinum
Soybeans	Soybean Meal	Palladium

This raises another important difference between trading in stocks and commodities. When a stock is purchased, the stock certificate is delivered and the transaction is completed. It can be held indefinitely or resold, let us say, ten years later. Obviously, this is not true of commodities. As has been pointed out, a contract is bought or sold for delivery in a specified month. That contract must be liquidated or fulfilled by the end of that month. A contract of May soybeans will expire in May. It must be liquidated before that time. Trading stops sometime before the end of the delivery month. The final trading day within the delivery month varies with the commodity and is determined by the rules of each exchange. *Before* the first day of the delivery period arrives, a trader with a long position in that month should notify his broker whether or not he intends to accept delivery. The contract is liquidated by either reselling the contract or accepting delivery of the soybeans.

NO, the soybeans are not dumped in the trader's back yard. He receives a warehouse receipt turning the ownership of the soybeans over to him. However, settlement of contract by delivery is not the common practice. Less than 1% of all futures are settled this way. The usual procedure is to resell the contract of May soybeans some time after it was purchased. This can be done one second later, or any time before trading in the May contract ceases (toward the end of May). Since a May contract was first purchased and then sold, the trader has offset his commitment. He need not receive delivery of the commodity. His obligation is completed. The difference between the price at which he purchased and at which he sold is his profit or loss, before charges for commissions.

Theoretically, perhaps, it might be expected that the trader who has bought a contract of May soybeans and then sold a contract for May delivery, should first take delivery of the soybeans from whoever sold it to him and then redeliver them to the person to whom he has sold. By having *purchased* a contract, he has legally obligated himself to *accept delivery* of soybeans in May. However when he *sold* the contract, the new buyer assumed that obligation. Actually the exchange clearing house eliminates any necessity for intermediate deliveries by ultimately delivering the soybeans to the last buyer of the contract. How this is done will be explained in a subsequent chapter where the role of the clearing house is more fully explored.

Notice in the above discussion that emphasis has been placed on the fact that both the purchase and sale must be made in the same delivery month (May) for the trader's position to be liquidated. He cannot sell a March or a September contract against his purchase of May. If he did, he would merely have assumed another obligation, that of delivering soybeans in March or September *in addition* to having to accept delivery in May. Trading in different delivery months is like trading in different markets.

Needless to say, in addition to having to buy and sell in the same contract month, it is also necessary to buy and sell the same amount of the commodity to liquidate a position. If a trader has purchased five contracts, he must also resell five contracts to settle his account. However, he can do this one contract at a time, or sell all five contracts at once, depending upon his wish.

Job Lots

The Chicago Board of Trade and some other grain exchanges at times permit trading in "job lots", which are units smaller than one full contract. These, however, are traded separately from the full contact. A word of caution is, therefore, necessary. Except under very special circumstances, the purchase of one full contract cannot offset the sale of several jobs or vice versa. All purchases of full contracts must be offset by a sale of full contracts and all purchases of job lots must be offset by the sale of an equal number of job lots. It thus differs from odd lot trading in stocks.

Selling Short

In the discussion above, we have assumed the trader first buys a contract and subsequently resells it. This was merely a matter of convenience. There is nothing to prevent an individual from doing the reverse, i.e., "selling short."

The whole process of selling short needs some further amplification. It is merely selling first and buying later to cover the sale. The question has often been asked, "How can I sell something I don't own?" Actually, this is not a situation unique to commodity futures trading, but common practice and standard selling techniques in many lines of endeavor. Textile manufactures, for example, make up samples of various types and patterns of cloth. These samples are used by salesmen to obtain orders for later delivery. After these orders are received, the mill buys the raw material and weaves the goods. In other words, the mill had sold short on its textiles.

Selling short in commodity futures trading is merely an extension of the same procedure. By selling first, the seller is obligating himself to deliver the commodity at a later date. But he need not necessarily do so. By subsequently rebuying a contract in the same delivery month, his original obligation is offset. He does not have to make delivery.

The difference between the price at which he sold and at which he bought is his profit or loss, excluding commissions.

Selling short in commodities is simpler and much more common than in stocks. In stocks a short sale can be made only on an "uptick." That is, the price of the stock must have rallied from the previous level before a short position can be instituted. Thus, an order to sell short in a stock "at the market" could result in an execution at a price below the intended level. If the price of a stock declines without any rally, no short sale is possible. There is no such problem in commodities. Whether a selling order is liquidating a long position or a new short sale does not matter in commodities. There is no need to wait for an uptick. A "market order" will be executed at the existing price without delay.

In the case of stocks, when a short sale is made, stock certificates must be borrowed. If during the period that a trader is short a dividend is declared, he must pay it. There are no such problems in commodities. There are no stock certificates (commodity warehouse receipts) to borrow nor any dividends to pay.

How An Order Is Placed

Commodity futures prices are quoted on the basis of their lowest selling unit. Thus, grain prices are quoted at the price per bushel, eggs in cents per dozen, and meal in dollars per ton. All other commodities, i.e., cotton, coffee, oils, rubber, etc., are quoted in cents *per pound.*

Another important distinction between grains and other commodities is in the placing of orders. Grain orders are placed *in bushels,* other commodities *in contracts.* Thus, if a trader places an order to buy one contract of November soybeans, the proper method of notification is: "Buy 5,000 bushels of November Soybeans," or more simply "Buy 5 November Soybeans." A contract unit of grains is 5,000 bushels.

On the other hand, orders for cocoa, rubber, soybean oil, etc., are placed in contract units. Thus, "Buy one May Cocoa" means the purchase of a full contract of 30,000 lbs. of May Cocoa.

The Order As It Leaves The Broker's Office

An order form, in addition to the above, would also contain the price at which the order is to be executed, the number of the account (not the name, which is kept confidential), and the name of the broker. The order is then given to the order clerk to be telephoned or wired to the exchange for execution. Immediately after the order is given to the order clerk, it is time-stamped. In case of subsequent dispute concerning whether or not the order could have been executed, there is an exact record of the time the order was placed. If the order is to be executed on an exchange other than the one normally or primarily used, the name of the exchange or its symbol is also placed on the order. For example, if a cotton order is to be executed on the New York Cotton Exchange, the initials N. Y. are added at the end of the order. Unless otherwise specified, an order is considered to be given for execution only in the single trading session during or before which it is received.

Ticker Symbols

Although many firms do not permit the use of symbols in writing commodity futures orders, symbols are used in reporting sales and giving quotes on some tickers. If one is following a ticker which uses symbols, it is essential to know what they stand for. Two designations are used together: one for the commodity and one for the month. For grains, the first letter is used: "W" for wheat, "S" for soybeans, etc. Commodities other than grains are usually written out or abbreviated.

The symbols for various trading months are standardized. They are:

January	F	April	J	July	N	October	V
February	G	May	K	August	Q	November	X
March	H	June	M	September	U	December	Z

Thus, November Soybeans would be written out as: "SX."

Where The Order Is Executed — The Exchange Trading Floor

All exchange trading floors are organized on a variation of the diagram shown below.

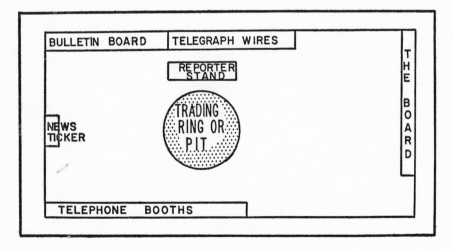

The central point is the trading ring or pit. This is a circular area around which the floor brokers will do their buying and selling. All bids and offers are made openly, by outcry or hand signals, so that all have an equal opportunity to obtain the best possible prices. During a period of active trading, the cries of bids and offers become deafening and an outsider wonders how it is possible to make any sense out of what appears to be a welter of confusion.

As the trades are consummated, the prices are recorded by an observing reporter and are marked up in chalk on the quotation board. They are simultaneously telegraphed to other markets or trading centers throughout the country, and are made available to market centers abroad. The floor brokers write the purchases and sales they have made on cards which they carry for this purpose. How much was bought or sold, from whom, and the prices paid are all recorded. They then telephone the confirmation of the trade back to their customers. Most floor brokers are usually self-employed and execute the orders for a floor brokerage fee. Their customers are the large stock and commodity brokerage firms with whom the public deals, or the firms which deal in that specific commodity in the spot market. Each floor broker usually has several telephone lines, each a direct wire to his customer's office.

The sequence of events, then, is for the customer to place an order to buy or sell a commodity with a firm which is a member of the exchange. The brokerage house telephones the floor broker on its direct wire. The floor broker executes the order by open outcry in the trading ring, and telephones back the confirmation. The entire process should take only a matter of minutes in an active market for an order placed "at the market." Of course, orders placed at prices not at the market must wait until market prices reach the specified level, i.e.— the limit specified in the order. These are called limit orders.

The exchange floor also has a series of bulletin boards on which important information is posted. There may be a weather map showing the latest reports on rainfall and temperatures which might affect a growing crop. Spot price quotations, shipments to and from major terminals, prices of competitive products, government announcements and similar items are also publicly displayed. In addition, a news ticker may be available so that no delay will occur in receiving information which might be important in determining price trends.

Executions on the Chicago Board of Trade

The following pages are an edited version of a Chicago Board of Trade release issued in response to various complaints concerning inability to obtain executions of orders at certain times and other problems.

Nothing outlined here is intended to condone poor service from a floor broker. When volume is normal, one has the right to expect efficient execution and prompt reporting. When there is a surge of abnormal volume, certain things are physically impossible and it is such conditions which cause complaints because the circumstances are not understood. The first part of this bulletin explains how it is possible for special situations to arise; the second part answers specific questions.

NOT LIKE STOCK EXCHANGE. Some of the misunderstanding about the execution of commodity orders occurs because of a belief that the procedures are the same as on stock exchanges. This is not true. The physical layout of the trading floor, the concentration of trading, reporting of trades on the tape are all different as is the fact that there is no specialist's book in commodities,

CONGESTION AT TRADING AREA. Much of the misunderstanding about execution of orders will be cleared up if one understands the physical environment in which futures orders are executed on the Chicago Board of Trade. The trading is done around 7 "pits" or "rings." The pits for the more active commodities are large, measuring 30 to 40 feet across. In the very active times, 150 or more floor brokers are crowded into one pit, all shouting and waving (by hand signals) their bids and offers. In very active markets, it is not uncommon for an offer at one price to be made in one part of the pit, while, at the same time, another offer for the same month is being made at a slightly different price in a different part of the pit. This means that a broker, in accepting an offer he hears, might miss a better offer that he could not see or hear which was made and executed in another part of the same large, crowded and noisy pit. This does not happen with quiet or even normal trading activity, but in sudden bursts of activity, in hectic markets, especially at the opening or closing, it does occur. It is no one's fault, but merely the characteristic of the trading and because of a broker's location around the pit.

The Chicago Board of Trade is the largest commodity futures market in the world. In recent times, orders to buy 4,000,000 contracts plus orders to sell 4,000,000 contracts have been executed in one year. 450 to 500 brokers are on the floor plus about 225 messengers and clerks. It is a very busy place, at times hectic, in which a huge volume of orders from all over the world are executed with dispatch.

TAPE NOT AT ALL TIMES AN EXACT RECORD OF EVERY TRADE. This is an important fact that is not always realized and consequently causes misunderstanding. In each pit, there are two or more exchange employees whose duty is to note each new price at which trading is done and report to a teletype operator (sitting above the pit) for transmission on the tape. With normal trading activity, the tape does show every change in price accurately. However, it is characteristic of the grain markets that, at times, there are very rapid changes in price coupled with high volume. A price-affecting piece of news breaking during market hours can make violent "surges" in the market. At such times, it is a physical impossibility for the reporting clerks to see every transaction. In such violent surges, the price has gone up 7 or 8 cents in a few seconds accompanied by unusual confusion. To keep the public informed of the market's action, it is necessary to give approximate quotations of what actually transpired, to feed a stream of prices to the ticker to show over what ground the market traveled and where the market is. For example: If there are a large number of trades made in a market that moves from 2.50 to 2.58½ in a minute or so, the tape will show a list of prices moving over that range and include the word "FAST." There may have been sales at each price shown and there may not have been sales at every price shown. The only thing that can be said was that the market moved over that range in that length of time. What has been mentioned about the action of the tape during market surges, of course, applies to quotations on the electric boards because they are merely a reflection of the tape.

PROMPT REPORT OF EXECUTIONS NOT ALWAYS POSSIBLE. For the same reason given above, it is not always possible for a floor broker to give a prompt report of an execution to a brokerage firm. With normal volume, executions are reported promptly. But in market surges, a floor broker is concentrating on handling a flood of incoming orders and there have been occasions when it has been physically impossible for him to report executions already made until an hour later or even until the market closes.

PRICES CAN VARY ON OPENING. On the Chicago Board of Trade there is *not* an opening call for each month in turn as is true on some other exchanges. Trading in all months opens at the same time. And trading in all grain pits opens at the same time. Another point to remember about the opening is that, on the Chicago Board of Trade, brokers cannot "cross" orders as on some other commodity exchanges. If a broker has orders to sell and also orders to buy, even though they are both at the same price, he must offer all of them at auction in the pit by open outcry or by hand signal; he cannot offset ("cross") such buying orders against selling orders in his deck.

For such reasons, it is easy to understand that duplicate orders can be filled at different prices and that opening prices are often reported as taking place over a range of prices. Openings are usually moments of great activity and some people advise that market orders for execution "at the opening" are dangerous ones, and for similar reasons, market orders for execution "at the close" are equally dangerous.

NO SPECIALIST-BOOK SYSTEM IN COMMODITIES. There is no "specialist-book" system on any U. S. Commodity Exchange as there is on the floor of the New York Stock Exchange. All orders are offered or bid for by open auction.

NOT ALWAYS ONE DEFINITE BID. Some people feel that there is always one very definite bid and asked at any minute of trading. This is not true. Because the futures market is an open auction market and there is no specialists' book as in stocks, the exact price at which business can be done is not known at every moment. As has been explained, at moments of abnormal activity, with a large, crowded and noisy pit, there might be simultaneous bids, in different parts of the pit, at different prices. On the other hand, if the market is abnormally quiet, there isn't any price until bids and offers come in and an execution is made to show exactly where the market is.

No Recourse Under Specific Circumstances

In periods of large volume and rapid price fluctuations, there is no recourse if an:

(A) Order was filled at a price not shown on ticker, but within range of prices quoted;

(B) Order was not executed at price named in a limit order although other orders were executed at said price.

These situations are covered on page 16-R in the rear of the Chicago Board of Trade Rule Book, a paragraph of which reads:

"That, whenever price fluctuations of the commodities dealt in on the Exchange are rapid and the volume of business is large, it is of common occurrence that different prices are bid and offered for the same delivery in different parts of the pit at the same time. The normal result of such conditions is, at times, the execution by members of orders at prices not officially quoted, or the inability of a member to execute an order at a limited price. This is unavoidable, but is in noway the fault of anyone; and it is not permissible for members to readjust the price at which orders have been filled, nor to report as filled orders that have not been filled. To do so is a grave offense."

Complaints on such circumstances in normal markets "may be made to any member of the Market Report Committee."

Limit Orders

A strict limit order, i.e. orders to be executed only at specified prices without leeway, will not be filled unless they can be done at the exact price named. At certain price levels it is not uncommon to have a concentration of limit and of stop orders for one reason or another. If there are limit orders on various brokers' cards to buy 200 contracts at a certain price, and there are sellers willing to sell only 150 contracts when the market reaches that price, there will be orders for 50 contracts unfilled at that limit. To overcome this, to some degree, limit orders with a leeway are commonly given. To indicate this, some firms use the word "with," others the word "use": BUY 5 NOV SOYBEANS LIMIT 2.50 WITH ¼! SELL 5 NOV SOYBEANS LIMIT 2.60 USE ⅛.

Adjustments of Prices Due to Errors

To make an adjustment to a customer because of an error made in handling his order, approval of the Exchange is needed. Regulation 1871 (Page 453) of the Rule Book reads:

"Price of Execution Binding. The price at which an order for commodities or securities is executed shall be binding and no member shall make any adjustment with his customer because of an error in handling the order without first obtaining permission from—

1. the Floor Practices Committee, if the error occurred on the Floor of the Exchange, or
2. The President or the Secretary, if the error occurred elsewhere, who shall report each case to the Rules Committee."

(Also see Regulation #1021, pages 222-3; Regulation #1718, pages 386-7; 1843 (b) page 450.)

CHAPTER 3

UNDERSTANDING THE COMMODITY QUOTATION BOARD

Because commodity futures are traded for delivery in many different months, a commodity board (in a brokerage firm's "board room") will list prices for these different trading months. The section of the commodity board devoted to Chicago wheat will look something like the illustration below. An explanation of this table will afford us an opportunity to examine several important relationships in commodity futures trading.

Chicago Wheat

Contract High & Low	170-144	173-148	172-146	158-141	162-145
Trading Months	Dec.	Mar.	May	July	Sept.
Previous Close	168	170	169½	158	161
Opening Today	167	169	168¾	157	160
Today's High	167	169	168¾	157	160
Today's Low	164	166	165⅞	154	157
Ticker	165	167	166⅝	155	158

To the left of the entire table is a column explaining each line. The top line contains the highest and lowest prices, in cents per bushel, at which that particular contract has been traded since its inception. Thus, over the word "Dec." (which represents December Wheat) is: 170-144. This means that at sometime during the period in which this particular contract has been trading, it sold as high as $1.70 per bushel and as low as $1.44 per bushel. The March contract has traded as high as $1.73 per bushel and as low as $1.48 per bushel—and so on for the other trading months. At any particular time, these prices will show the range within which a particular contract has traded. Naturally, if during the course of a day's trading, a contract has sold at a higher price than at any previous time, the life of the contract high would then be appropriately adjusted. For example, if December rallied to $1.80 per bushel, the present listing on our table of $1.70 would be changed to $1.80.

The Active Trading Months

The next line shows the trading months. Wheat is one of those commodities which can be traded as far ahead as one year. You will notice in our table, however, that not every month is listed. The months in which trading in a specific commodity becomes concentrated are those which correspond most closely to the needs of the particular industry served. Thus, the months in which the wheat industry found the greatest need for hedging became more active. There is another advantage to concentrating trading in various months instead of having it spread out over every month of the calendar year. By concentrating trading, the volume of sales in each of the active months becomes greater. This makes it easier to get into or out of the market at the trader's discretion, and without necessarily affecting the price level. If an elevator operator wishes to sell 50 contracts as a hedge, it will be much easier to do so in a month in which the daily trading volume is 500 contracts, rather than only 250. The price-depressing influence of the sale would also be reduced. Anyone who wished to buy 50 contracts would find it easier to do so, and would not necessarily force the price up.

The marketing practices of each commodity vary. The time of harvest, the distance to market, the degree of availability over the calendar year, and the seasonal pattern of processing and converting the raw commodity into a final consumer item are all different. Therefore, each commodity developed its own pattern of active trading months. Unlike soybeans, wheat is not actively traded for delivery in November and January. On the other hand, it has active trading in a December contract, while soybeans does not. Maine potato futures were originally traded for delivery from November through the following May. This corresponds to the period from the initial harvest until the time when practically the entire crop has been sold and moved into consumption. With remaining stocks small, there was a reduced need for hedge protection, and therefore trading for delivery, in the period from June through October. It was also found that little trading took place in December and February contracts. Consequently by a vote of the membership on the Exchange in 1957, these two contract months were removed from the active list.

How The Day's Price Changes Are Recorded

The third line on our table labeled "Previous Close" indicates precisely that. It is the final price at which each contract traded during the previous trading day. At times, trading may be very active during the closing seconds with the result that there is a "split close." That is, trading may have taken place simultaneously at two slightly different prices, say $1.70 and $1.70¼. In certain commodities or in some trading months when trading is not very active, the closing price

— 26 —

is sometimes listed as nominal. That represents the average between the bid and asked price. The closing price on such a day would be labeled "N" for nominal. At other times there might only be a bid price at the close, or only a contract offered at a specific price. The closings may therefore be labelled "B" for bid or "A" for asked.

The next line on the table shows the opening price. That is the first trade of the day. The next two lines are the high and low prices recorded for that contract during the particular trading session. As trading proceeds during the day, these highs and lows will change in accordance with price fluctuations.

The final line on the commodity board shows the "current" price as established by the most recent trade. At the end of the trading session the final price at which that particular contract traded, or the bid and/or offered price, will be shown.

Minimum Fluctuations

The minimum price fluctuation in most commodities is one one-hundredth (1/100) of a cent. Thus, if the last transaction in December cotton took place at 26.27¢ per pound, the minimum change would be to either 26.28¢ or 26.26¢. The principal exceptions are wool and wooltops where the minimum price change is one-tenth (1/10) of a cent per pound; silver 5/100ths of a cent per ounce; eggs 5/100¢ per dozen and meal which is 5¢ per ton. A fluctuation of 1/100th of a cent is spoken of as "one point." Thus, the minimum fluctuation in eggs of 5/100¢ is spoken of as "five points." Fluctuations in grains are in eighths of a cent rather than in points. Since a full contract of any grain involves 5000 bushels, the minimum fluctuation of ⅛¢ per bushel is equivalent to $6.25 in the value of the contract (⅛¢ x 5000 = $6.25).

Maximum Daily Fluctuations

At intervals news developments appear such as crop catastrophies, war scares, and the like that are so sensational as to be followed immediately by exceptionally sharp price movements. To prevent sudden demoralization, the exchanges have adopted laws fixing definite trading limits during the course of a day. For example, the daily limitation for wheat fluctuations is ten cents per day above or below the previous day's closing. Proponents of these daily trading limits contend that they prevent unnecessary fluctuations caused by hysteria or exaggerated hopes or fears.

CHAPTER 4.

PREMIUMS AND DISCOUNTS

When you look at commodity futures price tables, it immediately becomes apparent that the prices listed vary for each trading month. This should not be too surprising. Since it is probable that supply and demand conditions for any commodity would vary at different times of the year, the price of that commodity would reflect these differing circumstances. On examining the line of previous closing prices in the table, it will be seen that the prices listed for December through May become progressively higher. The more distant months are selling at premiums over the nearer months. This is called a "normal market." Were the situation reversed, with premiums on the near months as opposed to the more distant positions, we would have an "inverted market."

The determination of whether there will be premiums or discounts on the distant months depends primarily upon such factors as size of stocks, the actions taken by the buyers and sellers of the actual commodity as well as their opinion of future price movements and the costs of carrying the commodity in storage.

Development Of A Premium (The Normal Market)

Using wheat as an illustration, under normal conditions (with an average size crop, no international crisis, etc.), marketing pressure begins with the harvest. Farmers ordinarily sell a fairly large part of their crop within a matter of weeks. They need cash to pay for the added harvest labor and machinery, as well as to repay bank loans and other debts which periodically mature after the harvest. The harvest begins in the southern areas and works gradually northward until the crop harvest is practically complete, say ten to twelve weeks after the initial movement begins. This means that there is continued pressure on prices of the actual commodity, due to the harvest movement for a period of roughly three months. If the crop is sufficiently large to satisfy normal requirements, buyers are not particularly anxious to accumulate supplies quickly. They assume there will be no difficulty in obtaining supplies somewhat later. Consequently, there will tend to be a seasonal price decline, normally concommitant with, or shortly after, the harvest. As cash prices weaken (cash or spot prices are the prices of the actual commodity in regular commercial channels), so do the near month futures, to keep them in alignment with market conditions.

Farmers and dealers who are seeking to sell the actual commodity within a few months will tend to hedge in the near months. As the commodity moves into the major terminal markets from the outlying country points of production, stocks will tend to increase. If the price of the near future did not decline to the level of the spot market, the owners of these stocks would sell near month futures at the existing higher price and deliver their stocks against their sale of futures contracts. They would make a greater profit by doing this than by selling the commodity through the normal commercial channels. Normally, the process of selling the near month will continue until the price has declined to the level of the spot market. This tends to depress the price of the near future relative to the more distant positions.

The more distant positions, of course, are not under this type of selling pressure. Furthermore, once the major part of the harvest movement is out of the way and country selling diminishes, prices can be expected to firm. With prices expected to be higher later in the season, the distance futures will also tend to receive buying support while still at premiums to the near month.

Another reason for the development of premiums on the distant months is the cost of storing and carrying commodities over a period of time. Storage space must be built or rented, the commodity must be moved to storage, it must be insured against fire and other hazards, and interest must be paid on the capital borrowed to finance its ownership. These expenses often are called "carrying charges."

Since it is expensive to carry commodities, many dealers, processors, etc., will not buy commodities to be stored for later sale or use unless they are fairly certain that prices will be higher later in the season, or unless they can somehow offset the carrying charges. Theoretically, prices should increase as the season progresses by the equivalent of carrying charges. However, because of the many other factors that enter into the formation of commodity prices this development is highly problematical. Some inducement is, therefore, necessary for an individual or firm to buy commodities for storage and later sale or use. One such inducement is the opportunity to sell futures at a premium which covers all or most of the cost of storage.

This develops when the harvest pressure (as explained previously) or the anticipation of it causes near months to decline to discounts compared to the distant months. When these discounts are close to the carrying charge costs, the actual commodity can be bought and a distant month future sold at a higher price as a hedge.

The sale of futures at the premium equal to carrying charges (or nearly so) induces purchases of the actual commodity because:

a) The futures market in effect pays the storage cost. In the unlikely event that it becomes necessary, the actual commodity could eventually be delivered against the sale of the futures (assuming it equals contract grade and weight). Since futures were sold at a price high enough to cover nearly all or full storage costs, there would be little or no loss. (Why the actual commodity is rarely delivered will become clear later in the text when hedging is discussed in detail.)

b) The sale of futures protects against any major loss on the inventory of the commodity purchased. Should the spot price decline, the futures may be expected to go down also. Therefore, the inventory loss on the commodity purchased is expected to be offset by the profit on the sale of futures.

The cost of storing commodities, therefore, tends to induce the development of premiums on distant month futures. This, in turn, tends to induce demand for the actual commodity since little or no risk is involved and it may prove profitable to own commodities later in the season.

Premiums On The Near Months

The development of premiums on the near months is generally brought about as a result of conditions that are the opposite of those listed above.

a) If a crop is short there is the possibility that users of the commodity will have difficulty in obtaining the specific grades that they need. Thus, a strong demand develops for near term shipment. A rising spot price trend leads to purchases of the near future. If the near futures did not rise with the spot market, but remained underpriced, a trader could buy the near future, take delivery and resell the commodity in the spot market for a profit. Those who had sold short in futures would be anxious to rebuy their contracts as delivery time approached since they could not profitably deliver the higher priced actual commodity against their short sale of futures. This process of new buying and short covering in the near month tends to bring it to a premium over more distant positions.

b) If stocks in deliverable position are small, it will be difficult for shorts to obtain commodities to deliver. Consequently, aggressive short covering of the near month should develop particularly as delivery day approaches.

c) If a large new crop is expected, particularly if the current supply situation is tight, distant month futures will tend to discount the anticipated lower new crop prices.

The Crop Year —"New Crop Months" And "Old Crop Months"

Most commodities are discussed in terms of a "crop year" basis, rather than the calendar year. The crop year is considered to begin with the harvest and run until the beginning of the next harvest. For wheat, the crop year begins July 1. Thus, when someone refers to the 1971/72 wheat season, it means the period from July 1, 1971 to June 30, 1972. This period is also sometimes referred to as the 1971 crop year, since the harvest occurs in 1971.

In our illustration of the commodity board (Chapter 3), you will note that the price for the July delivery is at a discount to May. This is the crop year break. July is the first of the new crop months. It sells at a lower price than May anticipating substantial new supplies as a result of the harvest. The premium of May over July also reflects the possibility that a tight supply situation could develop at the end of the old crop year, before the new crop supplies are available. The September delivery is shown at a premium over July. A new crop year has started with July. The factors previously listed will determine whether subsequent months (Sept., etc.) will sell at premiums or discounts. The fact that September is at a premium to July indicates that normal market conditions are expected; a good crop, etc.

When near months are selling at premiums, factors are set in motion which tend to eventually force a realignment of prices to a normal market. Premiums on the near months usually mean that prices have been advancing for some time. There is a tendency for those who have previously accumulated substantial inventories (particularly merchants such as grain elevator operators) to sell them at the higher prices. At the same time, they buy distant futures at the existing lower prices to replace their inventory position. This combination of increasing spot supplies as well as increasing demand for distant futures tends to force down the price of near months while bringing up the price of distant months.

This illustration will serve to emphasize the important relationship between the spot and futures markets.

Relationship Of Futures Prices To The Spot Market

Futures prices cannot move far out of alignment with spot market prices, because of the possibility of making delivery of actuals against the sales of futures or of demanding actual delivery against purchases of futures, when the contracts mature. Suppose soybeans were selling in Chicago at $2.30 per bushel in mid-December and the January contract on the futures exchange was selling at $2.40 per bushel. Anyone who owned soybeans in Chicago would make an extra 10 cents per bushel profit by selling the January future and delivering the soybeans against this sale of January futures in January. It would be the obvious thing to do since he could obtain more for his soybeans on the futures market than in the spot market. Heavy selling pressure would, therefore, develop in January futures forcing the price down to the level of the actual commodity. Conversely, if the January future were selling at a discount to the spot price, many traders would buy the January future and hold for delivery, since this would be the cheapest price at which they could be purchased. This buying power would force the price of futures up to the level of the spot market. Therefore, barring some technical difficulty, the mere possibility of making delivery, or demanding delivery, tends to keep the futures price level of the nearest delivery month in line with the spot market. There may be some divergence in the weeks between delivery periods, but the two markets must be brought together during the actual time that delivery can take place.

This explanation largely corresponds to that advanced to show how and why the near month will go to a premium or discount to the more distant deliveries. The same factors which tie the spot market to the futures market also help determine the price relationships between the various future delivery months. Both markets are intertwined and anything which affects one will in all probability affect the other.

Maximum Premiums (On Distant Months)—The Carrying Charge

In grains and other non-perishable commodities various delivery months can sell at premiums or discounts to each other. There is a maximum premium above which distant months cannot sell over near months for any length of time. The maximum premium is equal to the cost of carrying commodities. For our purposes, this would include the cost of renting insured storage space which in 1971 was about 2¢ per bushel per month, plus interest on the necessary working capital borrowed from banks and commissions, which averaged about ¾¢ per bushel per month for grains. The higher the price of cash grains, the greater the amount of money that will have to be borrowed to finance inventory purchases and, therefore, the higher the per bushel interest cost. However, taking 2¾¢ per bushel per month would appear to give the maximum carrying charge for wheat and soybeans. The cost would be slightly lower for corn, oats and rye. Larger firms which have their own storage space, or can borrow money from banks at lower rates of interest, could carry the grain at less than the 2¾¢ per bushel we have used. (If they are Exchange and Clearing House members, commission expenses are greatly reduced.) But we are considering the more general case of grain traders.

The maximum premium of December wheat over September wheat, therefore, would be 8¼¢ per bushel. This is arrived at by multiplying the 2¾¢ monthly cost by the number of months the grain would be carried, which in this case is three. We use three months instead of four because the grain could be delivered against the December contract on December 1. The maximum carrying cost, therefore, would be from September 1 to December 1. (To be more accurate, the carrying charge period would be from first notice day on the September contract to first notice day on the December contract. An explanation of first notice day will be given subsequently.)

This cost of carrying the grain becomes the maximum premium of December wheat over September wheat because of the possibility of taking delivery in September and redelivering the same grain in December against the futures contract. If the December premium was 12¢ over September, then anyone could buy September wheat and sell December wheat at the 12¢ premium for December and reap an automatic profit. That person could accept delivery on his long September future, hold the grain until December, and then redeliver. It would cost 8¼¢ per bushel for carrying the grain from September to December. Subtracting this from the 12¢ premium at which the December was sold leaves a profit of 3¾¢ per bushel, less the costs incidental to making delivery.

The possibility of such redelivery makes the carrying charge a maximum premium over which distant months cannot sell for long. Too many large firms and traders would automatically buy the near month and sell the distant month at the premium. This would help raise the price of the near month (September) and lower the price of the distant month (December) until the automatic profit was eliminated.

This maximum, however, does not hold for the more perishable commodities such as potatoes and eggs. These commodities would require reinspection before they could be retendered. Because of their perishability, they could deteriorate in storage, and might not pass reinspection for delivery on the later month. In that case, no automatic profit could develop. Therefore, it is possible for distant month futures of perishable commodities to sell at a premium that is somewhat higher than the full cost of carrying the commodity from one delivery month to the other. In addition, if no storage space is available, spot prices can decline excessively. This has happened once or twice. Finally, in December 1967/January 1968 silver futures widened beyond carrying charges during a period of hectic silver trading involving many technical problems as well as the uncertainty created by rumors of imminent U.S. dollar devaluation. These, however, are quite rare exceptions to the rule of a maximum premium of a distant month to a near month.

No "Automatic" Limit On Possible Premiums For Near Months

While this maximum premium exists for the more distant month over the nearer month in non-perishable commodities, the reverse does not hold true. There is no limit to the possible premium of a near month over a more distant month.

For example, the September future could sell at almost any conceivable premium over the December in the cases described above. There is no point at which we can say the premium is high enough and cannot go higher. In fact, if a shortage of supplies in deliverable position exists, a "short squeeze" can develop.

A"short squeeze" occurs when those who are short in the delivery period cannot obtain supplies to deliver on futures. They must, therefore, cover their short positions. This forced buying of the near month causes it to steadily increase its premium over the subsequent month. The premiums of the near month over the distant month could widen out day after day until trading ceases in the near month.

There is no point at which the speculator or general trader can enter the market with an automatic profit possibility. Even if the near month is at a 25¢ premium to the distant month, a trader who sells the near month (at the big premium) and buys the distant month (at the discount) still takes a risk. The premium might widen out to 30 cents or more by the time the last trading day comes around for the near month.

In summary, there is a maximum premium above which the distant months cannot go over nearer months. This does not hold true for perishable commodities. There is no maximum premium of nearer months over distant months.

CHAPTER 5.

THE COMMODITY FUTURES CONTRACT

The question has often been raised as to why some commodities, but not others, are traded on organized futures markets. There are certain fundamental conditions which must be met before standardized futures contracts can be established for specific commodities and futures trading can be successfully instituted. These include:

(1) Competitive market conditions must exist in production as well as distribution. This implies production by numerous individuals spread over a wide area, as well as many buyers, so that no individual can control prices by withholding supplies or refusing to buy except at his own price. It also means an absence of rigid government controls over prices, production and marketing. While the government support program (as discussed in a subsequent chapter) has limited the need for futures markets in certain instances, it has not yet become rigid enough to eliminate all price fluctuations and hence price risks.

(2) The commodity must be subject to specific grading. Since buying and selling futures contracts involves trading in a commodity sight unseen, it must be certain beyond a reasonable doubt that the grade called for in the contract will have fairly exact, specific qualities with little tolerance for variation. It must not be necessary for a buyer to examine specific lots of a commodity individually. For example, all #2 Soft Red Winter Wheat must have the same characteristics.

(3) The commodity must be in the raw or semi-processed state. A completely manufactured item is subject to production increases or decreases at the will of the manufacturer. It is also subject to grading difficulties.

(4) The leading members of the trade must be willing to participate in, or at least not actively oppose, futures market trading. Widespread trade participation is necessary to supply the hedging contracts and the large volume of trading needed for a liquid market.

(5) The commodity must be storeable, under proper conditions, through at least the major portion of the marketing year. If it were not storeable it could not be traded in for delivery at some time in the future. Certain commodities are, of course, more perishable than others. These will therefore require more frequent inspection to insure that their quality has not deteriorated.

Attempts have been made to institute trading in commodities (such as tobacco) whose inherent characteristics or marketing practices fail to meet all the conditions outlined above. They have not been able to prosper or survive.

While these conditions may be modified to some extent for some successful exchanges, elements of all appear to be essential.

Once a commodity fulfills the conditions discussed above, the organization of a futures exchange requires the establishment of a contract and rules of trade, spelling out in detail the methods of operation and trading procedure.

How Futures Contracts Are Standardized

The contract is standardized for two reasons:

1) To attract risk capital and avoid the pitfalls of the "to-arrive" contract,

2) To allow instantaneous trading.

Shown on the next page is a facsimile of the "B" coffee contract.

As can be seen, only:

1) The names of buyer and seller,

2) The price, and

3) The delivery month

need be filled in. All other terms and conditions are uniform and are fully covered by the remainder of the contract and the trade rules. The size of the contract, the grades that are deliverable, the premiums and discounts for grades other than the basic one, the point of delivery, etc. are all previously determined.

The names of the buyer and seller written on the contract will not be the names of the speculator or trader who is the client of a brokerage house. The brokerage houses themselves will appear as the parties to the transaction. The members of the Clearing Association are directly responsible for the fulfillment of the contract. The trader dealing through a brokerage house does not have to sign anything except the original ordinary margin forms and papers used to open an account. Thereafter, he is responsible only to the brokerage house through whom he deals.

Premiums And Discounts For The Different Deliverable Grades

The contract calls for delivery of Santos No. 4 with additions or deductions for grades, ports and quality according to the differentials established by the Rules. With few exceptions, the contracts of futures

CONTRACT "B" (new)
(BRAZIL COFFEE CONTRACT)
(Variable Differentials)

New York..19.......

.... (has)   this day   (sold)
                                                         (have)   (bought)

and agreed to (deliver to) ....
               (receive from)

32,500 lbs. (in about 250 bags) of Brazilian COFFEE shipped through
the ports of Santos, Paranagua, Angra dos Reis or Rio de Janeiro, grading from No. 2 to No. 6 inclusive, provide the average grade shall
not be above No. 3, nor below No. 5. Nothing in this contract, however, shall be construed as prohibiting a delivery averaging above No. 3
at the premium for No. 3 grade. No premium shall be allowed for
Softish Coffee grading above No. 4.

At the price of .... cents per pound for Santos No. 4, Strictly
Soft, Fair to Good Roast, Solid Bean with additions or deductions for
grades, ports of shipment and description (quality) according to the
differentials established or to be established by the Committee on Coffee
of the New York Coffee and Sugar Exchange for the delivery month
specified below in accordance with Section 88(8)(a) of the By-Laws of
said Exchange. The delivery must consist of Coffee from one port only.

The Coffee to be Fair to Good Roast, Solid Bean, and the description (quality) to be Strictly Soft, Soft, or Softish. No delivery permitted
of Hard Coffee.

Deliverable from licensed warehouse in the Port of New York between the first and last days of...
inclusive, the delivery within such time to be at the seller's option upon
either five, six or seven days' notice to the buyer as prescribed by the
Trade Rules.

Either party may call for margin as the variations of the market for
like deliveries may warrant, which margin shall be kept good.

This contract is made in view of, and is in all respects subject to, the
By-Laws, Rules and Regulations of the New York Coffee and Sugar
Exchange, Inc.

(Across the face is the following): ....
                                                         (Brokers)

For and in consideration of One Dollar to.................................
in hand paid, receipt whereof is hereby acknowledged,......................
accept this contract with all its obligations and conditions.

— 37 —

exchanges will call for delivery of one grade (called the basic grade), but allow the seller to deliver several other commercially desirable grades at discounts or premiums to the contract price. This is done to enlarge the quantity of a commodity which could be available for delivery and thus prevent a cornering of the market by a group which may be able to gain control of one particular grade of a commodity. Because of weather conditions or other factors, the supply of one grade may be small. If only that grade were deliverable, an individual or group that bought up the limited supply could refuse to sell except at very high prices—prices which would be far out of line with prices of other grades. This would force the shorts in the futures market either to buy back their contracts or pay an exorbitant price for the particular deliverable grade (which might be monopolized) for delivery against their short sales. In either event, the "shorts would be in a squeeze" and the price of futures would rise sharply. To prevent such a short squeeze and a possible corner on the market, the seller is allowed the option of delivering other specified grades. These other grades, however, must be limited to those which are commercially desirable. Otherwise, the contract would be useless for hedging purposes. As long as the trade knows that only desirable grades are deliverable, the price of futures will normally move up and down with the spot market. If undesirable qualities could be delivered, price movements in futures would not be governed by the usual commercial market, but by the depressed prices of the off-grades of the commodity. As it is, the lowest quality of the deliverable grades is the one most likely to be tendered.

The seller therefore usually has the choice of several grades to deliver against the contract. He also has the choice of the exact day within the delivery period on which to deliver the actual commodity. This gives him the necessary time to move his supplies into deliverable position. Were delivery at buyer's option, it is possible that all longs would demand delivery on the first day, again allowing a short squeeze to develop.

Because of the possibility of grades other than the basis grade being delivered, the premiums and discounts at which these deliveries can be made become of great importance. These premiums and discounts are established at a level that is designed to correspond with those existing in the commercial market. Of course, as conditions of supply and demand in the commercial market vary, the price differentials between grades change. Consequently, it becomes necessary for the differentials on futures to be changed by the commodity exchange. When differentials vary from those under the existing contract, the premiums and discounts for delivery on subsequent futures contracts are changed to conform to the new commercial market levels. All exchanges have provisions for changes in the contract to conform to the commercial market or to make other changes deemed necessary. Other than possible changes for grade differentials, the salient terms of a contract may not be changed during its life.

Provisions Made For Deliveries

The contract calls for delivery within a certain month (say December): ". . . the delivery within such time to be at the seller's option upon either five, six or seven days notice to the buyer as prescribed by the Trade Rules. . . ." The amount of notice that the seller gives to the buyer varies among the different exchanges. With the exception of the Merchantile Exchanges, at least one day's notice must be given before delivery of the physical commodity is made. "First Notice Day" therefore will be from one to seven business days prior to the actual delivery month (except for sugar). The exact calendar day will vary from month to month and one must check to see exactly when first notice day occurs. From first notice day onward, any trader who is long the near month (which now becomes known as the "spot month") is liable to receive a notice that the actual commodity will be delivered to him.

If a trader who is long accepts delivery, he must pay the full value of the contract (not just the margin of about 10%). He must arrange for warehousing if he wishes to store the commodity, or for transportation if he wishes to utilize it, or find a buyer if he does not. This obviously presents difficulties that can prove to be both time-consuming and expensive. Unless there are some special circumstances prevailing, a speculator would be well advised to avoid taking delivery. If a trader finds it necessary to remain "long" after first notice day, prior instructions should be left with his broker to sell and pass the notice if it is received and if it is possible. This is possible on most exchanges, but to do so the long position must be liquidated within a matter of minutes. The notice is then passed on to the new buyer.

At times, the notice may be received too late in the trading session for it to be passed on. This is generally true for grains. In that event, the trader has no choice but to accept the notice. He can then resell (and redeliver) at the next trading session. This also involves new problems and expenses. On most exchanges the resale transaction involves an extra commission. The trader is also responsible for storage costs for at least one day and, under some circumstances, a full month.

For some commodities reinspection may be necessary to see that the product is still of deliverable grade. The cost of the reinspection must be paid and the commodity may fail to pass for redelivery. In that case, the trader may find himself the unwilling owner of (let's say) a carload of potatoes which he must then sell in the cash market at a discount.

Advice To Traders — Liquidate Before First Notice Day

Strange as it may seem, shorts may, under certain conditions on some exchanges, find themselves the unwilling owners of the actual commodity, also. When a short covers his position, he may find he has bought from a long who hands him a notice, and if there is not sufficient time to pass the notice as provided in the rules, the short may be forced to hold the notice overnight, and have the same risks and added expenses as the long in the previous paragraph.

It is highly recommended to non-trade accounts that all positions be liquidated before first notice day, thus avoiding all possible expenses and difficulties attendant upon deliveries. Customers who are not prepared to accept delivery should not trade in the spot month. There are more than ample trading opportunities in other delivery positions which generally offer the same profit possibilities without the potential added problems.

The last *trading* day is the last day in which open positions can be liquidated by buying and selling. The last *tender* day is the last day to issue notice of intention to deliver. On some exchanges, the last trading day and the last tender day are the same day, so that at the end of the day all shorts have either covered their positions or tendered notices, and all the longs have either liquidated their positions or accepted the notices of delivery. All that remains then is for the actual documents of ownership to be delivered for cash. On some exchanges, for example, the Chicago Board of Trade, New York Produce and New York Mercantile, the last trading day occurs before the last tender day. Therefore, anyone who has not liquidated his position before the cessation of trading, will have to make or take delivery as the case may be.

CHAPTER 6.

THE CLEARING HOUSE

Each commodity exchange has its own clearing association. It is an important adjunct to the smooth flow of commodity futures transactions, as follows:

a) A trader can liquidate his contract whenever he wishes, without the necessity of obtaining the agreement of the other party to his contract.

b) The actual delivery of the commodity against the sale of a futures contract is simplified.

c) The fulfillment in accordance with the rules of all contract obligations to a clearing member is assured even if one party to a contract has become bankrupt or otherwise defaults.

Those who have bought seats on an exchange are not automatically clearing house members. Owning a seat on the exchange entitles a person to trade on the exchange floor and pay less than non-member commission rates. They must still, however, deal ("clear their contracts") through a clearing house member. A clearing house member pays no commission except the clearance fees and floor brokerage fees if he uses an independent floor broker. To become a member of the clearing house, rigid financial and other qualifications must be met. One of these is having an office within a short distance of the exchange so that margins, delivery notices, etc. can be quickly handled.

At the end of a trading session, the floor brokers exchange slips confirming their transactions. These slips then go to the commission houses or brokerage firms who are members of the clearing house and for whose account these transactions were made. Each such clearing-member firm then makes up a tally sheet and files its report with the clearing house. Once these transactions are checked to see that they agree with the trading recorded in the ring, an important change is made. *The clearing house substitutes itself as the "other party" in all trades.* Thus, the clearing house becomes the buyer from everyone who has sold a contract and the clearing house also becomes the seller to everyone who has purchased a contract. Once the trades are completed in the ring and accepted by the clearing house, the buyers and sellers deal directly with the clearing house in regard to any specific contract and not with each other. Under this procedure, an individual trader who has bought a contract through the regular brokerage house procedure can liquidate his contract at his discretion. He need not wait until the other party to his contract decides that he also wishes to liquidate. He can sell out to *anyone* through the regular trading procedure. This liquidates his position. Since the clearing house will become the purchaser of his sale (liquidation), and had been substituted previously as the seller in his earlier purchase, the trader's obligations are fulfilled through his broker. He has bought from the clearing house and sold to the clearing house, thus liquidating his position. The difference between his purchase and selling price is his profit or loss, not including commission expense.

How Deliveries Against Contracts Are Simplified By The Clearing House

The actual delivery of the commodity against the sale of a futures contract is simplified by the use of a clearing house. Suppose Mr. A has sold a March contract to Mr. B, who subsequently resells to Mr. C, who later resells to Mr. D, who resells to Mr. E, etc.

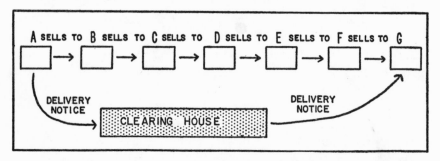

When first notice day on the March contract arrives, Mr. A issues a notice of his intention to deliver the actual commodity. Instead of this notice having to be passed to Mr. B, who sends it on to Mr. C, etc., it is given to the clearing house who has been substituted as the buyer in Mr. A's contract. The clearing house consults its records and passes on the notice of delivery directly to the clearing firm or individual who is still long the March contract, thus eliminating all the intermediaries. Mr. G who receives the notice can (as explained previously) sell out his long position and pass on the notice, or he can choose to accept delivery.

Messrs. B, C, D, E, and F, who had both bought and then resold their contracts, are not involved since their purchase and sale had eliminated each of them from the market previously.

Delivery notices are apportioned by the clearing house in three different ways depending upon the exchange. First, as is the case with potatoes on the New York Mercantile Exchange, the holder of the oldest long position on the books will receive the notice. All subsequent notices are in turn given to the holder of the then existing oldest long position. The second method is for the clearing house to apportion the notices according to the percentage of the gross long position in the delivery month held by the various clearing firms; the firm holding the largest long position receives the most notices, etc. The third method is by *net* long position of each clearing member.

The Financial Strength Of The Clearing House

The clearing house guarantees performance of all contracts under the exchange rules. The financial strength of all of its members can be mobilized for this purpose. The clearing house requires an original margin deposit on the net long and short position of each member. In addition, each day, variation margin must be sent by each member to the clearing house on each net contract outstanding on which there has been a loss for that day. (*Note:* this would be the brokerage house, not the individual customer.) For example, if a commodity price had advanced 15 points during the day's trading, all those who had sold or were net short that commodity previously, would have to deposit additional margin equal to that 15 points with the clearing house. In addition to the original and variation margins, protection against failure of a member is provided by a Guarantee Fund to which each member must contribute and which the clearing house keeps as a reserve. Finally, most commodity exchanges charge clearance fees and the surplus from these fees, over the expenses of running the clearing house, can also be utilized. In summary, in the event of financial failure of a member who cannot fulfill his contracts, the following procedure for protection would be generally followed:

1) All contracts held by the member would be liquidated.
2) If, as a result of this liquidation, his account with the clearing house is in deficit, his margin deposits would be used to cover the deficit.
3) If this were not sufficient, his contribution to the Guarantee Fund would be utilized.
4) If still in deficit, the surplus fund would then be used.
5) If necessary, final recourse could be had to the contribution of all members in the Guarantee Fund.

Since the inauguration of modern commodity clearing associations, it has never been necessary to resort to the various funds other than the margins deposited, but they are always available in the unlikely event they should ever be needed.

Should an individual trader who is an account of a brokerage house be unable to fulfill his obligation and be in default of funds, that particular brokerage house must make good that loss with its own money. That is why the brokerage houses insist that margin calls, when necessary, are promptly met. It is also the reason that the margin agreements signed by the individual trader give the brokerage house the right to liquidate the position of its customer, in the event that margin calls are not promptly met.

CHAPTER 7.

THE COMMODITY EXCHANGE AUTHORITY

Just as the Securities and Exchange Commission is organized to supervise trading in stocks and bonds, the CEA is organized to supervise and regulate trading in certain commodities, under the Commodity Exchange Act. This supervision now covers all domestically produced agricultural commodities traded on organized exchanges, with the exception of hides. The act does not cover imported commodities, coffee, cocoa, sugar, rubber or metals, since the Authority could not regulate activities in countries outside the United States and its territories.

The object of the act is to maintain fair and honest practices in futures markets. The exchanges are self-managed institutions. No federal official sits on the governing board, nor does the federal government write rules and regulations.

The major functions of the Commodity Exchange Authority as authorized by the act include:

1) Licensing of Futures Exchanges,
2) Registration of all brokers and commission merchants,
3) Audits of commodity brokerage firms,
4) Surveillance of trading, investigation and compliance activities,
5) Regulating the total position that may be held by any one speculator,
6) Make public certain market analysis, surveys and market information reports.

Through these functions the CEA works to prevent the unlawful practices of:

1) Price manipulation and market corners;
2) The dissemination of false and misleading crop and market information, which can affect prices;
3) Fraud, cheating and manipulation practices such as false records of trades, deception with regard to execution of an order, or the offsetting of an order by brokers without proper execution on an exchange;
4) Improper brokerage practices and misuse of customers' funds for the broker's own business.

Before an exchange will be licensed for futures trading in regulated commodities, the exchange rules must provide for the prevention of malpractices. The exchange must keep written records of all transactions, as well as minutes of meetings, etc. These records, as well as all books and records of the exchange itself, must be kept at least three years and are subject to inspection by an agent of the U.S. Department of Agriculture or the Department of Justice.

The active exchanges and commodities subject to regulation under the act are:

ACTIVE MARKET	REGULATED COMMODITIES
Chicago Board of Trade	Wheat, corn, oats, rye, soybeans, cotton, cottonseed oil, soybean oil, grain sorghums, soybean meal, cattle
Chicago Mercantile Exchange	Broilers, eggs, potatoes, turkeys, hogs, pork bellies, cattle
Chicago Open Board of Trade	Wheat, corn, oats, rye, soybeans
Kansas City Board of Trade	Wheat, corn, bran, shorts, middlings, grain sorghums, cattle
Minneapolis Grain Exchange	Wheat, oats, rye, soybeans, flaxseed
New York Cotton Exchange (and Wool Associates of)	Cotton, wool, wool tops
New York Mercantile Exchange	Potatoes
New York Produce Exchange	Cottonseed oil, soybean oil

How The CEA Regulates Commodity Trading

In addition to licensing exchanges, the CEA requires all brokers or commission merchants soliciting business for regulated futures trading to register with the agency. The CEA also audits the books of all registered brokerage firms to insure that no fraud or deceit has been practiced, no false trades recorded, no speculative positions in excess of allowable limits have been incurred, and that customers' funds have been segregated from those of the brokerage house and given "trust fund" treatment.

The latter point receives particular attention. These funds cannot be used by the broker for his own business purposes. They must be kept in a separate account, and deposited under specified rules and limits. This insures that they will be kept available for their primary purpose, and not misused.

The CEA has established limits as to the maximum number of contracts of a particular commodity, long or short, that can be held by speculative accounts in either any single delivery month, or in all months combined. These limits vary with each commodity, and are kept small enough to prevent a corner on the market.

A system for reporting positions to the CEA is in effect for purposes of market surveillance and investigations. The exchange clearing members file daily reports showing their trading and open positions; and in addition must report the name, address and occupation of any customer, hedger or speculator, whose position in a particular delivery month reaches a specified size. Thereafter, the clearing member must make a daily report on that position until it is reduced below the reportable status; meanwhile, the customer must file reports showing all his positions in that commodity on all markets for all delivery months.

COMMODITY FUTURES CONTRACTS TRADED 1969-1973

Jul 1 - June 30	Per Contract	1972-73	1971-72	1970-71	1969-70	1968-69
*Corn	5,000 bu	3,481,001	1,549,987	2,734,435	1,270,576	1,706,577
Iced Broilers	28,000 lbs	141,483	29,002	76,216	138,583	16,590
*Live Choice Steers	40,000 lbs	- - -	11	367	25,309	46,068
*Oats	5,000 bu	73,264	37,542	76,482	104,101	136,864
Plywood	69,120 sq ft	274,533	146,914	180,296	15,098	- - -
*Rye	5,000 bu	- - -	- - -	208	10,802	26,892
Silver	5,000 ozs	1,237,642	633,641	469,752	103,929	- - -
*Soybean Meal	100 tons	723,404	485,789	634,184	717,504	405,644
*Soybean Oil	60,000 lbs	1,636,845	1,365,595	1,464,212	1,672,031	426,416
*Soybeans	5,000 bu	3,649,635	3,890,354	2,652,911	1,271,613	932,815
*Wheat	5,000 bu	1,335,775	514,566	582,359	540,827	1,119,659
Stud Lumber		6,018				
CHICAGO BOARD OF TRADE		12,559,600	8,653,401	8,871,422	5,870,373	4,817,525
*Corn	5,000 bu	56,072	7,431	13,832	9,321	10,506
*Oats	5,000 bu	3,357	1,593	511	3,125	5,729
*Rye	5,000 bu	- - -	- - -	3	404	258
Silver	5,000 ozs	114,636	71,128	35,286	5,535	3,939
*Soybeans	5,000 bu	79,185	70,022	33,282	15,454	9,936
U.S. Silver Coins	$5,000	128,133	10,407	- - -	- - -	- - -
*Wheat	5,000 bu	47,082	7,088	9,591	18,604	29,489
MIDAMERICA COMM.EX.		428,465	167,669	92,505	52,443	59,857
*Corn	5,000 bu	- - -	- - -	- - -	3	57
*Grain Sorghums	280,000 lbs	2	40	433	791	2,247
*Wheat	5,000 bu	402,163	129,871	201,309	141,443	171,373
KANSAS CITY BOARD OF TRADE		402,165	129,911	201,742	142,237	173,677
*Corn	5,000 bu	- - -	30	36	- - -	- - -
*Oats	5,000 bu	- - -	- - -	4	- - -	- - -
*Pork Bellies, Fzn	36,000 lbs	- - -	4,574	1,057	- - -	- - -
*Rye	5,000 bu	- - -	- - -	- - -	- - -	34
*Wheat	5,000 bu	167,472	55,393	53,765	41,882	65,510
MINNEAPOLIS GRAIN EXCHANGE		167,472	59,997	54,862	41,882	65,544
*Butter	40,000 lbs	- - -	- - -	- - -	4	9
*Fresh Eggs	22,500 doz	652,541	374,248	523,863	629,471	256,712
*Frozen Beef	36,000 lbs	- - -	- - -	648	1,064	- - -
*Frozen Eggs	36,000 lbs	61	30	5	58	2,058
*Grain Sorghums	400,000 lbs	1,367	5,682	3,511	- - -	- - -
*Hams, Fzn, Sknd	36,000 lbs	- - -	77	156	493	193
*Idaho Potatoes	50,000 lbs	6,314	7,250	32,725	90,246	88,347
*Live Cattle-Midwest	40,000 lbs	2,105,272	961,314	605,717	860,982	609,621
*Live Feeder Cattle	42,000 lbs	15,522	3,501	- - -	- - -	- - -
*Live Hogs	30,000 lbs	791,823	366,378	191,043	119,708	12,744
Lumber	90,000 bd ft	119,476	69,339	132,582	3,661	- - -
*Pork Bellies	36,000 lbs	1,639,199	2,038,653	1,525,755	2,287,172	1,658,073
Turkeys, Tom	30,000 lbs	- - -	- - -	- - -	20	10
British Pound	50,000	30,626	2,929	- - -	- - -	- - -
Canadian Dollar	200,000	43,158	16,749	- - -	- - -	- - -
Deutschemark	500,000	27,937	6,693	- - -	- - -	- - -
Italian Lira	50,000,000	607	110	- - -	- - -	- - -
Japanese Yen	25,000,000	124,930	1,759	- - -	- - -	- - -
Mexican Peso	1,000,000	19,973	66	- - -	- - -	- - -
Swiss Franc	500,000	28,294	3,626	- - -	- - -	- - -
CHIC. MERC. EXCH.		5,607,100	3,858,404	3,016,005	3,992,879	2,627,767

COMMODITY FUTURES CONTRACTS TRADED 1969-1973

Jul 1 - June 30	Per Contract	1972-73	1971-72	1970-71	1969-70	1968-69
Aluminum	50,000 lbs	- - -	- - -	2	- - -	- - -
Apples	840 ctns	- - -	- - -	75	392	- - -
*Butter	30,000 lbs	2				
*Imptd Bneless Beef	30,000 lbs	1,596	1,137	- - -	- - -	- - -
Nickel	2,000 lbs	- - -	- - -	60	323	- - -
*Potatoes-Idaho	50,000 lbs	2	27	- - -	654	- - -
*Potatoes-Maine	50,000 lbs	385,616	152,607	205,694	334,755	478,410
Palladium	100 ozs	1,424	92	233	2,791	23,811
Platinum	50 ozs	152,919	139,186	104,062	103,856	95,890
Plywood	70,000 sq ft	- - -	13,128	524	6,040	- - -
*Shell Eggs	22,500 doz	- - -	- - -	113	- - -	- - -
Silver Coins	10 bags	40,501	25,699	5,214	- - -	- - -
NEW YORK MERCANTILE EXCHANGE		582,058	331,876	315,977	448,811	598,290
*Coconut Oil	60,000 lbs	6,150				
*Shell Eggs	22,500 doz	2,770				
PACIFIC COM. EXCHANGE		8,920				
*Cotton #1	50,000 lbs	- - -	- - -	- - -	- - -	388
*Cotton #2	50,000 lbs	433,638	410,756	165,516	33,000	153,800
*Orange Jce, Fz, Con	15,000 lbs	119,300	132,585	116,879	86,637	179,906
*Wool (Old & New)	6,000 lbs	4,811	3,157	3,756	4,924	7,859
*Wool Top	5,000 lbs	- - -	- - -	40	83	103
Propane	100,000 gal	3,578	681	991	- - -	- - -
Tomato Paste	26,500 lbs	- - -	257	65		
N.Y. COTTON EXCHANGE & ASSOC.		561,327	547,436	287,247	124,644	342,056
*Cottonseed Oil	60,000 lbs	6	- - -	50	- - -	38
Fishmeal	100 tons	10,361	51	311	695	861
Foreign Currency		18,417	24,766	3,026	28	- - -
Pepper	11,200 lbs	- - -	1,733	- - -	5	5
*Pork Bellies	18,000 lbs	- - -	54	- - -	- - -	- - -
INTERNATIONAL COMMERCIAL EXCHANGE		28,784	26,604	3,387	728	904
Cocoa	30,000 lbs					
NEW YORK COCOA EXCHANGE		389,956	210,433	280,336	337,040	475,760
Coffee "C"	37,500 lbs	19,980	94	175	- - -	- - -
Coffee "U"	32,500 lbs	- - -	- - -	1	5	137
Molasses	40,000 gal	- - -	- - -	- - -	445	- - -
Sugar #8 World	112,000 lbs	- - -	- - -	76,105	442,383	564,227
Sugar #10	112,000 lbs	22,049	15,791	7,132	15,044	9,499
Sugar #11	112,000 lbs	1,018,591	652,344	286,644	1,710	- - -
NEW YORK COFFEE & SUGAR EXCH.		1,060,620	668,229	370,057	459,587	573,863
Copper	25,000 lbs	434,847	216,008	227,824	138,201	36,486
*Hides	40,000 lbs	- - -	- - -	- - -	70	680
Lead	60,000 lbs	- - -	- - -	18	56	233
Mercury	10 flasks	87	97	550	539	1,952
Propane	100,000 gal	- - -	1	800	520	1,624
Rubber	22,400 lbs	- - -	- - -	- - -	40	53
Silver	10,000 ozs	1,090,679	619,269	682,065	667,236	533,380
Tin	11,200 lbs	- - -	2	37	103	254
Zinc	60,000 lbs	- - -	- - -	- - -	29	129
COMMODITY EXCHANGE, INC.		1,525,613	835,377	911,294	806,794	574,791
Cocoa	15,000 lbs	3,929	6,828	3,719	- - -	- - -
Coffee		1,982				
Copper	25,000 lbs	5,118	5,545	2,103	- - -	- - -
Diamonds	20 carats	2,678	896	- - -	- - -	- - -
Gold	200 ozs	- - -	475	- - -	- - -	- - -
Silver	5,000 ozs	118,603	54,338	28,193	- - -	- - -
Silver Coins	$5,000	- - -	493	391	- - -	- - -
Sugar	56,000 lbs	52,015	24,748	3,856	- - -	- - -
WEST COAST COMMODITY EXCHANGE		182,343	93,323	38,262	- - -	- - -
TOTAL ALL FUTURES CONTRACTS		23,504,598	15,582,660	14,443,096	12,277,418	10,310,034
CHANGE FROM PREVIOUS YEAR		+50.83%	+7.89%	+17.64%	+19.08%	+17.20%

NOTE: Above figures are in terms of full contract units. The number of trades (buys plus sells) are twice the above figures and also should be increased by an allowance for job lots.

 * Asterisks denote futures contracts trading regulated by the C.E.A. Association Bulletin 1124.

 Source: Association of Commodity Exchange Firms, Inc.

VOLUME OF FUTURES TRADING
FISCAL YEARS TOTAL 1942-1943 — 1971-72

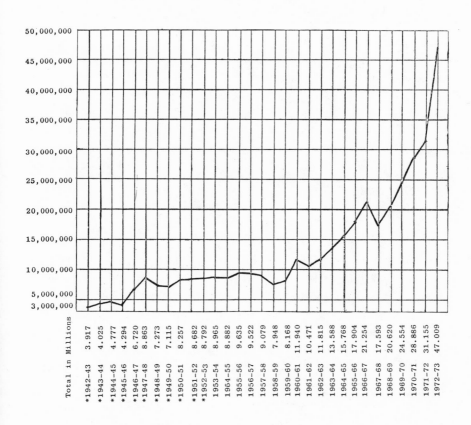

Number of Trades (buys plus sells) (i.e. Number of full contracts traded times two).
* Figures for 1942-43 through 1952-53 represent only CEA regulated commodities.
Source: Association of Commodity Exchange Firms, Inc.

The enclosed chart indicates the rapid expansion of commodity futures trading in the past ten years. Trading volume grew only modestly in the first fifteen years following World War II. The U.S. public was rediscovering the stock market in those years. Securities markets had been anathemas since the 1929 collapse. Now a new generation was looking to the speculative potentials. In the years to 1960, the public learned to trade first in common stocks, then into more sophisticated procedures such as new issues, convertible bonds and warrants. The years of experience and prosperity developed a major pool of sophisticated speculators familiar with trading techniques who also had risk capital and the desire for leverage opportunities well beyond those offered in the securities markets. The result was an explosive growth of commodity futures trading. This growth, as with securities markets, should continue as long as prosperity continues to generate sufficient income to provide for continuous availability of risk capital. Percentagewise, the growth of futures trading volume should exceed that of the securities markets.

CHAPTER 8.

SOURCES OF COMMODITY INFORMATION

Surprisingly little background information is necessary for successful trading in commodity futures. There is no need to be a farmer or other specialist. Most traders would probably not recognize a kernel of wheat if they saw one.

Price movements, after all, result from *changes* or *expectation of changes* in current conditions. A grasp of the current picture of "supply and demand" therefore is the starting point for successful trading. In this respect, 1) prospective crops; 2) carryover stocks; 3) domestic use; 4) exports and imports; are a basic beginning. These statistics are easily obtainable. All brokerage houses which deal extensively in commodity futures will watch for these reports and keep them on file along with comparison figures for previous years.

Government Reports

The U.S. Department of Agriculture issues periodic reports and estimates of all statistics affecting commodity prices. The dates for the issuance of these reports are listed well in advance, so that all who are interested can be alert to their release. The markets are particularly responsive to crop reports during the growing seasons. *Nobody can obtain the crop reports in advance.* Special governmental precautions are taken to insure this. Before a government crop estimate is released, the sealed reports from the County Agents throughout the country are assembled. The building in which these individual reports are to be opened and compiled into a single estimate, is then sealed off. All communications are cut. Nobody can leave the building. Communications are reestablished only after the report is officially released to the waiting press.

In addition to these releases, the Department of Agriculture also publishes a host of weekly, monthly, bi-monthly and quarterly bulletins on the various commodities. The most important of these are listed below.

WEEKLY GRAIN MARKET NEWS—An excellent little bulletin listing weekly price changes, CCC sales, stocks and exports. Comparisons with previous years are also shown. In addition, all crop estimates, loan entries, domestic consumption and export figures are released. If a person had time to study only one report on grains, this would be a good choice; nor would it take much time. Only a few minutes spent examining these figures will tell one whether prices, stocks, etc. are rising or falling; also how they compare with the preceding year. These figures are current.

THE "SITUATION" REPORTS — Most of these are issued monthly during the most important part of each season, and bi-monthly or quarterly thereafter. They are magazines containing extensive reviews of major price-making influences, and will give opinions as to probable price movements, domestic use, exports, etc., as well as the statistics upon which these estimates are based. A representative list of these follows:

The Demand and Price Situation	The Cotton Situation
The Wheat Situation	The Poultry and Egg Situation
The Feed Situation	The Vegetable Situation
The Fats and Oils Situation	The Farm Income Situation
The Wool Situation	The Livestock and Meat Situation

FOREIGN AGRICULTURE BULLETIN — These reports cover world production, trade, and price prospects, emphasizing foreign output and its relation to world market conditions. They are particularly important for such commodities as coffee, cocoa and sugar. American embassies in the major producing centers make their own surveys of crop and demand prospects. These are then gathered and published by our Department of Agriculture. Many times, these estimates conflict with the estimates officially released by the producing countries themselves, but have proven to be quite accurate in most cases.

The Futures Exchange Daily, Weekly and Monthly Sheets

The futures exchanges, themselves, are major sources of information concerning the commodities traded there. All major exchanges issue statistical information. Some are extremely thorough. The Kansas City Board of Trade's daily newspaper covers grain conditions, news and relevant statistics very completely. The Cocoa Exchange sheet gives complete coverage on exports from major centers; cocoa loading or afloat to the U.S.; daily, monthly and annual arrivals; licensed warehouse stocks; and major news items. These are published daily, are current, and shown in comparison with previous years. The N.Y. Coffee & Sugar Exchange also has fairly complete coverage.

Newspapers

One of the best overall sources of daily information on all commodities is the *New York Journal of Commerce*. It has a specific section devoted to futures trading, daily price tables and individual stories on each commodity. These are indexed on Page 1. In addition, it covers all the major business and financial news which can affect all commodity prices. Periodically, there are whole sections of the newspaper devoted to specific industries and commodities, as well as supply and demand studies. Its purchasing guide carries excellent reviews of the supply, stocks on hand, and prospective levels of demand for each commodity, as well as a conclusion regarding probable price trends.

Other newspapers, such as *The New York Times* and *Wall Street Journal,* also contain daily commodity market comments and reports which are very helpful. There are trade journals for many of the commodities which provide information on individual markets.

"Services" and Commodity Research Organizations

There are a number of commodity advisory services or publications. Some offer comprehensive price analyses, complete with statistics and charts. Others merely give buy and sell recommendations. The largest and best-known of the services is the weekly FUTURES MARKET SERVICE published by Commodity Research Bureau, Inc. This organization also publishes the annual Commodity Year Book series which presents important data and statistics on more than 110 basic commodities as well as up-to-date research studies on forecasting price movements.

The Brokerage Houses

The partial listing above should indicate that there is no dearth of reliable commodity information available to those who wish to engage in commodity trading. The amount of time required to maintain a working knowledge of the basic statistical information is not great. Once the background figures are obtained, it only takes a little time each day to keep abreast of developments in any particular commodity. The customers' representative in the brokerage house reports significant changes in the commodity market picture to the customer. (This parallels the standard stock trading procedure where customers' representatives watch for and report developments in specific stocks and make recommendations.) The final responsibility and decision relative to entering into a transaction must always be that of the individual trader.

Most of the brokerage houses that do any significant amount of commodity business have a commodity research section, which issues periodic bulletins outlining the various important market influences.

CHAPTER 9.

PRICE MAKING INFLUENCES — HOW TO ANALYZE THEM PROFITABLY

In addition to the changes in supply and demand as shown by statistical information, commodity futures prices are affected by more general considerations. Of prime importance are the following:

Changes In Government Agricultural Policy

With the government determining acreage allotments, marketing quotas, subsidies, loan levels, export programs, certain selling prices, etc., it has become a major, if not *the* most important, factor in determining (within broad limits) the selling prices of commodities.

A comprehensive review of government programs now in force comprises a later chapter of this text. With this section as background (and an ever-ready reference source), the importance and meaning of any proposed changes should not prove difficult. On the other hand, such changes will probably be of major importance to prices.

International News

Commodity prices are very sensitive to news concerning the prospects of war or peace. This is particularly true of the imported commodities: sugar, wool, copper, lead, zinc, rubber, and (to some extent) coffee and cocoa. The prospect of war leads to hoarding, a greater demand for raw commodities for defense and stockpiling purposes, and the possibility that imports will be cut off (or at least curtailed) through either lack of available shipping space or blockade. The result is a general rush by consumers and manufacturers to get supplies quickly in order to build their inventories. The increase in demand soon causes the price level to advance.

The sequence of events for domestically produced commodities which are dependent to a large extent upon export markets is not the same. While an actual war will eventually stimulate a sharp upward price movement, the initial effect can be the reverse. The prospect of a loss of major export markets can temporarily, at least, depress prices.

A revolt or civil war in a major producing country will, of course, also cause prices for that commodity to rise because the prospects of curtailed production and interruptions of shipment are great. Again there will probably be aggressive bidding for available supplies, and a resultant higher price level.

Weather Developments

Perhaps this should not properly be included as a separate factor, since its results would show up in production estimates. Still, it is important enough to consider alone. The primary effect of weather conditions takes place during the growing season, since it affects crop yields and quality. A drought, of course, results in a decline in crop prospects. Dust storms blow away the top soil and seed, as well as cut the stalks and stems of growing crops. These are fairly obvious. What might not be so obvious, however, is the fact that weather conditions outside our borders may also prove to be an important price making influence in our markets. For example, the European winter of 1956 was for a period of time quite severe, damaging the wheat crop in France and killing a considerable number of olive trees in Spain, Italy and Portugal. The result was an increase in our wheat exports and the demand from Spain and Italy for our vegetable oils jumped sharply. The world is now basically one market area, and developments in any part of it can have widespread repercussions.

Devaluation Of Money

When a nation imports much more than it exports, the value of its money in international trade declines. This outcome develops because that nation is under special pressure to obtain foreign moneys to pay for its imports. For example, a Brazilian importer of U.S. wheat must pay the U.S. exporter in dollars. Although this is done through a complicated banking procedure, it simply comes down to the Brazilian buying dollars (for his cruzeiros) to send to the U.S. exporter. Dollars are earned in Brazil through her exports to the U.S. If the value of Brazilian imports is larger than exports, there will be a greater demand for dollars than the available supply. As each Brazilian importer tries to compete with others to get the dollars to pay for his imports, the price of dollars goes up. He will have to pay, let us say, 1,500 cruzeiros for each dollar rather than 750. This is an extreme hypothetical example, but shows that as the need for and price of dollars goes up, the value of the cruzeiro goes down. Conversely, a dollar could then buy twice as many cruzeiros (1,500 instead of 750), or twice as large a quantity of commodities exported from Brazil. In other words, as the price of the cruzeiro is cut in half (devalued), so is the dollar price of Brazilian export commodities such as cocoa or coffee.

Let us see how that happens. Naturally, Brazilian exporters selling cocoa or coffee want to get paid in their own money — cruzeiros. Suppose they had been selling coffee for 750 cruzeiros per lb. When they cannot earn enough dollars through their exports to pay for U.S. imports, they must attempt to stimulate exports. Originally an American importer would have had to pay $1.00 to get the 750 cruzeiros to pay for this pound of coffee. Now, with the devaluation outlined above, he would only have to pay half a dollar for this pound of coffee (which is still selling for 750 cruzeiros). Thus, the price of coffee, in dollars, has fallen from $1.00 to 50¢.

If the U.S. ever devalued the dollar it would mean that U.S. importers must pay more dollars for commodities and therefore higher futures prices would be seen in the U.S. Thus one method of hedging against U.S. dollar devaluation might be to be long U.S. futures of imported commodities.

The explanation above is somewhat complex. However it is only necessary to keep in mind that ordinarily, *Devaluation of foreign currency means lower prices for commodities exported to the U.S. and therefore lower futures prices.* It means higher prices within the country whose currency is devalued.

On November 18, 1967, the United Kingdom was forced to devalue the pound sterling by 14.3% from $2.80 down to $2.40. The table below indicates what happened to prices on London futures and in New York futures. We have used prices just before the devaluation and prices just after the devaluation. Contracts are for March, 1968.

Commodity	London		New York	
	Before	After	Before	After
cocoa	247/6	274/6	28.79	28.44
sugar	24.30	26.30	2.63	2.61
wool	97.7	103.	114.0	112.0
copper	478	547	56.95	56.90

As can be seen, the pattern worked out according to the theory. Prices on London futures rallied sharply. Since there had been some prior expectation of the devaluation, there had been some advance buying which had already begun to put futures higher in London. Therefore, in some instances the immediate post-devaluation London price rises did not total the full 14.3%.

In the U.S. prices were only slightly affected but they went down a little. The U.K. is not a major producer of these commodities but they are major consumers and distributors. Their devaluation meant some cut-back in their consumption of these commodities was likely and therefore, greater supplies would be available for other areas.

General Business Conditions

Over the long run, general business conditions play a major role in commodity prices. If we have a supply of a given size during a depression year such as 1932, the price of the commodity would be much lower than the price we could expect if we had the same supply during a good business year such as 1967. However, since each commodity futures transaction will ordinarily be limited to a matter of weeks or months, the overall influence will not be too great. Nevertheless, whether we are in an inflationary or deflationary period must be taken into account.

If economic activity is running at a high rate, if business conditions are good, if unemployment is low, and inflationary tendencies are still intact, a given set of supply and demand conditions will tend to find commodity prices moving upward. However, if business activity is slowing down, if there are tendencies for recessions to develop in various individual industries, if unemployment begins to increase, or if there are fears of a general business setback, the very same supply and demand conditions would lead to the absorption of commodities at a somewhat lower price level.

Since the 1930's the public, the government and the newspapers have become very conscious of general business conditions. The ordinary run of newspaper stories keep the public informed on this topic. More specifically, an indication of general business conditions can be obtained by watching for changes in unemployment, automobile production, construction, and retail sales.

The General Price Level

As to the general price level, there are several figures that receive widespread publicity when issued. The most notable is the Consumer Price Index, more popularly known as the "cost-of-living" index. Another is the Wholesale Price Index issued by the Bureau of Labor Statistics. Of major importance for purposes of futures market analysis, however, are those indices more closely related to the commodities traded on organized exchanges. These are the Farm Price Index, the Dow-Jones Spot and Futures Price Indexes, (The last two are published in the Wall Street Journal), the Reuters Spot Index, and the Commodity Research Bureau Futures Price Index.

Seasonal Price Patterns

In addition to the general trend of prices, each commodity usually follows a certain price pattern of its own during the various seasons of the year. In farm crops for example, the period during the harvest movement is ordinarily one of declining prices. Consumers delay buying, reducing demand, waiting for the anticipated flood of new crop offers. On the other hand, farmers must sell at least part of their crops immediately to get enough cash to pay for the added farm labor and machinery hired for the harvest, to pay off loans which usually fall due around harvest time, and for other expenses. Thus supply offered on the market tends to be heaviest during the harvest and the early post-harvest period. We thus have a combination of decreased demand and heavy supplies. This usually tends to depress prices around harvest time every year. Once the harvest movement has passed and the crops not to be sold immediately are moved into storage, a resurgent demand tends to raise prices until this demand is temporarily fulfilled. Thereafter, price variations depend upon the factors previously listed: i.e., size of crops, stocks on hand, the level of domestic demand, exports, imports and various news events.

A General Method Of Price Analysis

Commodity traders use many techniques to determine whether or not to buy or sell specific commodities. Some are said to depend upon the phases of the moon or sun-spot activity, but most traders use methods that fall into two general categories. One is the analysis of supply and demand conditions known as "trading on the fundamentals." The second is chart trading. The latter technique is extensively treated in another section of the text. We shall here concentrate on the "fundamental" approach.

Actually, that entire approach has been developed throughout this chapter. What remains to be done is to summarize the factors to be watched and establish an itemized check list for easy reference.

1) Determine the general climate of business conditions. Are we in a recessionary or inflationary period? Is unemployment rising or falling? How are retail sales holding up?

2) Check the trend of commodity prices. Are the indexes mentioned earlier in the chapter rising or falling?

By thus appraising the general economic context, you can determine whether the price of the commodity in which you are interested will be moving with an upward or downward bias.

Following this general appraisal there are specific things to determine for each commodity.

1) Is the price level of the specific commodity higher or lower than a year ago? Is it rising or falling?

2) What is the seasonal pattern of prices for this commodity? (This is discussed more fully in the next chapter.) When does the

high and low usually occur? Have prices been following the seasonal pattern in the past few months or have they been moving counter-seasonally?

3) What about the government loan level (if any)? What is the exact dollar and cents price? Is it higher, or lower than last season? (An ensuing section will deal with this in detail.)

4) Are there any other forms of government support, direct or indirect? Is this commodity helped by government export subsidies?

5) What are the figures on U.S. production and stocks, relative to a year ago?

6) What are demand prospects domestically — better or worse than last year? Check the number of animal units if it is a feed grain, or the level of demand for the major industry in which the commodity is a raw material. (For example, check the supply and demand prospects for shoes if you are attempting to forecast the price of hides.)

7) Is production outside the U.S. better than a year ago? Where —in normally importing or exporting countries? How do export prospects look?

8) Is the production of competitive products larger or smaller than the previous season?

9) News events.

Certain news events profoundly affect price prospects for a particular commodity. While some tend to come as a surprise, others develop over a period of time, with attendant heavy publicity. Appropriate market positions can be taken to meet the situation. Changes in government agricultural policy, political crises in major producing countries, and devaluation of currency are recurrent factors of special significance.

The above check list should help the trader determine whether supply and demand conditions warrant higher or lower prices than the previous year, around what price levels government or other support should develop, and during which months prices can be expected to rise and fall. It will also help indicate whether the general economic situation is likely to help push prices higher or act as a price depressing influence.

CHAPTER 10

SEASONAL PRICE TRENDS, SPECIAL CHARACTERISTICS & FACTS ABOUT THE INDIVIDUAL COMMODITIES

Successful trading can be aided by: (1) knowing current conditions in a commodity, (2) knowing what changes to look for, (3) knowing how to interpret major news items, (4) and, as will be explained later, the proper handling of one's position in the futures market.

Nevertheless, most traders need some background information on each commodity: where it is produced, how important U. S. production is compared with world output, how important are exports and imports, what the major uses are, the price level at which little or no competition from other commodities may be expected, and any unique characteristics the individual markets might have. Such knowledge is valuable in interpreting news items. The more important aspects of this information are detailed below.

Seasonal Price Patterns

The seasonal price pattern of some commodities is one of the most important factors to be considered in attempting to forecast price movements. As mentioned earlier in the text, because of the peculiarities of production and marketing, each calendar year most commodities repeatedly tend to have the same periods of rising prices as well as periods of declining prices. While there are exceptions, knowing the usual pattern is of great assistance in determining whether or not a futures market position should be established.

The table of seasonal highs and lows which follows is a composite of a number of studies. It deals with spot commodity prices. The price of futures contracts will, ordinarily, closely follow the trend of spot commodities. However, remember that there are premiums and discounts between the different delivery months and that these, to some degree, can anticipate changes in spot prices. This is particularly true of new crop months. That is, a tight supply situation in the final months of a crop year can cause the near months (still old crop) to advance sharply while the more distant months (new crop) will advance only moderately, if at all. This anticipates the increase in supply to be available at harvest time. In choosing the futures month in which to trade, the seasonal pattern of prices should be studied, but the choice of the par-

Seasonal Pattern of Spot Commodity Prices[1]

COMMODITY	HIGH	LOW
Barley	May	June
Broilers	July	December
Cattle	April	November
Cocoa	December-January	September
	May	March
*Coffee	January-February	April, November (double bottom)
Corn	August	November-December
Cotton	July	October-December
*Cottonseed Meal	March	December
*Cottonseed Oil	June	October
Eggs	November	March-April
Flaxseed	May	October-November
Hides	August, October	March
Hogs	June	November
Oats	**(January) May	August
Pork Bellies	July	November
Potatoes	June-July	October
Propane	February	June
Rye	February	July-August
Soybeans	**(January) April	June, October (double bottom)
Soybean Oil	July	October
*Soybean Meal	April	December
*Sugar (World)	September	March
Wheat	**January, May	August-September
Wool	December	June

[1]Some commodities such as the metals do not have clearly defined seasonal price patterns.
*More than the usual number of exceptions to the seasonal pattern.
**These grains have often been subject to sharp reactions in February (known as the February break) after which a good rally sometimes has occurred.

ticular month in which a position is established can have a real bearing on the ultimate profitability of the transaction.

With this in mind, several studies have been made of the results of trading in particular futures months with a view towards choosing a particular day on which to establish positions. The Commodity Research Bureau, Inc. (in its weekly "Futures Market Service") periodically issues such studies for grains. In one such report the May contract for each grain was studied for a series of years. A particular day was selected upon which positions were theoretically instituted. The results were then calculated for each season. The wheat study of July 27, 1962, will indicate the methods used. We have added data for more recent years.

"The following data analyze a seasonal tendency in price movements of the May wheat delivery that occurs with a high degree of consistency. It shows that:

1. May wheat prices rose at some time after the beginning of August in each of the past 19 seasons.

2. The May delivery experienced a net gain from about the beginning of August to the following April 1, in 9 out of the 11 seasons studied.

The Seasonal Price Rise After August 1

Marketings of wheat usually reach their seasonal peak in the month of July as the winter wheat harvest draws to a conclusion. A smaller marketing crest occurs in the month of August when a large part of the spring wheat crop is harvested. Prices often establish their seasonal lows during the summer marketing period.

For the purpose of analysis, we selected August 1 (or a day close to it if it fell on a non-trading day) as an approximate period when wheat prices often are near their season's lows. The following table shows the extent of advances after August 1.

May Wheat Delivery (Chicago Board of Trade) 1962-63 to 1969-70

(Cents per bushel)

Season	Aug. 1 Close	High After Aug. 1 Price	High After Aug. 1 Date	Maximum Net Advance	Maximum Percent Advance
1951-52	242⅞	265½	12/10/51	22⅝	9.3
1952-53	244⅛	249⅜	11/12/52	5¼	2.2
1953-54	209⅞	231¼	3/15/54	21⅜	10.2
1954-55	207¼	230¼	12/29/54	23	11.1
1955-56	196¼	240¾	4/20/56	44½	22.7
1956-57	221¼	244½	10/31/56	23¼	10.5
1957-58	215⅝	229⅜	5/20/58	13¾	6.4
1958-59	194¾	212⅜	4/ 3/59	17⅝	9.1
1959-60	197½	211	5/ 2/60	13½	6.8
1960-61	195½	215	2/ 2/61	19½	10.0
1961-62	210¾	217	5/16/62	6¼	3.0
1962-63	220	228⅝	5/21/63	8⅝	3.9
1963-64	180¼	219⅞	1/13/64	39⅝	21.8
1964-65	150¾	157⅞	11/13/64	7⅛	4.7
1965-66	154¼	173	12/14/65	18¾	12.2
1966-67	194⅞	207	9/14/66	12⅛	6.2
1967-68	166	169⅝	8/ 4/67	3⅝	2.1
1968-69	139⅜	142¼	11/18/68	2⅞	2.8
1969-70	133¾	153	4/30/70	19¼	14.4

From the foregoing it can be seen that the maximum net advances from August 1 to the expiration of the contract ranged from 5¼ cents to 44½ cents and averaged 19.2¢ during the past 19 seasons. Maximum percentage advances ranged from 2.1 to 22.7 percent and averaged 9 percent. There is a double peak; once in April/May (7 times) and once in November/December (6 times). There was never a high in June or July.

The Price Gain from August 1 to the Following April 1

In most years under review, prices of the May futures contract have shown a tendency to gain from about August 1 to the following April 1. This can be ascertained from the following table which shows closing prices on August 1, the following April 1, and the net advances in the seasons 1951-52 through 1961-62.

May Wheat Delivery (Chicago Board of Trade)
1951-52 to 1961-62

Season	(Cents per bushel)		Net Advance	Percent Advance
	Aug. 1 Close	April 1 Close		
1951-52	242⅞	250	7⅛	2.9
1952-53	244⅛	223	—21⅛	— 8.7
1953-54	209⅞ 1)	219¾	9⅞	4.7
1954-55	207¼ 2)	211¾	4½	2.2
1955-56	196¼	227½ 3)	31¼	15.9
1956-57	221¼	223½	2¼	1.0
1957-58	215⅝	216⅞	1¼	0.6
1958-59	194¾	210½	15¾	8.1
1959-60	197½ 1)	208¼	10¾	5.4
1960-61	195½	196⅜ 4)	⅞	0.4
1961-62	210¾	207⅞ 3)	— 2⅞	— 1.4
11 Year Avg.	212.3	217.8	5.5	3.0

1) Aug. 3   2) Aug. 2   3) April 2   4) April 3

From the preceding table it can be seen that prices experienced net gains from August 1 to the following April 1, in 9 of the 11 years.
In reviewing this study in 1968, the pattern still held, although, perhaps, April 10 may have proven to be a slightly better mechanical liquidation date.

This type of study has many advantages. It also suffers from several shortcomings which are to be expected with any method that is so mechanical as to pick a particular day on which to establish and liquidate a position every year. Conditions simply are not precisely that similar every year. For example, as shown in the Commodity Research Bureau's table, prices moved counterseasonally in 1952-53 and a serious loss could have occurred had the position been held until the April 1st liquidation date. A study of price movements indicates that at other times the market declined for some time after the purchase date selected before the upward trend began. At still other times, the April 1st liquidation date was either too early or too late.

Nevertheless, the study clearly shows that there is a marked seasonal pattern to wheat price fluctuations, and that at some time during the summer conditions are generally favorable to the establishment of a long term long position. The exact date would depend upon the action of the market. The clue to the exact date for liquidating the position is also to be taken from the action of the market each year. The originators recognize the limitations of this type of study and indicate that the dates should not be followed blindly. Subsequent research may indicate better originating and liquidating dates than those mentioned.

Studies for other commodities indicated that purchases and sales made on the following dates for the May contracts had the following results:

	Theoretical Buying Date	Liquidate	No. of Times Profitable
Cocoa	September 25th	November 30th	13 out of 15 years
	March 15th	May 15th	8 out of 10 years
Cottonseed Oil	September 30th	April 10th	11 out of 11 years
Rye	September 20th	(no liquidation dates given but figures did indicate advances at some time after the initial date.)	
Soybeans	October 1st		
Soybean Meal	October 5th	February 5th	8 out of 11 years
March Wheat	June 15th	January 15th	12 out of 14 years

As with May wheat, these buying and selling dates should not be taken too literally. They should only be considered as guides. Each crop year must be considered individually.

It is interesting to note that the March wheat purchase and sales dates vary somewhat from those of May wheat. The purchase date for March is at the beginning of the harvest while that for May is towards the end. The selling dates show a greater disparity. Nevertheless, if you refer to the seasonal spot price table a few pages back you will note the wheat seasonal highs as "January, May" with a footnote to the effect that this commodity is subject to a February break. March wheat (sell January 15) is apparently more susceptible to this break than the May (sell April 1).

Studies apparently made along similar lines are responsible for one of the legends which is prevalent in commodity circles. The story (which may be true) goes that following the death of a successful commodity trader, a search of his papers revealed a list of dates upon which to buy and sell wheat and corn. These dates are known today as those of:

"The Voice from the Tomb"

They are:

	BUY	SELL
Wheat		January 10th
	February 22nd	
		May 10th
	July 1st	
		September 10th
	November 28th	
---	---	---
Corn	March 1st	
		May 20th
	June 25th	
		August 10th

These dates are still believed to be used by some traders as sign-posts for trading directions.

Grains

By far the most important futures markets (judged by the volume of transactions) are the grain exchanges, particularly the Chicago Board of Trade. While the general use of statistics has been avoided, the following table is the easiest method of indicating concisely the U.S. share in world production, as well as the relative domestic and export use of U.S. produced commodities. The figures were chosen to depict what could be considered a "normal" relationship and are not precise averages for any particular years. Thus the U.S. soybean production figure includes an adjustment for the sharp and rapid expansion of the early 1960's. A precise average would understate the importance of United States production in the world picture.

U. S. Production, Consumption and Exports of Leading Commodities Compared with World Production

(APPROXIMATE AVERAGE FIGURES FOR YEARS PRIOR TO 1971)
(millions omitted)

Commodity	World Production	UNITED STATES Production	Domestic Use	Exports*
Wheat (bu.)	10,000	1,350	700	750
Corn (bu.)	9,000	4,200	3,800	500
Oats (bu.)	3,000	850	875	25
Rye (bu.)	1,200	33	25	5
Flaxseed (bu.)	125	25	21	5
Soybeans (bu.)	1,600	1,100	700	400

* These are not net figures. Imports are not included in the table, and there is an allowance made for long term trends.

Wheat

Wheat production in the United States ordinarily exceeds the one billion bushel mark. Since this is well above the domestic use of about 700-750 million bushels, the U.S. export market and government support programs are of extreme importance as price making influences. Under the support program, the Department of Agriculture has accumulated stocks of this grain. It is prohibited by law from selling these stocks in the domestic market at less than 115% of the current season support price plus "reasonable carrying charges." It must sell at the higher of the market price or the statutory minimum. The government is not required by law to adhere to any minimum price when selling in the export market.

Under the current support program wheat prices in the U.S. should approximate world price levels. They had been kept artificially high by the old style price support schemes. It is important to remember that despite all the various payments the farmer receives under the new support program (discussed in a subsequent chapter) the market price is most influenced by "the loan" level. The free market price should tend to fluctuate around this level unless a serious shortage is created due to a crop failure, or other cause.

The government still exports wheat directly from its stockpile under barter agreements and through relief donations.

The P.L. 480 program is explained in the chapter on price supports. Through it, the United States government makes dollar grants to foreign governments for purchases of U.S. surplus commodities. This has been a major factor contributing to the substantial U.S. wheat exports of recent years.

Wheat is grown in practically all states, but the Great Plains area is the commercial bread basket. Kansas, the largest producer, usually has a crop of winter wheat more than double that of Oklahoma, its nearest rival. Nebraska runs a close third. North Dakota leads the spring wheat states, with Montana and South Dakota second and third, respectively. Harvesting begins in the most southerly areas in May and June and works its way northward through the summer. By Labor Day the harvest is generally almost complete.

Principal competitors of the U.S.A. in the wheat export market are Canada, Argentina and Australia. Because Argentina and Australia are below the equator, their harvest is approximately six months later than that in the U.S. Competition from their offerings in the world market, therefore, is felt most heavily around February.

Winter wheat, which accounts for approximately three quarters of the total U.S. production, is planted, takes root and begins to sprout in the fall. During the winter months, the plants lie dormant, protected by an insulating cover of snow. When spring comes, growth is resumed with the result that the crop is ready for harvesting early in the summer. Actually, the first carload of the new harvest sometimes moves by the end of May. However, the quantity coming to market usually is insignificant at that time. Spring wheat is planted in the spring and is harvested late in the summer.

In addition to the breakdown into winter and spring wheat, this commodity is also classified as soft wheat, hard wheat and durum wheat. Generally speaking, the soft wheat is used for cake flour, the hard wheat for bread and the durum wheat for spaghetti and similar products.

The distinction can prove important, since soft wheat is deliverable against contracts only on the Chicago Board of Trade. The Kansas City and Minneapolis Exchanges only permit delivery of hard wheat varieties against their contracts. Durum wheat is deliverable on the Duluth Exchange. At times, therefore, when the price of Chicago wheat futures may seem low relative to the other exchanges, it is probable that the cause is an overabundance of soft wheat for that crop year.

The crop year for commodities begins with the major harvest movement and runs until the beginning of the next harvest. For wheat, the crop year officially begins July 1st and runs through June 30th of the following year. Thus, the 1971/72 season begins on July 1st, 1971 and continues to June 30th, 1972. The first new crop month on the futures exchange is therefore the July delivery.

The basis grades of the Chicago contract, deliverable at the contract price, include #2 Hard Winter, #2 Red Winter, #2 Yellow Hard Winter and #1 Northern Spring. Other grades are deliverable at specified premiums and discounts. The most common class of wheat tendered on contract at Chicago is #2 Soft Red Winter.

The volume of trade in wheat futures normally is very large with by far the greatest volume of trading on the Chicago Board of Trade. The wheat contracts on the Kansas City Board of Trade and the Minneapolis Grain Exchange are also significant. This commodity has a wide speculative following.

Corn

The United States produces approximately half of the world output of corn. Approximately 70%-80% of this crop is consumed domestically as livestock feed. Most of the corn is consumed directly on the farm where it is grown, with roughly only 30% of the crop moving into commercial channels. The corn price level is an important determinant in the production of hogs. The hog-corn ratio is the number of bushels of corn equivalent in price to a hundred pounds of live hog. If the price of hogs is relatively high while corn prices are low, farmers will feed more of their corn to their hogs and sell their hogs rather than their corn. The price of corn, therefore, is a major determinant of the size of the hog population, and thus of meat and (indirectly) pork belly prices.

As with wheat the government has over the years accumulated a stockpile of corn through defaults on government price support loans. The government must theoretically abide by a minimum selling price in the domestic market equal to 115% of the latest current support price plus carrying charges. There are, however, exceptions to the minimum. The government can sell at the going market price if the commodity is in "danger of deterioration." With this provision, the U.S. Department of Agriculture has sold large quantities of corn in the domestic market. There have been many times when over half the carload arrivals of corn for sale at Chicago were government owned corn.

Government programs in the form of acreage allotments and lower support prices have been ineffective in the past insofar as curbing production is concerned. Attempts to increase usage have taken the form of grants under Public Law 480 and an export subsidy program begun in mid-1958. (See section on Government Support Program.) The latter returned export demand to the free market after years of government monopoly. With only 30% of the crop moving into commercial channels, renewed free market export demand now plays an important part in determining price levels. As of 1959 corn exports can no longer be ignored as a potential market factor.

Corn, like wheat, is very widely grown. Two states, Iowa and Illinois, together produce approximately one-third of the U.S. crop. Other major producers are Minnesota, Indiana, Ohio and Nebraska.

The basis grade for the Chicago futures contract is #2 Yellow Corn but other grades are also deliverable. The grade most frequently tendered is #2 Yellow.

Corn trading volume at times is relatively heavy, although price movements have been restricted in recent years because of government action. The loan level, when effective, tends to limit price declines. On the other hand, frequent sales of government corn "in danger of deterioration" tend to increase supplies and limit price advances.

The corn crop year runs from October 1st to September 30th, with the December delivery the first active new crop month on the futures board. However, in years of an early harvest, some new crop corn may become available for delivery on September contracts.

Oats

The United States produces between 25% and 35% of the world oats crop, and consumes just about all of it domestically. Oats are used primarily as an animal food. They are directly competitive with corn. The feeding value of oats is actually a little less than corn on a pound for pound basis. However, a bushel of oats weighs more than half that of a bushel of corn. Therefore, oats prices should run a little higher than half the price of corn. There is considerable switching back and forth between corn and oats in feed mixes used by farmers and feedlot owners. This reflects price trends. If corn prices are more than twice the price of oats, there is a tendency for the demand for oats to increase. The reverse is true when corn prices are moderately less than twice the price of oats. There are some uses, of course, for which the corn-oats interchangeability is not very great.

Oats are grown in a wide area of the country which includes the corn belt, the Northeast, and the Pacific Coast. The most important oats producing states are Iowa and Minnesota, with Illinois ranking third. Wisconsin and South Dakota are also important. Oats are planted in the spring and harvested during the summer. The crop year begins on July 1st.

Imports from Canada at times play an important price-making role on the Chicago Board of Trade, particularly in the May through September deliveries. Canadian oats usually carry a price premium because of quality, but Winnipeg prices must be watched closely. When our prices rise, it is possible to ship Canadian oats to Chicago over the Great Lakes. This is not true during the winter months when navigation usually is closed.

The volume of trading in oats, though not substantial, is still sufficiently large to warrant interest. Price movements have been narrow in recent years. Oats prices reflect corn prices, but tend to move only half as much, since a bushel weighs only approximately half that of corn.

Oats, unlike wheat and corn, are not classed as a basic crop under the federal price support program. But the loan program does have an important price influence. It has been relatively effective for this commodity. Also of possible importance is the export subsidy program established for feed grains. Because of the restricted price movements, margin requirements for oats futures trading tend to be low. Consequently, the percentage return on an investment in this commodity can be quite high.

The basis grades for the Chicago contract are #2 White Oats or Special Red Oats. The grades usually delivered are #1 Heavy White oats and #3 extra heavy white oats.

Rye

Rye production in the United States is relatively small, both in comparison with other grain crops and in terms of the U.S. share of world rye production. This is so despite the fact that there are no acreage restrictions on this crop. The primary producers of rye are Russia, Germany and Eastern Europe.

Rye is a minor bread grain crop. It is also used in feed and the manufacture of alcohol and whiskey. The Dakotas, Minnesota and Nebraska are the major producing states. Because the size of the crop is relatively small, changes in demand or supply which would be minor for other commodities can cause major disturbances in the prices for rye. Consequently, rye price movements are usually quite wide and at times erratic.

Rye futures trading volume on the Chicago Board of Trade is good with #2 rye the basis grade. The crop year begins July 1st.

Imports from Canada at times are of major price significance, with the major movement coming over the Great Lakes. In some years import quotas have been in effect, on a first-come first-served basis, beginning July 1st. Imports therefore tend to pour in heavily during July to get in before the quota is filled.

Federal price supports have been relatively effective in rye. Here too an export subsidy program went into effect in 1958.

Soybeans

Strictly speaking, the soybean is not a grain but an oilseed. However, in futures markets it is generally discussed with the grains and we shall continue that convention.

U.S. production, prior to the World War II period (1935-1939), averaged approximately 56 million bushels. But the post-war period has witnessed a phenomenal expansion, partly because of acreage limitations on other crops. The U.S. soybean crop now is about twenty times as large as the pre-war average. Current production places the United States first in world output, replacing the traditional leader, China (including Manchuria). The United States and China produce virtually the entire world output between them.

The rapid growth of this crop in the United States has been caused primarily by two factors. First, the embargo on trade with China cut off our supplies from that source. Second, the acreage restrictions on production of cotton, corn and wheat released much acreage which could be planted to other crops such as soybeans. The reduced cotton acreage commensurately reduced the supplies of cottonseed, the primary oilseed crop of that period. Soybeans made up this deficiency. The forced reduction in plantings in grains and cotton gave the necessary acreage for expansion.

Many new varieties of soybeans have been developed so that the crop is now grown in virtually all sections of the country. However, the principal producing states are those close to the Great Lakes. Four states—Illinois, Iowa, Indiana and Minnesota—normally account for two-thirds of the U.S. crop.

The soybean is not used directly as such but is crushed to obtain oil and meal. A bushel of soybeans will produce about 11 lbs. of oil and about 47 lbs. of meal. The meal is a high protein feed used largely for chicks as well as livestock, while the oil is used primarily in the manufacture of food products. It is also a low grade substitute for linseed oil in the manufacture of paint, and is used in making printing ink as well.

Soybeans are planted in late spring and early summer. The crop year officially begins September 1st, and all the statistics and government reports are on the basis of a crop year beginning September 1st. Because of new varieties and wider distribution of planting, the harvest period has gradually moved forward. Weather permitting, a substantial amount of soybeans usually is harvested in September. If general rains are received late in August, the harvest will be delayed until the plants have absorbed this added moisture. The difference of a few weeks in harvesting can be very important for the September futures contract. The starting time of the harvest will determine whether the price of the September contract will reflect new crop or old crop prices. If the harvest is early, new crop soybeans should be available in time for delivery on the September contract. It will then tend to reflect new crop prices. The size of the old crop carryover will also be important in this respect. Only since the 1956/57 season has any important carryover developed.

Once the harvest begins, it proceeds very rapidly. The bulk of the harvest movement pressure is felt during the last half of October and in early November.

The loan program has been very effective in soybeans, although they are not in the "basic crop" category. The small quantities the government has acquired occasionally, as a result of defaulted loans, have usually been disposed of in the final quarter of each crop year. The government selling price has been the existing loan level plus carrying charges, or the market price, whichever is higher. Prior to 1964, soybean prices have averaged well above the loan. Whether the tremendous expansion of production in recent years will allow this situation to continue, remains to be seen.

The basis grade for soybean futures on the Chicago Board of Trade is #2 Yellow Soybeans. Volume of trading is usually extremely active with price movements about twice as wide as those for wheat. The soybean market has a large speculative following.

Flaxseed (Linseed)

Flax is a minor crop in the United States. Total output of seed rarely reaches 50 million bushels, with the Dakotas and Minnesota producing virtually the entire output. Nevertheless, the U.S. is the primary producer, accounting for close to 25% of the world output. The U.S. flax crop is harvested in late summer and early autumn in most states.

Flaxseed is crushed to obtain linseed oil and meal. The meal is used as a high protein feed. It is competitive with the other oilseed meals.

The oil from flaxseed, however, is not used for edible purposes. It is the principal drying oil used as a basic ingredient in the production of paint and varnish, linoleum and printing ink. The straw from the flax varieties used for obtaining oilseeds has not proven useful for the manufacture of linen. Low oil-yielding varieties of flax are used for this purpose.

Because flaxseed output is concentrated domestically within a small area, and because production is small, weather conditions normally play an extremely important role in price movements. The swing of flaxseed price movements tends to be wide.

Flaxseed futures are not traded in Chicago, but are concentrated on the Minneapolis Grain Exchange. (They are also traded at Winnipeg,, Canada.) Trading volume is not heavy. The support program has been important in the past as a factor in maintaining price levels.

Broilers

Iced broiler futures are traded on the Chicago Board of Trade. While previous attempts at various types of poultry futures contracts failed, the volume of trading being attracted by this new variation indicates a successful development.

Broiler production and consumption has risen steadily in the United States. From 1.8 billion birds in 1960, the number has grown to 3 billion in 1971. Consumption has kept pace with per capita utilization growing from 23.3 lbs. in 1960 to 35.3 lbs. in 1969.

There is a modest seasonal in production with cold storage stocks an important indicator of supplies. The pattern indicates increases in storage stocks to a winter peak, then a reduction to a low in the summer months. This is also the key to the seasonal price pattern. Prices tend to be weakest in the late fall and early winter, (November-December) as surplus production begins to move into storage while they are strongest in the summer (July) as storage stocks are absorbed.

The Government support program here comes via direct purchases for school lunch programs and the armed forces. In addition, the USDA has a subsidy program for exports.

As with eggs, hogs and bellies, government statistics are excellent. They permit an analyst to trace the development of the bird or animal from its inception (broiler egg placings for hatch) through to its marketing. From the pattern, it is possible to forecast with a reasonable degree of accuracy the size of the flocks some months later and thus anticipate the general level of marketing. Of course, there are always new developments that help alter the picture. Extreme periods of heat or cold affect the size of flocks, new export orders, changes in government buying policies, etc. However, these tend to cause variations around the trend rather than alter the basic trend pattern. However, there is a close correlation between chicks placed for hatch and the price movement of broilers.

Broilers are produced primarily over the whole range of Eastern states in the area roughly paralleling the Appalachian Mountains range. It takes about eight weeks to bring broilers to marketable weights. The designated processing plants for delivery are in Arkansas, Alabama, Georgia and Mississippi with a freight allowance to Chicago.

Cattle and Beef

There are seven cattle and beef futures contracts in existence at this time and an eighth might be established very shortly. There is a dressed beef and frozen beef carcass contract, two live cattle contracts traded on the Chicago Mercantile Exchange with delivery points in the Midwest and the West Coast. The Chicago Board of Trade has a live cattle contract and one for carcass beef. The Kansas City Board of Trade has a live feeder cattle contract. The only one with major activity is the live cattle contract with Midwest delivery points on the Chicago Mercantile Exchange. However, in view of the widespread interest in cattle in the United States, we do expect to see an expansion of trading in these contracts as time progresses.

Cattle account for about one-third of the entire U. S. farm income and are produced in practically every state of the Union. The leading states are Texas, Iowa, Nebraska, Kansas and California. For cattle on feed, however, Iowa is the leading state followed by Nebraska and California.

The importance of cattle on feed for the futures contract cannot be overestimated. It is only a fed steer that can reach the choice grades on Government meat ratings and the futures contract calls for live cattle that can meet the "choice" standard when the carcass is cleaned and graded. When cattle are permitted to roam the hills and ranges of the country and feed on grass at will, they can increase in weight but only to a limited extent. Their meat is lean and of commercial and utility grade. To fatten them up and bring them to market weights and of the palatability desired by the American consumer, the cattle must be fed in feed lots on various different rations. These are largely corn and other grains but also will include high protein supplements such as soybean meal and cottonseed meal or urea.

Certain terminology should be understood to properly follow the important Government reports. First, "Feeder" steers are those animals that will be bought to be placed on feed lots to be fed. After they are fed they become "Fed" steers or "Slaughter" steers. The slaughter steers are, of course, the cattle that are finished and ready for marketing. Cows need no definition but Heifers are female cattle that have not yet had calves. A distinction is made in marketing between heifers, cows and steers in terms of price and marketability.

There is unfortunately no single clear seasonal pattern to cattle prices as there is to hog prices. There are a whole series of price patterns differing by type and area in which the cattle are developed and also whether they are grass fed or feed lot finished cattle. On a national basis the cattle slaughter seasonal appears pretty well defined. Starting with a low point in February slaughter tends to expand fairly steadily to a peak in October and then decline rapidly to a low the following February. The number of cattle slaughtered in October will tend to be about 20 to 25% higher than the slaughter numbers the previous February. This pattern follows some logic since the animals can be let out to pasture during the warmer months to put on weight on grass at relatively cheap cost. In the autumn, however, as they must come in from the range, they must either be sold or put on winter feed. Since putting them on winter feed and caring for them over the winter months is relatively expensive, there is a tendency for slaughter to increase in the autumn months and to decline rapidly during the early winter months. In the early Spring the pattern tends to be reversed. The weather warms up. The cattle are taken out of winter quarters and are marketed. The cycle is then ready to begin again.

Price patterns tend to differ. The grass fed animals that are brought in from the ranges in the fall force lower prices for these stockers and feeders at that time. Fed cattle, however, can be kept on feed from periods ranging from as little as three months to as long as one year. Consequently the price variations will depend upon the marketability at the particular location of these animals. The seasonal pattern appears to be one that calls for strength in the early spring with a peak around April followed by a decline into the mid summer and through the fall. The market then tends to bottom out and begin a slow rise again. There are, however, numerous exceptions to this cycle. Cattle prices in the last ten years have been extremely volatile with short term price movements of five dollars a hundred weight not unusual. This means the difference of fifty dollars in the value of just one head of cattle. Longer term moves of twice that amount can be expected.

To get prime or choice steer beef a typical pattern would be for the following: steer calves would be purchased in the fall when the large runs of feeder calves are marketed. They would be worked up to full feed concentrates as rapidly as possible and fed to weights of 900 to 1,000 pounds. Sometimes calves are started on concentrate feeds more slowly wintered largely on roughage or high quality silage and then worked up to full feeds only in March or April. They are then marketed in September or October without use of pasture.

Because of changes in weather the pattern of prices is different in the Far West than it is in the Mid West. The pattern however, is fairly consistent. Chicago prices tend to be at their highest premium over the Far West, at the turn of the new year. Prices then decline fairly consistently relative to the Far West right through June or July. At that time the pattern changes and prices begin to firm in the Mid West relative to the Far West until close to the end of the year. From a peak of about $2.50 a hundred pound over the Far West at the turn of the year Chicago prices usually go to a discount of as much as a dollar a hundred pounds by mid year before the pattern reverses again.

Despite all these variations the average trend throughout the country up or down is fairly consistent, i.e. when a major move is under way, up or down, all types of cattle will tend to follow, some with greater speed, some with less. Thus we must analyze markets in terms of a general long term trend. To do this we must look to the numbers of cattle on farms and the stage of the cattle cycle, i.e., whether or not the number of cattle on farms are expanding or contracting. These will indicate the total quantities of beef to become available in the year or years ahead. Beef consumption in the U.S. continues to improve on a per capita basis as well as on a total basis. Some discussions of this are included in the section on live hogs. Beef prices are influenced directly by supplies available without too much consideration needed for supplies of competing meats such as pork and poultry. When the price of beef increases ten percent demand tends to decrease by four percent. Imports in the past have played an important role in prices. However, the Government has restricted the imports of live cattle and beef and the situation remains fluid. The volume of imports appears likely to remain relatively small over the next two years. World cattle numbers exceed one billion animals with India, Brazil, the USSR and Argentina primary producers. Australia, New Zealand and Ireland are the major exporters of meat to the U.S. Exports are not yet an important price making influence. The American cattle tend to be too heavy and fatty for tastes elsewhere and the same is true of U.S. meat. Thus the price trends in the U.S. are largely dependent upon internal supply and demand conditions.

Cocoa

Cocoa is grown in tropical regions. The largest producer is the now independent state of Ghana (formerly the Gold Coast colony). Nigeria runs second in importance, followed by Brazil.

Cocoa production shows a marked seasonal pattern, with three-quarters of the year's output harvested in October-March (main crop). Most of the remainder is harvested in May through July (mid-crop).

The Ghana crop (Accra) is purchased from the cocoa farmers at a fixed price by the Cocoa Marketing Board through farmer co-ops in each region. This Board resells to all buyers at prices varying with world conditions. The Nigerian crop is similarly controlled, but Brazilian output is sold through regular free market channels. Nevertheless, the Brazilian Government does have the power to establish minimum selling prices and export quotas through the agency, "Cacex". These have proven, at times, to be very effective price support measures and they are frequently invoked.

The Accra (Ghana) and Bahia (Brazil) crops constitute half of the world's cocoa output. They, along with Ivory Coast, San Thome, Panama and Costa Rican growths, are the basis grades for the New York cocoa futures contract. Other growths are deliverable at premiums or discounts.

Cocoa from the Caribbean Islands has often been delivered. Many Bahia notices have also been issued in recent years, but Accra has been tendered less frequently.

During the late 1950's, the absence of an adequate inventory reserve was largely responsible for the wide price swings and the sensitivity of prices to changes in crop estimates. With the development of substantial carry-over stocks, the amplitude of price movements as well as their sensitivity to changes in crop estimates has been reduced.

This has also led the producing nations, under the auspices of the United Nations, to take steps toward an international agreement to establish minimum export prices. These agreements take years to establish but even in the discussion stage they can influence prices. The dates of the international meetings and the agenda should be taken into consideration.

The United States is the largest importer and consumer of cocoa, utilizing 265,000 to 290,000 long tons annually, depending upon price and consumption patterns. When the price of cocoa is high, substitutes and fillers (milk, nuts, fruits) are used in candy, and the size of the chocolate bar is reduced. When prices are low, the reverse is true. However, it takes many months for these changes to be instituted.

Germany is the second largest consumer, utilizing approximately half the U.S. quantity. Holland is third, followed by the United Kingdom and France.

Coffee

Between 75 and 85 percent of world coffee production comes from Latin America. Almost half the world crop is produced in Brazil. Colombia, the second largest grower, produces from one-third to one-half as much as Brazil. In recent years coffee production in Africa has expanded sharply, given added impetus by the increasing use of instant coffees which use African coffees more freely. Total production of coffee in Africa is now roughly equivalent to that of Colombia, but the flavor and aroma do not appeal to American tastes. For this and other reasons, African coffees usually are the low-priced varieties. Brazilian coffees are in the medium price range. Colombian and Central American coffees, falling into the "mild" category, comprise the high-priced varieties.

The United States consumes approximately 50% of the world output of coffee. Europe takes most of the remainder.

After years of negotiations a new International Coffee Agreement was finally ratified and became effective prior to the end of 1964. For the first time it also included the major consuming nations. The latter led by the U.S., promised to help enforce the regulations.

The Agreement establishes export quotas for each producing nation. Consuming nations are to check certificates of origin on all imported coffee to see that no "above quota" shipments take place. Thus the importers are enforcing the regulations which are to keep prices higher. Minimum and maximum price ranges are establisted for four basic different classes of coffee. If prices stay above or below these levels for 15 days, appropriate export quota adjustments are to be made to bring prices back within the range.

The history of the various coffee support programs has been one of sporadic success.

The coffee crop year begins July 1st but there is no marked seasonal price pattern.

Citrus (Orange Juice)

December is the beginning of the processing season (oranges begin harvest in the fall) and receipts at processing plants continue heavy into the summer. Shipments are heavy year round.

In citrus, as in agriculture generally, weather becomes of prime importance. Occasional freezes cut into the crop substantially. Between 1901 and 1968, there were 30 years during which major cold spells hit Florida. Of these 30 cold spells: 3 hit during November; 7 during December; 12 in January; 7 in February and 1 in March. When it occurs prices rally sharply and swiftly. With futures margins as low as they are, the risks of being short in a frost period are extreme. Of these "cold spells" there was only one that can be considered severe. That was in 1962 when temperatures fell below 20 degrees on one night and stayed low for four and a half hours. Usually a cold spell can be, say, around 26 degrees at ground level and 34 degrees just above the tops of the trees—this is known as a temperature inversion. Wind machines are used to mix the temperatures. This type of equipment added to the usual heaters (smudge pots) and damage preventing methods can help preserve the crop on cold nights. Temperatures can differ from point to point and within a given area depending on whether the tree is on high or low ground or close to water. A "hard freeze" is defined as twenty-six degrees or lower for four hours or more.

Orange and orange juice demand is fairly elastic for agricultural commodities. This means that consumption responds more readily in this luxury item to changes in price than, say, a more basic commodity such as wheat. In fact, the USDA says that "the coefficient of elasticity of demand with respect to price for frozen concentrated orange . . . was —1.0." Translated into more meaningful terms—at a given point, if prices decrease one percent, demand will tend to increase by one percent.

The real key to price is production. There is an inverse relationship between Florida production and the price of a box of oranges which is a tight statistical fit. This means that when annual production is low the annual average price tends to be high. The frozen concentrate price tends to follow in the same direction as the box price. The dominance of this relationship carries through to the rest of the nation. The reason for this is that Florida produces the major share of the nation's oranges. Thus, the California box price is more closely related to, say, the Florida concentrate price than to California production. The problem of over-production has been recognized by the USDA. A purchase program for school lunch programs and charitable institutions is being initiated.

Cotton

The United States normally produces 40 to 50 percent of the world cotton output. Russia and China are also major producers, as are India, Egypt and Brazil. Cotton is grown throughout the southern half of the United States. In recent years, California has become a major producer of the highly desirable longer staple varieties. Texas is the largest producer of the shorter staples. The Southeast is, of course, the traditional cotton belt.

Until 1966, the federal government loan program had been the major determinant of the domestic cotton price level and had kept it well above the world price level. This allowed foreign producers to expand acreage and absorb a major part of the export market the U.S. formerly enjoyed. They needed only to sell at slightly below U.S. prices. As a result of the support program, the U.S. Government has been forced to acquire very large quantities of cotton. It therefore instituted new export plans to dispose of these holdings. The government catalogues its cotton and sells it to exporters on a competitive bid basis. The exporters bid for it at the world price level since that is the price at which they can sell.

Details of the cotton loan program are given with the Government Support section of this text. Suffice it to point out here that the government domestic market selling price for its acquired stockpile of cotton is 10% above the existing loan.

Because of the major role played by the federal government, cotton price fluctuations and the volume of futures trading have become quite restricted. Cotton used to be one of the most active trading markets, and may become so once again.

The basis grade and staple for the active New York futures #2 is middling $1\frac{1}{16}$-inch cotton, with certain other grades and staples deliverable at commercial market premiums and discounts.

The crop year begins August 1st and the first active new crop futures month is the October delivery.

Currency

The International Currency Exchange was organized as a separate entity by the members of the New York Produce Exchange. They have hopes of organizing an active market in foreign currencies independent of the large banking institutions that now control this market. Currency price variations normally are rather modest and limited by international agreements as much as possible. However, year after year there have been monetary crises in one nation or another caused by adverse balance of payments, revolts, coups d'etat, bank failures, nationalization, invasions, etc., etc. Each of these has an effect on the value of the money of the nation involved causing fears of devaluation in one instance, or revolution in another. Prices for forward delivery of these currencies fall sharply during periods of crisis, while the spot price can remain virtually unchanged. Thus despite limits on spot price fluctuation, distant month values of the currency can fluctuate widely. For example, when fears of sterling devaluation occur, the price of the London pound falls to a level at which the Central Bank (Bank of England) steps into the open market. It buys up all the pound sterling being offered at the minimum support price thus halting the decline. Sterling being offered for a year later, however, does not obtain this support and sinks in price to a much lower level. When the momentary panic is over these distant month positions snap back to a more natural relationship to the spot value.

The major international banks make markets in all currencies, much like markets are made in over-the-counter securities by brokerage firms. They will permit their large customers to buy and sell currencies as needed. It is a very important adjunct to international trade and all firms engaged in international trade will want to cover their currency risks at most times. A good sale of cocoa, for example, can turn into a loss if the currency value changes drastically. Thus when England devalued in November, 1967 and Nigeria did not, most of the London cocoa dealers found themselves in serious financial trouble. It took the Bank of England to bail them out.

However, the banks fail to provide the needed currency protection in times of extreme stress and also refuse to permit many of the general public to trade through them. In times of stress, banks, at times, refuse to make markets over week-end or holiday periods—or even overnight. Thus, at the most crucial times, they have been found wanting. The International Currency Exchange is trying to alter this picture. However, the margins required for this and the continuity of the market are still problems that the Exchange has not yet adequately solved. The next time a monetary crisis arises in a primary currency, we shall see a test of its effectiveness.

The currencies involved at present are the British Pound Sterling, Swiss Franc, French Franc, Deutche Mark, Italian Lira and Japanese Yen all traded in terms of U.S. dollars.

Eggs

Egg futures prices ordinarily move over a fairly wide price range during any year. In the post-war period, a swing of 20¢ per dozen has not been unusual.

There are two egg futures contracts on the Chicago Mercantile Exchange, one for frozen eggs and another on which primarily fresh eggs are deliverable. The latter is by far the most active. Deliveries are based on Chicago prices, but can be made in many other cities in the United States, with freight deducted to Chicago.

Storage egg holdings traditionally increase during the March to July period, then decline from August into February. This movement corresponds with the months in which fresh egg production is greater than consumption (Spring), and when production is traditionally below demand (Autumn). In recent years, however, improved production methods have resulted in a tendency to flatten out the seasonal pattern of output. Monthly fresh egg production is tending to become more and more equalized each season. Nevertheless, the movement into and out of storage remains of great importance in determining egg futures prices.

There is no standard government support program for eggs. However, when the price is low, the government on occasion attempts to stabilize or raise prices by purchasing fresh or dried eggs in the cash market for use in school lunch programs and for donation to institutions.

Exports play a relatively minor role in total demand. Because this is so, a substantial export order can have a sharp and immediate price firming influence at certain times of the year. The government, therefore, has made use of occasional export grants to help the egg price structure.

Almost 90% of total egg usage each year is accounted for by direct consumption of shell eggs for household and restaurant use. Egg breakers, who process shell eggs into forms suitable for use in mayonnaise, salad dressing, baking, ice cream, candy, noodles, and dried eggs, absorb approximately 5 to 6 percent of production. Hatcheries absorb the remaining 4 to 5 percent.

Hatchery demand for eggs is largest in the spring, and tends to vary directly with the price of eggs. If feeding ratios are favorable, there will be a strong demand for hatchery chicks to increase flocks.

Egg breakers usually buy in the spring also, for this is usually the period of low prices. In addition, breakers require spring pack eggs for certain quality characteristics, such as color. However, should they have underestimated demand, there can be a secondary buying movement in the autumn. Since this is the period when out of storage movement is normally heavy anyway, the added breaker demand can use a sharp advance in egg prices.

In addition to the production reports and storage movement statistics, it is important to watch the monthly federal government reports on hatchery production. These provide the best indication of the probable number of layers on farms six months later, and hence of coming production.

Hides

Until 1953, the United States had normally been a net importer of cattle hides. The situation, however, has since changed. The U.S. is now an important net hides exporter, alternating with Argentina as the largest supplier for world trade.

Cattle hides are a by-product of beef production. The supply depends largely upon the size of the cattle population, the size of the calf crop and the trend of slaughter.

Demand depends primarily upon shoe production, which is the major end use of cattle hides. The luggage, upholstery and the belting industries are of secondary importance. The lighter weight hides are used for shoe uppers and the heavy hides are tanned into sole leather. In the post-war period there has been a major change in the shoe industry, with rubber and composition soles (such as neolite) now being used on over half the shoes produced. As a result, the demand for heavy hides has been sharply curtailed. Consequently they are forced to sell at sharp price discounts from the lighter weight hides.

This has major significance for hide futures. The futures contract is a weight contract. It calls for delivery of 40,000 lbs. with the basis grade Domestic Standard Packer Native Cow and/or Steer Hides of 52-53.99 lbs. each. It also allows delivery of other hides at fixed premiums and discounts. For heavier hides, a discount applies. If the hides are branded, an additional discount applies since part of the hide cannot be used. Because of the lessened demand for heavy hides, most deliveries against futures prove to be of these varieties and futures prices now tend to reflect the price movement of the following varieties:

Heavy Native Cows and Steers
Heavy Butt Branded Cows and Steers
Heavy Colorado Steers

The season of take-off (slaughter) is also important in hide prices. Hides produced in the summer sell at premiums to winter-kill hides. The summer hides contain less hair and grubs and are therefore easier and less expensive to tan into quality leather.

Slaughter of cattle, and therefore hide production, follows a seasonal pattern. The heaviest period of production is in the October to December quarter, followed by a decline into the Spring months. Thereafter, there is a slow but steady increase during the remainder of the calendar year.

The post-war price pattern has been rather erratic. Nevertheless purchases of futures around the end of February frequently have led to excellent profit possibilities by summer.

There is no federal government support program for hides. Europeans consider U.S. hides less desirable than those from Argentina and Uruguay, but U.S. hides have moved freely in the export market at a discount to those of South America. In view of the level of current U.S. hides output, rather large exports are needed to keep demand and supply in approximate balance.

Live Hogs

Trading in live hog futures began on the Chicago Mercantile Exchange early in 1966. This followed the successful introduction of trading in live cattle futures the previous year. The delivery point is approved live stock yards in Chicago. However, deliveries may also be made in other mid-western cities at a discount of 75¢ per hundred weight. These cities are listed in the rules of the Exchange.

Demand for red meat has been expanding rapidly throughout the world. This is largely believed attributable to the higher levels of income which have been noticeable throughout the world in recent years. As the income of a nation rises there is a tendency to increase per capita consumption of red meat. Of course, this is true only to a certain point. In the highly developed nations and those with the highest standard of living the percentage spent on food as a total tends to decline. Nevertheless, the percentage spent on red meat appears to increase. From 1957 to 1964 consumption of red meat expanded rapidly in the U.S. but the expansion was more rapid for beef than for lamb or pork. Beef consumption increased by 18% while pork consumption increased by only 3% per capita in the same period. An examination of other studies indicates that pork, unlike beef, receives little of the benefits from expanding personal incomes. That is, pork consumption in high income families in the U.S. appears to be about the same as that in lower income families. Beef consumption, however, expands rapidly with income.

With this "income effect" largely eliminated, the price analysis for pork, and therefore live hogs, becomes somewhat simplified. We find a much closer relationship between the price of pork and live hogs and the supply available. When we add in the supply of competing meats we tend to get a very close approximation of near term price movements. An expansion of beef and lamb production will have an adverse effect on pork and hog prices. However, the reverse effect appears to be much smaller. That is, the expansion of pork and hog supplies will have only a small adverse effect on beef prices.

In looking to forecast the price of hogs, therefore, we must look closely at those factors influencing the long term and short term supply of hogs. The long term supply is forecast for us through the government's pig crop reports. These come out in the spring and fall and indicate what the anticipated change for the supplies six or seven months thereafter will be. Closer analysis of these two reports will permit fairly accurate forecasts of the amount of pigs coming to market in each of the months for the ensuing year. Between the two major government pig crop reports are intermediate reports for the corn belt states. These can be used as checks on the anticipated supplies forecast by the two major government reports.

The number of sows farrowing during the spring period has been substantially larger than those farrowing during the last half of the year. At present spring farrowings are about 15% larger than fall. This has been a declining percentage increase indicating that the hog farrowing cycle has been evening out. However, it will take many more years before the spring and fall farrowings will be approximately equal.

There are two important seasonal factors in the hog analysis picture. First, there is a very marked seasonal pattern to hog marketings within the calendar year.

Utilizing the figures for hog slaughter under federal inspection, we find that the low point in each year is mid-summer and the high point appears to be October-November. This pattern has been very consistent over the years. Furthermore, the degree of variation in weekly slaughter is quite large. Thus the slaughter in mid summer might be 40% below the levels toward the end of the calendar year.

The second seasonal factor is directly related to the first, and that is the seasonal price change. Hog prices follow a beautifully traditional supply-demand relationship, i.e. the price of hogs tends to be highest in mid-summer when supplies are the lowest, and conversely, tends to be the lowest during the October-November period when supplies are highest.

Longer term price patterns also play a significant role. The most consistent one appears to be a four year cycle of hog prices. Highs were established in 1954, again in 1958, again in 1962, in 1966 and in 1970. Declines of about a year and a half duration tend to follow and these appear to be pretty steep. Thus the lows for the previous cycles have been at the end of 1955, 1959, 1963 and 1967. This will call for prices to turn up in 1972.

Another determinant of longer term hog supplies is the hog-corn ratio discussed earlier in corn. The corn itself can be marketed either as corn or can be fed to hogs and marketed as hogs. Obviously the price relationship between feed and hogs will determine whether or not the hogs will be kept on the farm and fed or whether both they and the corn will be sent to market early. The economic ratio between hogs and corn have varied over time. Under current prosperous conditions and the expansion of large hog farms, the hog-corn ratio necessary for a break even point appears to have advanced substantially. For many years a ratio of 13½ bushels of corn equal in price to 100 pounds of live hog was sufficient to permit a break-even point for hog raisers. In 1968, however, it appears likely that a ratio of 16 bushels of corn equal to 100 pounds of live hogs might be necessary for a break-even point. Some industry spokesmen claim that 17 bushels might even be more like it. In other words, if corn prices are down to a dollar a bushel, live hog prices of at least $17.00 a hundred, would be necessary to continue in the hog business.

At present there are no Government support programs for live hogs. Exports are also negligible, as are imports, as a market factor.

Metals

Futures in copper and silver are traded on the Commodity Exchange Inc. (New York). Normally the volume of trading has been limited. Trading on the London Metal Exchange has been more active. Modest trading in platinum and palladium has begun on the New York Mercantile Exchange. Tin, lead and zinc are traded on the London Metal Exchange.

Speculators generally are advised to limit their operations in these markets when trading volume is low.

Copper production in the United States accounts for approximately 30% of world output. The U.S. is the largest producer. Chile and Zambia are next in importance, but their combined production still does not reach the level of the United States. Despite its large production, the U.S. is a net importer of this metal. Copper is consumed primarily in the form of wire and brass. Automobiles and the construction industries are important outlets. The basis grade for copper futures is electrolytic copper, but fire-refined and lake copper are also deliverable.

The United States is the largest lead producer, but must also import heavily to meet consumption needs. Australia, Mexico and Canada are also relatively large producing countries. Storage battery production accounts for 30% of U.S. lead consumption. Tetra-ethyl gasoline accounts for another 15%. Thus, the use of lead is highly dependent upon the automobile industry.

Tin is produced principally in Malaya and Indonesia. Their combined production accounts for well over half the world output. Bolivia is the third largest producer. There is one tin smelter in the United States at Texas City, Texas. It was government built as a protective war measure, but since has been sold by the government to private industry. No tin ore has been found in the United States in commercial quantities. Tin consumption in the United States is dependent to a great extent upon the plating industry. Solder, bronze and brass are next in importance as tin consuming products.

An International Tin Agreement, encompassing virtually all producing countries except China and Russia, has been organized. Under the Agreement, a "buffer stock" is established, as is an International Tin Council. The Council determines policies with respect to the buffer stock. As now constituted, when tin prices fall below a specified price, tin *must* be bought for the buffer stock. Buffer stocks *must* be sold above a specified price.

Tin futures are traded on the London Metal Exchange but have become inactive on the Commodity Exchange Inc. of New York. However, from time to time efforts are made to revitalize New York tin futures, usually by moderate changes in the contract.

Because tin is produced in areas of basic political unrest, and must be transported thousands of miles to consuming centers, prices tend to be very sensitive to international events.

As with copper, the United States is a major producer of zinc but must still import heavily both zinc ore and slabs. U.S. mines supply only three-quarters of U.S. smelter needs. Principal suppliers of the U.S. market are Canada, Mexico and Peru. Over 40% of U.S. zinc consumption comes from galvanizing (coating) steel. A close second is zinc die-casting. Brass production (30% zinc) accounts for around 10% of total use.

In the post World War II years, the United States Government stockpiled copper, lead and zinc as a price support and defense measure. The U.S. government not only purchased domestic output but entered into barter agreements under which this country received foreign surplus zinc and lead in exchange for our surplus U.S. wheat and other commodities. This government absorption of the world surplus constituted the major price supporting influence. Barter deals are still possible, though on a reduced scale. It is important when trading in metal futures to continuously watch developments along these lines.

Silver trading began in 1963 on the Commodity Exchange Inc. and subsequently was introduced on the Chicago Board of Trade as well. Since this is one of the most valuable of metals and widely used as a medium of exchange, the outlook for active trading is excellent in coming years.

Silver production is largely a by-product of the mining of other non-ferrous metals. Hence, much of its supply is based on the demand and price for other metals rather than itself. This complicates the supply picture considerably. Over half the world production comes from the Americas with Mexico the largest supplier. The U.S. is usually second in production with Peru and Canada a close third and fourth. The USSR is fifth, averaging about 25 million ounces per year compared with Mexico's 44 million. Total world production averages about 230 million ounces but varies widely.

World consumption on the other hand has averaged about 100 million ounces above production in the 1960's. The basic sources of additional supply have been the sale of U.S. Treasury stocks, the demonitization of coinage, dishoarding by speculative holders, sales by Communist China and recovery by secondary industries from old uses such as silver plate and photo film.

By far the most important source has been the U.S. Treasury— once it withdrew offers at the statutory 91¢ per oz. in November 1962, the market shot up to the level approximating the $1.2929 per oz. redemption for U.S. silver certificates. After remaining there for a time, the Treasury was forced to limit its sales and prices rose to about the $2.00 level and have been fluctuating freely. In mid-1968 the Treasury ceased redeeming silver certificates with bullion. The bulk of their remaining supplies could therefore be available for public sale. These Treasury sales and the waves of hoarding demand that occur from time to time based on fears of U.S. dollar devaluation, were the prime market factors through 1970. Now, however, no treasury silver is left and world prices must adjust to this change beginning in 1971.

Silver use is now about three-quarters by industry and the arts and one quarter by coinage. Of the former, use in photography is by far the greatest. Use in jewelry and silver plating is still a major outlet while consumption by the electrical industry is growing.

Platinum and palladium trading has become active on the New York Mercantile Exchange. Both precious metals have caught the public fancy as a hedge against possible increases in the price of gold or devaluation of the dollar. This factor can cause waves of buying and selling that will overshadow the more usual supply and demand trends.

Production of platinum and palladium together comprise 95% of the six platinum group metals, the other 5% is composed of iridium, rhodium, ruthenium and osmium. As shown below the Soviet Union accounts for almost 60% of world output. The Union of South Africa is a poor second with Canada a distant third.

WORLD PRODUCTION 1967
(troy ounces)

Nation	Palladium	Platinum	Others	Total
U.S.S.R.	1,080,000	540,000	180,000	1,800,000
South Africa	200,000	575,000	25,000	800,000
Canada	152,000	152,000	76,000	380,000

Production continues to expand in Russia and South Africa.

While Russia produces 70% of world palladium production, the U.S. consumes over 60% of the total output. Russia produces just under half the world platinum production while we consume somewhat over half. You can well see what a peculiar situation this can be. We are in the dubious position of being subject to possible erratic political decisions for supplies of these strategic metals. Variations in Russian willingness to sell these metals can be the dominant price influence for years to come.

Platinum's primary use is in oil refining as a catalyst with other chemical uses second in importance and electrical industry use third. Palladium is hardly used in petroleum refining but finds its chief use in the electrical industry with chemical uses second.

Prices for both metals have increased steadily since 1958 when palladium producer prices were down to $15 and platinum $55 per oz. At the beginning of 1968 palladium producer prices were $39 and platinum $115 an ounce. However, secondary dealer prices, those at which the general public could buy were double the platinum list price but only 25% above list on palladium. Wide price swings can be expected in both.

An attempt to introduce nickel trading in 1971 on the New York Mercantile Exchange proved fruitless.

Plywood

The trend in developing new commodity futures contracts has been towards semi-processed and finished products rather than primary agricultural ones. The development of futures trading in plywood is now typical. It is widely used, has a widely distributed marketing area, is highly competitive and has wide price fluctuations.

The first panel was shown at the Portland, Oregon 1905 trade fair. This was just for demonstration purposes. Output and acceptance grew slowly until the post World War II period. It then emerged as a leading building material. In 1955, output exceeded 5 billion square feet. By 1970 it had trebled!

The bulk of plywood production in the United States is in the Pacific Northwest so that the basing point for the Chicago Board of Trade Contract is Portland, Oregon. A secondary production area is in the Southeast where southern pine is utilized.

Primary factors to watch on the supply side are the number of trees permitted to be cut from the forests under Federal regulation, and mill output. On the demand side, the general level of construction particularly new home building is most important. Timber exports, too, have become at times a dominant influence. With the number of trees felled limited by decree, a U.S. housing boom augmented by heavy timber exports can create a severe shortage. This occurred in 1967 and 1968. Timber exports were very heavy, particularly to Japan. This made the difference between an adequate supply and a shortage. Prices zoomed, actually doubling in that period. However, since 1969 was a year of general U.S. recession, and there was a major slowdown in housing construction, prices broke sharply and in half the time lost the entire gain. Extremely high interest rates during the 1969/70 period also were instrumental in hindering housing starts. This too is a major factor to watch. As in so many commodities, labor strife and the renegotiation of industry contracts must be considered and railroad strike prospects or other transportation interruptions can be very crucial in short-term price movements.

A New York Mercantile Exchange plywood contract and a Chicago Mercantile lumber contract exist but have not been able to get off the ground as yet.

Pork Bellies

Trading in frozen pork bellies, the very unglamorous name for unsliced bacon, began in 1962 and has become one of the most active futures markets now being traded. Since the pork bellies are a by-product of hog slaughter the same factors that will influence hog prices should have a major influence on the price of pork bellies. Thus, the seasonal marketings of hogs and the seasonal price trends of hog prices become the major consideration. These are discussed elsewhere in this chapter under "live hogs." There are, of course, some unique characteristics of pork bellies themselves that must be studied to determine the particular price trend for this commodity.

Pork belly prices tend to follow the same seasonal price pattern as live hogs. Peak prices tend to be reached around mid-summer followed by a rather rapid decline to an October-November low. Prices tend to stay low through the winter months and begin rallying sharply in the spring and early summer.

The best indicator of demand is the report on weekly bacon slicings. Also of very major importance, is the storage movement of pork bellies. The pattern of production and consumption is such that a serious deficiency in production tends to arise during the summer and one therefore finds the need to have storage stocks on hand which can be drawn down as needed during these deficit months. The into-storage movement begins very modestly in November-December and expands to a peak about April or May. The storage movement into and out of warehouses around the Chicago area can be obtained daily and are watched for any significant changes in the major storage. They give a clue as to the very important monthly government reports as of the first of each month.

The very significant factor in the pork belly demand picture appears to be that it has very little elasticity relative to price. That is, people tend to utilize relatively the same amount of bacon whether prices are high or low. It takes a very rapid and sharp advance in price to induce a reduction in utilization and equally important it takes a very sharp break and a very low price to induce a significant expansion in consumption. This is quite different than the price effect of pork products. With other pork products, the price has a significant effect on demand. For bellies then, the important price making influence is the change in supply.

There is no significant export movement or import movement of pork bellies and there is no government support program in effect for pork bellies at this time.

Potatoes

Potatoes are grown in virtually every state of the Union. However, the contract of the New York Mercantile Exchange, which is the most active potato futures market, calls for delivery of Maine grown potatoes exclusively. An Idaho potato futures market has developed modest volume on the Chicago Mercantile Exchange.

Over two-thirds of the U.S. potato crop is produced in the so-called "late states." Maine is one of these, and is the largest producing state. Its harvest begins in late autumn and the crop is marketed through May. The active futures delivery months are, therefore, limited to the November-May period.

Potato futures prices are dependent to a large extent upon the size of the Maine crop, but not exclusively so. Maine potatoes are distributed widely through the states east of the Mississippi, and are therefore competitive with other types grown along the East Coast—all the way down to Florida. A freeze which can ruin a good part of the crop (in Alabama or the Eastern Shore districts of Virginia, for example), can have a major effect on prices for Maine potatoes, as could a bumper crop in those states. Frost possibilities during the growing season have proven to be important price-making influences. Some California and Idaho potatoes also compete in the Eastern markets, but mostly with specialty types such as baking potatoes.

Weather also affects demand and shipments. Normally, demand is best during the cold winter months. But heavy snows can prevent loading and shipment. The result is a somewhat erratic minor day-to-day price fluctuation depending upon weather, but these fluctuations usually tend to be about a clearly defined trend.

Potato imports and exports play a relatively minor role in price-making. However, the U.S. does import potatoes, primarily from Canada, and exports go largely to areas in Latin America. When some unexpected export orders are received, prices may firm for a few days. But export orders are rarely large enough to create more than a minor influence.

In 1954, potatoes again became eligible for federal price supports. However, the government, rather than instituting the standard loan type of support program, has chosen to use a diversion program instead. The government pays the farmer a subsidy for shipping his potatoes to starch factories or diverting them to animal feed. The U.S.D.A. also authorizes producers to enter into State Marketing Agreements through which minimum size and quality requirements for shipment are established.

Potatoes are rather perishable and, therefore, are not carried over from one marketing year to the next. Because of this perishability, reinspections of deliverable stocks are frequent to insure the maintenance of quality. While this practice guarantees good quality deliveries, the perishability of potatoes also increases the risk of taking delivery for anyone who cannot market the commodity commercially. The potatoes may not pass reinspection and may not be redeliverable. It is quite important that speculative long positions be liquidated in the near month before the delivery period begins.

Propane

Propane is the most important liquefied petroleum gas and has a higher heating value per cubic foot than manufactured or natural gas.

It is produced from both natural gas wells and oil wells.

Production follows the seasonal demand pattern being highest in the winter months and lowest in the summer. Some inventory building prior to the high heating months is normal. Thus inventories are built up in storage facilities during the late spring and summer with a rapid decline from October to March.

Price variations also follow a seasonal pattern very similar to the production and demand pattern. That is, prices are highest in the winter (Feb.) and decline normally fairly steadily to a June low.

Five states account for 70% of production. Texas produces about 3.4 billion gallons, well over one-third the U.S. total of 9.2 billion. Louisiana is second, Oklahoma third followed by Kansas and New Mexico.

Storage facilities of the liquid are largely underground due to economy reasons with Texas holding over half the storage capacity.

Sugar

The sugar market is actually two distinct markets, the domestic market and world market. They must be treated separately, and their price movements need not parallel each other.

The domestic market's sugar supply is governed by a quota established each year by the Secretary of Agriculture. This quota can be changed at any time during the season, at his discretion. Out of approximately 10 million short tons of sugar used each year in the United States, we produce domestically about 3,000,000 tons of beet sugar in the west, 500,000 tons each of cane sugar in Louisiana and Florida and 1,000,000 tons in Hawaii. The balance is imported. About 1,000,000 tons each come from Puerto Rico and the Philippines. Cuba used to send 3,000,000 tons but this quota has been suspended and divided among other world producers. Quotas are adjusted annually, depending upon our needs and production in the various districts.

The whole purpose of the quota system is to insulate the domestic sugar market from erratic world price fluctuations. The object is to keep sugar prices at a high enough level to satisfy domestic growers and yet prevent sharp price upturns for consumers. This is achieved by the Secretary of Agriculture setting an initial quota below the level of normal requirements. After a while, as supplies begin to tighten, the quotas are increased, usually in 50,000 or 100,000 ton stages. The result is believed to be a more stable price level than could be obtained without the quotas. Ordinarily the quota system results in higher prices in the domestic market than in the world market (even allowing for deductions of excise taxes, duties and transportation costs). This induces exporting areas to fulfill their quotas to the U. S. The domestic market sugar futures contract is the #10 and ordinarily sells above the world contract, the #11.

About 35% of world sugar production is comprised of beet sugar, primarily European and U.S.S.R. output. The remainder is produced from cane. Eastern Europe generally has a beet sugar export surplus. Cane and beet sugars are chemically identical, and can be used completely interchangeably at will.

The world sugar futures contract (#11), however, is a cane sugar contract having sugars of many origins as a basis and allowing delivery in virtually all parts of the world. It is the closest we have yet come to a universal contract. Cuban sugar, however, is not deliverable except under special circumstances including a vote by the appropriate Exchange Committee. This resulted because of the fears of expropriation.

Also important is the International Sugar Agreement, which was organized by most of the sugar export nations and subscribed to by the important consuming nations. It was designed to keep the price of sugar between previously specified levels. Each producing nation is given a basic export quota. If the world price falls below the minimum, provision is made in the agreement for contraction in the export quotas until such time as the world price again increases. Similarly if the price level exceeds the maximum all quota restrictions are automatically eliminated, and the various producers are free to take advantage of the high prices by selling as much sugar as they can until the price again declines below the maximum. The quotas and price range under the Agreement are adjusted periodically by holding an international meeting. The Agreement has been effective in recent years because Cuba agrees to accept the restrictions.

Sugar prices are very sensitive to war prospects. When the possibility of a shooting war develops, nations scramble for supplies and a hoarding movement sometimes develops. What may have been a world sugar surplus supply situation suddenly, with the outbreak of war, can turn into one of scarcity.

Political developments in Cuba must be watched. These can alter their production, sales policies and their relationship with the United States. This in turn can alter the disposition of the U.S. import quota and the world price level.

The London sugar market has become very active in recent years with excellent arbitrage opportunities presented against New York.

The London #2 contract calls for delivery in London or Liverpool of sugars of the same origins called for in the New York #11 contract. However, the N.Y. #11 contract is on an F.O.B. basis. That is, the N.Y. contract is priced at the loading port aboard ship while the London contract includes the cost of shipping the sugar to London or Liverpool. The London #2 contract therefore should sell at a shipping cost premium to the New York #11. This varies of course, but approximates 40 to 60 points per lb. Thus, London should sell 40 to 60 points over New York.

Vegetable Oils and Meal

Cottonseed oil and soybean oil are the primary edible vegetable oils. They are, however, competitive with several others such as peanut oil (produced domestically as well as in India and Africa) and olive oil (produced in the Mediterranean countries). As a consequence, prices and production of these other oils must also be considered. Cottonseed and soybean oils account for approximately 40% of the world production of edible vegetable oils. To a major extent, therefore, their price movements are leaders of the entire group.

Both of these oils are by-products of other major crops, cotton and soybeans. About twice as much soybean oil is now produced in the United States as cottonseed oil. Both oils can be used interchangeably in their major uses. These include the manufacture of shortening, margarine, salad and cooking oils. Historically, crude cottonseed oil has sold at a ½¢ to 1¢ per lb. premium over crude soybean oil. This was due to the fact that soybean oil had a tendency to develop a distinctive flavor if it was stored for long periods after refining. Also the refining loss of soybean oil in weight was greater than cottonseed oil. Today, however, improved refining methods have largely eliminated these soybean oil shortcomings. Nevertheless, the tendency for crude cottonseed oil to sell at a small premium over crude soybean oil persists.

It should be emphasized that, in futures trading, the cottonseed oil contract calls for delivery of a semi-refined oil while the soybean oil contract represents crude oil. This difference, as well as the difference in delivery points, should make the cottonseed oil futures contract sell for around 175-200 points above soybean oil futures—when both crude oils are selling at the same price.

Crushed cottonseed and soybeans yield approximately the following quantities of by-products:

PER TON OF COTTONSEED	PER BUSHEL OF SOYBEANS
313 lbs. of oil	11 lbs. of oil
822 lbs. of meal	47 lbs. of meal
182 lbs. of linters	2 lbs. loss
573 lbs. of hull	
110 lbs. of loss	

Cottonseed meal and soybean meal are also competitive to a large extent. However, because of a certain chemical content in cottonseed meal, it cannot be readily used in poultry feed.

Linters are the fuzz which adheres to the outside of the cottonseed hull. The seed is removed from the cotton boll through ginning but the fuzz remains. This is removed by a delinting machine. The linters are used for rayon, paper and cellulose. The hulls are practically worthless, although they are sometimes used as a filler in animal feed mixes.

Crushing shows a definite, marked seasonal pattern. The low point in crushing of both oils in the U.S. is the May through August period. Heavy crushing usually occurs in the period just before and after the turn of the calendar year. The production of oil and meal is, of course, directly related to crushing and follows the same seasonal pattern.

The United States has become the major export nation for cottonseed and soybean oils, particularly since the Public Law 480 dollar grant program went into effect. Since U.S. production of these products is well above domestic needs, the export market has become the dominant price-making influence. In alternate years, the olive oil crop in the Mediterranean basin is poor (a two year production cycle). Naturally, this affects our edible oil exports to Spain and Italy, two of our principal customers.

While there is a government support program in effect for cotton and soybeans (loans, purchase agreements, etc.), there is none on oils at present. There was a "package support program" in effect during the 1953/54 and 1954/55" seasons for cottonseed products, but this was discontinued because it resulted in large quantities of cottonseed oil being accumulated by the government while soybean oil took over a larger percentage of the regular commercial markets.

The government also contracted to purchase limited quantities of cottonseed oil during the 1958/59 season as a support measure. The government-acquired cottonseed oil stocks have since been liquidated and the P.L. 480 program has been used as a means of disposing of our surplus production in this country.

The crop year for cottonseed oil is August 1st to July 31st, while that for soybean oil is October 1st to September 30th.

Both oils are traded on the New York Produce Exchange and on the Chicago Board of Trade. By far, the most active trading of soybean oil, however, is at the Chicago market, while virtually all the trading in cottonseed oil is confined to the New York Produce Exchange.

The trading volume in meal futures has grown substantially. The Chicago Board of Trade has an active soybean meal contract.

Wool and Wool Tops

The largest producer of wool is Australia, which accounts for roughly one-third of the world's output. New Zealand and Argentina are next in importance. Although South African production is only as large as that of the United States, that country has a considerable surplus for export.

The United States, despite large subsidies to growers, produces less than half its wool needs and depends largely upon the Commonwealth area as well as Argentina and Uruguay for the remainder. These nations hold periodic auctions and the price trend, particularly at the Australian auctions, plays an important role in determining futures market prices. Changes in the auction prices are printed in the daily trade journals and are easily obtainable.

Wool, when sheared from the sheep, contains substantial quantities of oil, dust, grass, seeds, etc., and is called "grease wool". It must be scoured. During this process these oils and particles are eliminated, leaving "clean" wool. In the process, over half the weight of the original shorn wool is lost.

Wool tops is wool that has gone through the first stage of manufacture in the production of worsted yarn. The scoured wool is combed to place the fibres in parallel positions. It is then wound in a loose thick strand on a spool and is called "wool top." The fibres left in the comb are called "noils." The price of wool tops will generally move up or down with the price of grease wool, but not necessarily by an exactly identical amount. The price at which the "noils" can be sold must be taken into account.

The government support program used for wool is the "incentive payment system" described in the section on Government Supports. Despite the large payments to producers under this system, it has so far failed to produce any important increase in wool production.

There are two futures contracts traded by the Wool Associates of the New York Cotton Exchange, a grease wool contract and a wool top contract. The grease wool contract is quoted on the price basis of "clean" wool. The basis grade is a U.S. 64's standard. However, wools from all over the world are deliverable, with premiums or discounts depending on grade. Wool certified over three years old is not deliverable. Delivery is in licensed warehouses at Boston.

The wool tops contract also is based upon 64's quality wool and is deliverable at Boston. Both grease wool and wool tops are also traded in London, and grease wool in Sydney, Australia.

The table below is a handy reference to some major characteristics of each commodity.

COMMODITY CATEGORY TABLE

	U.S. Net Export Commodity	U.S. Net Import Commodity	Primary Product	By-Product	Major Competition From Substitutes	Marked Seasonal Price Pattern	Concentrated Production Period	Continuously Produced	Major Use — Animal Consumption	Major Use — Human Consumption	Major Use — Industrial Use (Non-Food)	Perishable Within A Year	Storable More Than A Year
Broilers	X		X		X	X		X		X			
Cattle		X	X		X			X		X			
Cocoa		X	X			X	X			X			X
Coffee		X	X				X			X			X
Copper		X	X					X			X		X
Corn	X		X		X	X	X		X				X
Cotton	X		X		X	X	X				X		X
Eggs			X			X		X		X		X	
Flaxseed	X		X			X	X				X		X
Hides	X			X	X	X		X			X		X
Oats			X		X	X	X		X				X
Orange Juice			X		X	X	X			X			X
Paladium		X	X					X			X		X
Platinum		X	X					X			X		X
Pork Bellies			X			X	X			X		X	
Potatoes			X			X		X		X		X	
Rye	X		X			X	X		X	X	X		X
Silver		X	X					X			X		X
Soybeans	X		X		X	X	X						X
Soybean Meal				X	X		X		X			X	
Soybean Oil	X			X	X		X			X	X		X
Sugar		X	X					X		X			X
Wheat	X		X			X	X			X			X
Wool		X	X		X	X	X				X		X

CHAPTER 11.

GOVERNMENT PRICE SUPPORT
AND SURPLUS DISPOSAL PROGRAMS

In view of the tremendous expansion of farm production in the United States during the past two decades, government action designed to maintain farm prices, reduce surpluses, and alter the pattern of agricultural output has become of ever increasing importance in determining farm prices and income. Many programs have been established over the years and they basically have fallen into three categories:

1. Direct payment for farm crops at a fixed minimum price or at the market price, (loan, purchase agreement, direct purchases, and incentive payment plans) ;

2. Payment to farmers for reducing production (the New Deal AAA, the Soil Bank); and land diversion payments.

3. Surplus disposal programs (P.L. 480, Section 32 of P.L. 320, International Wheat Agreement.

The farm program is under constant review by Congress, and changes in farm laws can be expected with virtually every new session. Yet, the basic patterns remain largely unchanged. This chapter is designed to explain the major provisions of the various programs, as they existed in early 1971. An understanding of these provisions should lay the groundwork for estimating the effects on farm prices and commodity futures prices of these programs as well as of any new policies which the government may institute. Since this study is designed for use by those interested in commodity futures, discussion will be confined to commodities for which futures trading exists.

There are four methods of direct price maintenance now used by the Department of Agriculture as part of its effort to raise or support farm commodity prices. These are:

1) Loans
2) Purchase Agreements
3) Direct Purchases
4) Incentive Payment Plan

Of these four, by far the most important is the loan program.

Loans to Farmers

Under the loan program, the Department of Agriculture seeks to establish a minimum price for a specified commodity for that crop year. This is accomplished by the government announcing a price at which it will lend money to farmers who pledge part or all of their crop as collateral. This loan price, in many instances, has been above the commercial market price for that commodity. Consequently, it induces farmers to accept government loans, pledging their crop as collateral, thus preventing its sale on the open market. The loan program, therefore, when effective, eliminates a large part of the supply from the open market and causes an artificial scarcity to develop. This in turn, causes prices in the open market to move higher; ultimately, it is hoped, to levels well above the loan price. The loan, therefore, is in effect an alternative market for the farmer's crop.

Whether or not the loan is ever repaid, is strictly up to the farmer. He has the choice of keeping the money borrowed and discharging the loan by permitting the government to keep his crop. Alternatively, he may repay the loan principal, plus interest and storage charges. If he repays the loan, the government returns his crop and the farmer can then sell it in the open market. Whether or not the farmer chooses to repay the loan will depend upon the market price of the commodity. If the price of the commodity has advanced in the open market to the point where it is higher than the loan price (plus interest and storage), then the farmer will repay the loan and repossess his commodity. He will then sell it on the open market for the higher price. If the open market price does not advance sufficiently, then the farmer does not repay the loan. He keeps the money and the government keeps the crop and his obligation under the loan is fully discharged. In this way, huge quantities of wheat, corn, cotton and other commodities were accumulated by the government.

How Farmers Obtain Loans

Obtaining a loan is a fairly simple procedure. A farmer applies to the County Agricultural Stabilization and Conservation (ASC) Committee for a loan on his farm-stored grains. They send an inspector to check on the farm storage facilities which must meet fairly rigorous requirements. He measures the quantity that is stored and takes a sample for grading to see that it is of a quality that can keep for some time without deterioration. The storage bin is then sealed. The farmer next signs a loan note and chattel mortgage for the grain. He receives his money from the local bank which acts as lending agency for the government. The farmer must then pay a service charge varying with the commodity and the amount of the loan.

Should his farm storage facilities prove unacceptable, or, if he does not have the space, the farmer must move the grain to a government-approved warehouse before he can obtain the loan. He then gives the warehouse receipt to the ASC (rather than a chattel mortgage) and obtains the loan in the same fashion as before.

Obtaining a loan on cotton and other commodities follows a similar procedure. The commodity must be in approved storage facilities, and must meet certain grade requirements to insure that it can be stored for a reasonable time without deterioration. Repayment of the loan and repossession of the crop can also take place the same way.

In the cotton trade, another method of loan crop repossession has become dominant—the farmer selling his loan "equity." The farmer will only repossess his cotton if the market price is higher than the loan. The difference between the loan price and the market price is the producer's equity. The cotton dealer or other person who wishes to buy the farmer's cotton pays the farmer this difference. The farmer then signs the equity transfer on the Producer's Loan Statement in the presence of an ASC authorized witness. The farmer now has the loan funds granted by the government plus the payment for the equity. The person who bought the equity has 15 days in which to pay off the government loan. If he does not, title to the cotton reverts back to the farmer, who then can again sell another equity transfer.

Basic and Non-Basic Crops

For purposes of the loan program, all farm commodities are divided into three categories:

(a) basic crops, which are wheat, corn, cotton, rice, tobacco and peanuts; (b) designated non-basic crops including wool, mohair, milk, butterfat, honey and tung nuts; (c) all other commodities.

Until the 1959/60 season, support through the loan program was mandatory for basic crops somewhere between 75% and 90% of parity; for designated non-basic commodities, between 60% and 90% of parity and for all other commodities at the discretion of the Secretary of Agriculture at up to 90% of parity. However, new legislation continues to change the support levels in relation to parity for each of the several crops.

Parity

Price supports on farm commodities are based upon a percentage of "parity prices." Parity prices are the theoretical levels at which farm commodities should sell to keep them in the same relationship to other prices as existed in some base period. For example, during 1910-14, a farmer could sell two bushels of corn and with that money buy a shirt.

If he could do the same today, corn would be selling at full parity. If he had to sell more corn to buy the same shirt, corn prices would be below full parity. The "other prices" used for comparison are the prices of commodities and services farmers buy, taxes and interest on farm real estate and indebtedness, as well as cash wage rates for hired farm labor.

How Support Prices Are Computed

A change in the factors included in computing the parity price took place in 1954, giving rise to the expression "new formula" as opposed to the previous "old formula." Parity prices are computed under the "new formula" as follows:

1) Divide the past ten years average farm price for a particular commodity by the average index of prices received for all farm products during these same ten years.

2) Multiply this by the index of costs covering goods and services farmers buy (1910-1914 base).

The support price for a particular commodity is then set at a percentage of this parity price.

For example, suppose the cotton loan is to be fixed at 75% of parity for a crop year.

$$1)\ \text{Parity} = \frac{\text{Average farm price of cotton for last 10 years}}{\text{Index of all farm prices for last 10 years (relative to a certain base period)}} \times \text{Index of what prices farmer pays (relative to a certain base period)}$$

$$2)\ \text{Parity} = \frac{32.75 \times 2.84}{2.64}$$

3) Parity = 12.40 x 2.84 = 35.22
4) Loan at 75% of 35.22 = 26.42

The average loan for cotton at the farm would be 26.42 cents per lb. A higher loan is established for better qualities with longer length fibres; a lower loan price for poorer qualities and shorter staple lengths. These premiums and discounts are determined by the commercial market. The loan price is then adjusted for planting location. The final result, therefore, is a whole series of prices listing the loan level for each grade and staple length of cotton in each county where grown.

Parity prices for each commodity are published monthly by the Department of Agriculture. There is usually a change in these parity prices from month to month. Since most prices in our economy are in a constant state of flux, the relationship of farm commodity prices to other prices is constantly changing. How then is a fixed dollars and cents support level to be established if it is based upon parity which is constantly changing? This is accomplished by the Secretary of .\griculture first announcing a minimum dollars and cents support. Subsequently, a second announcement is made, either confirming the first *or raising it.*

The first announcement of the intended support level will be made prior to the planting season of the next crop. Thus the first announcement of the 1968 crop wheat support level was made July 7, 1967. These announcements, so far ahead of actual planting time, allow the farmer to evaluate his probable returns from planting various crops, and thus helps determine which crops and the amount of acreage he will plant.

This first announcement will list the percentage of parity at which the crop will be supported, and the dollar and cents equivalent of that parity. *This dollar price becomes the minium support price. It cannot be lowered. However, if parity prices are higher when the new crop year begins, the dollar and cents support price will be raised.* For example, suppose the Secretary of Agriculture announces that soybeans will be supported next year (that is, loans will be available) at 82% of parity. At the time of the announcement, soybean parity is at a level which makes 82% equal to $2.00 per bushel. This price, $2.00 per bushel, becomes the minimum loan level for next crop soybeans. As the months go by, let us assume parity for soybean increases. At the beginning of the new marketing season, assume parity has advanced to the point where 82% is $2.15. The loan rate will be increased to this level. This becomes the fixed loan price for that year. Any further increases or decreases in parity no longer count. The critical support is the dollar and cents figure designated at the beginning of the corp year by the Department of Agriculture.

The above example illustrated what can occur if parity prices advance in the period between the first announcement and the beginning of the new crop year. What would have happened if parity prices fell during that interim period? The first announcement (made months before the crop year begins) gave $2.00 per bushel as the tentative loan price based upon 82% of soybean parity as it existed at that time. Now let us assume that parity prices declined sharply in the ensuing months so that at the beginning of the new soybean crop year, 82% is equal to only $1.75 per bushel. The loan price is *not* cut to $1.75 per bushel. It remains at $2.00. That was the *minimum* established by the first announcement and it, therefore, remains intact. Whether parity prices continue to decline, or rise sharply, after the new crop year has begun, does not matter. The support price is now fixed for that crop year.

Farmers have planted and grown certain crops based, at least in part, upon their respective announced support levels. This is the reason usually advanced for not allowing those support levels to be reduced if parity declines.

While the Secretary of Agriculture may not set the loan price below the minimum, he determines the actual level of support above that minimum. The Secretary is authorized to set price supports at levels up to 100% of parity if he determines, after a public hearing, that such a higher level is necessary for the following purposes:

1) to prevent to alleviate a shortage of a commodity essential to the national welfare,

2) to maintain or increase the production of a commodity in the interest of national security.

Acreage Allotments and Marketing Quotas

The accumulation of large surpluses through the loan program led to the search for a method which would limit production and still allow the farmer to receive the benefits of the loan program. This was accomplished by adding acreage allotments and marketing quotas to the loan program for basic crops. Acreage allotments limit the acreage that can be planted by individual producers, per given commodity. The Secretary of Agriculture determines the maximum desirable total acreage to be planted for a given crop, within the limitations set by law. This acreage is then apportioned amongst individual farms. Acreage allotments, by themselves, constitute a very mild form of restriction. Farmers who plant more than their allotments (if marketing quotas are not in effect) do not pay any cash penalties. The only penalty is that they are ineligible to receive price support payments for that commodity.

The ineffectiveness of acreage allotments alone, as a means of reducing production, was proven early in the life of the loan program. The penalty, loan ineligibility, was apparently not a sufficient deterrent to overplanting. A more stringent form of control was needed. Marketing quotas were established. Alternatively, in the newer support schemes following 1966, additional cash payments were made to those adhering to acreage allotments as part of additional support plans.

The marketing quota of a farm is the quantity of a crop that the farmer can grow on his acreage allotment. In other words, an acreage allotment is established and only what can be grown on those acres can be marketed; no specific number of bushels per farm is announced. Of all commodities traded on futures exchanges, marketing quotas apply only to wheat and cotton, when in effect.

Marketing quotas proclaimed by the Secretary of Agriculture, are a much stronger form of regulation than acreage allotments. Unlike the penalty on acreage allotment violation, there are severe cash fines for violation of marketing quotas. Producers marketing in excess of their quotas must pay the following cash penalties:

Wheat — 45% of the May 1 parity price during the harvest year;

Upland Cotton — 50% of the June 15 parity price during the year of production;

Extra-long Cotton — 50% of the June 15 parity price, or 50% of the support price on extra long cotton, whichever is higher.

These must be paid to the county Agricultural Stabilization and Conservation Committee (ASC).

The establishment of marketing quotas for a particular commodity must be approved by the growers in a referendum to be held before planting time. (Acreage allotments do not require farmer approval). The Secretary of Agriculture must proclaim marketing quotas for cotton by October 15th, and for wheat by May 15th, of the previous crop year. Following the announcement of marketing quotas, a referendum is held. Two-thirds of the farmers voting must approve the quotas before they can be instituted. They then become binding on all producers of that commodity. That is, all producers of that commodity who market in excess of their quotas will be fined, whether or not they personally voted for quotas. If the necessary two-thirds approval is not obtained, then the price support level for that commodity falls to 50% of parity.

The Soil Bank Act of 1956

The development of huge commodity surpluses and the declining level of farm prices gave rise to numerous legislative proposals. In his message to Congress on January 9, 1956, President Eisenhower outlined specific additional measures which he hoped would have the effect of:

1) disposing of the surplus commodities owned and stored by

the government,

2) reducing production of surplus commodities, and

3) raising the level of farm income.

This was the proposal for a "soil bank" consisting of two parts, an Acreage Reserve Program and a Conservation Reserve.

The Acreage Reserve Program

The Acreage Reserve was designed to immediately reduce production of wheat, cotton, corn, tobacco and rice. It applied only to the basic crops. Farmers were asked to reduce planted acreage to a point *below* their government-granted *allotments*. They agreed not to graze or harvest any crop on the unplanted acres. In return they received a certificate for commodities whose value was based on the normal yields of the acres held in this reserve. The farmer could either redeem the certificate in cash or turn it in for CCC owned surplus commodities at specified prices. Thus, it was hoped that the Acreage Reserve program would both reduce production and, through certificate redemptions, reduce the surpluses held in storage by the government.

However, in practice, the program proved to be ineffective and it was eliminated in 1959. It was found that the farmers removed only the low yield fields from production and increased their output on other fields by closer planting of rows, the use of irrigation, more fertilizer, etc. Various other ingenious practices were developed which, while sticking to the letter of the law, negated its crop reduction purpose. Despite large government payments for keeping land out of use, surpluses continued to develop. The principle of the acreage reserve program, however, was incorporated into the loan program and became a direct part of the loan program as will be shown in the later section on the Agriculture Act of 1970.

The Conservation Reserve Program

The Conservation Reserve is a long range program. Under the impetus of wartime shortages and postwar production incentives, large land areas have come into cultivation which otherwise would not have been used. The Conservation Reserve is designed to plant these marginal lands with forages and trees. The government pays a sufficiently high percentage of the costs of this development to encourage broad participation. All crop lands are eligible for the Conservation Reserve as opposed to the limitation of the Acreage Reserve to the basic crops. There is no maximum limit to the acreage on a farm eligible for conservation payments. The government is attempting to get whole farms under this program, removing their crops from the market.

The Secretary of Agriculture is authorized to enter into contracts with producers for a minimum period of three years, and a maximum period of ten years (15 years in the case of tree cover), under which the producer would devote a designated part of his cropland to conservation purposes. He would agree not to harvest any crop from the designated acreage and not to pasture it for a specified period, except in emergencies. The Secretary of Agriculture is authorized to pay a fair share of the costs of establishing the conservation use and, in addition, to make an annual payment to the producer which will provide a fair and reasonable annual return for the land diverted.

As the program is constituted, the government will pay 80% of the cost of taking land out of current production and planting grasses, trees or other water or soil conserving purposes. This averages around $12.00 per acre. In addition, the annual payments to be made are tending to average $13.50 per acre, with a range of between $7 and $20. The latter payments are supposed to approximate the land's rental value for the production of hay or feeds and, therefore, will vary from one farm to another.

The Soil Bank at first proved to be both expensive and ineffective. Farmers have put little land into the long term Conservation Reserve Program. However, when the program was incorporated together with acreage allotments as part of the eligibility for loans, the effect improved sharply. The basic solution to the farm overproduction problem apparently lies not in restricting output but in expanding demand. This has been shown in the years when Russian and Chinese crops were poor and demand turned to the West.

Under the Food and Agriculture Act of 1965 the program is renamed the Cropland Adjustment Program. The primary change is that payments cannot exceed 40% of the estimated value of the crops that might otherwise be grown on the land.

Non-Basic Commodities

Support for non-basic commodities is not mandatory (with the exception of the "designated non-basic" commodities—milk, butterfat, honey, tung nuts, shorn wool and mohair). The Secretary of Agriculture must consider the following factors in determining loan levels on non-basic commodities:

1) The demand-supply relationship for the commodity,
2) Levels at which other commodities are being supported,
3) Availability of CCC funds,

4) Perishability of the commodity,
5) Importance of the commodity in our economy,
6) Ability to dispose of stock acquired.

With the above considerations taken into account, the support level is established. However, the loan level may not exceed 90% of parity unless a higher support is necessary for national security or welfare.

Loan Entry and Maturity Dates

The government allows several months of the crop year for the farmer to obtain a loan on his crop, and several additional months thereafter for him to repay the loan and redeem his commodity. The extended period for loan entries gives the farmer time to wait for higher prices before selling his crop. If his judgment is wrong and prices react, he still has time to place his crop under the loan and obtain the support price. The loan matures, that is, it must be repaid, sometime before the crop year is over. Occasionally the government will extend loans into the following year, but it usually prefers to have all loan transactions completed during the same crop year. The table below indicates the last days of each year on which loans can be obtained and the usual last date on which repayment can be made. Loans can be obtained, of course, at any time up to the dates listed beginning with the time of harvest. That is, as soon as the commodity is stored and available for inspection and grading, a loan can be obtained.

Redemption can take place at any time thereafter up to the dates indicated:

LAST DATES FOR LOAN ENTRIES AND REPOSSESSIONS

	Entries	Repossession
Wheat	January 31	March 31
Corn	May 31	July 31
Soybeans	January 31	July 31
Oats	January 31	April 30
Rye	January 31	April 30
Cotton	April 30	July 31

In addition to the charges for the loan itself, except for cotton, the farmer must also pay for any warehouse or elevator charges while the commodity is covered by the loan. These charges are deducted in advance at the time the loan is obtained, and will cover the costs of storage to the loan maturity date. In other words, the earlier in the season the loan is obtained, the greater the deduction for storage will be. (Note: These deductions occur only if the farmer does not have his own on-farm storage but must use commercial grain elevators to store his grain.) This has given rise to the expression "net loan" as opposed to "gross loan." The net loan (or effective loan) is the gross loan minus storage costs from any particular day as shown in the example below:

NET AND GROSS LOANS AT TERMINALS (SPECIFIED)
(per bushel)

| | SUPPORT PRICE | |
	Net Loan as of July 17	Gross Loan
#2 Soft Red Winter Wheat at Chicago	$1.36	$1.46
#2 Rye at Minneapolis	1.13	1.23
#2 Yellow Milo at Fort Worth*	1.87	2.09
#1 Flaxseed at Minneapolis	3.15	3.15

*per cwt.

The net loan will increase as time goes on until it reaches the gross loan level at the time the loan matures (last repossession day). In other words, in September the net loan will be higher than the figures shown in the table for July 17th. Anyone putting these grains under the loan in September will receive this higher net loan. The reason is, of course, the fact that it costs less to store grains from September to the maturity date than it does from July to that same fixed date. Nevertheless, notice that the farmer can never get the *full* gross loan as long as the grain must be stored off the farm. The last wheat loan entry date is January 31st, while the carrying charge deductions last through March.

Since the net loan return increases as time goes on, why does the farmer not postpone putting his crop under the loan as long as possible? Actually he does, but there are two factors which cause at least part of the crop to be put under the loan early in the season. First, the farmer must obtain cash to pay for his harvesting expenses—the extra labor and machinery hired. The various personal loans and credits he has obtained also usually call for repayment shortly after the harvest. This need for cash can be met either by selling at least part of his crop or putting it under the loan. What he does will, of course, be decided by whether loan prices are higher than commercial market prices. Secondly, farm storage space is limited. If the producer has to store his commodity in a commercial warehouse or elevator, he will have to pay the storage costs anyway. He might as well put the commodity under the loan. Another reason that became important since World

War II is the possible tax advantage of selling part of the crop in one calendar year, and part in the next.

It may be noted that the support prices listed in the table are at specific terminal markets for specific grains. The government, while announcing the specific various county loan rates for all loan commodities, does not announce loan prices in specific terminal markets (Chicago, Minneapolis, etc.) for corn, oats or soybeans.

Each month, the Government also announces the loan entry and repossession figures for each commodity. This is an important indicator of whether any probable supply stringency will develop in the open market. Consequently, these announcements have an important effect upon prices and must be watched closely.

Why Farm Prices Are Often Below Loan Levels

Market prices for many commodities are often below their corresponding loan levels. While it would seem that support levels should set a floor below which market prices could not decline, developments in recent years have shown that this is not the case. There are a variety of reasons for market prices dropping below loan levels. These include:

1) The fact that market prices must go below the loan price before producers will be induced to take out government loans. If a probable supply surplus exists, market prices are likely to remain below loan levels until the loan absorbs this surplus and creates an artificial scarcity.

2) A lack of approved storage space can occur. Farm storage facilities quite often are either not sufficiently adequate to provide for storage of the complete farm crop, or do not meet requirements for loan approval. The local grain elevator, particularly during the period shortly after the harvest, may also lack space for the storage of the farmer's crop. The producer, rather than ship the grain to another locale where storage may be available, will sell all or part of his crop even if market prices are below the loan. The fact that farmers must prepay warehouse storage costs for the entire season is also a factor in limiting their use by farmers. Since this same situation is repeated in many communities throughout the country, substantial selling is concentrated within a few weeks at the time of harvest. Farmers are forced to dispose of their crops at prevailing market prices.

3) The crop may be of poor storing quality, or otherwise ineligible for the loan. For example, if there have been heavy rains around harvest time, the moisture content of grain may be too high for storage. This makes it ineligible for the loan. While grain could be dried mechanically, this process is expensive and, therefore, a considerable portion of the high-moisture commodity would be sold in the open

market. Alternatively, the grain kernels may not have filled out properly and will be hollow. This light-weight grain is also ineligible for loans. These factors force supplies into the market and create price pressure.

4) If prices are close to loan levels, producers may not feel the difference is worth the time and effort involved in getting a loan, particularly since there are some charges attached to it. Producers would market their crop, thus in effect, helping to force prices lower if free market prices are close to the loan.

5) Producers of small quantities of the crop may also feel that the price advantage to be gained from the loan is not worth the red tape and expense. The cumulative impact of many small farmer offerings, however, could well mean a substantial increase in supplies.

6) Misjudgment of demand is another factor affecting the loan-market price relationship. If, after last loan entry date, demand fails to hold to expected levels, supplies become burdensome. Since it would be too late to obtain a loan, prices could easily react below loan levels.

7) If the crop proves to have been underestimated, prices could decline.

8) At harvest time, some hedges are placed in the market regardless of price either because it is company policy to remain hedged at all times, or because banks insist on it as a condition for loans.

Other factors could also be demonstrated, but the list presented covers the major reasons why commodity prices often go below the loan. They all come down to the fact that marketable supplies remain in excess of demand, or probable demand, at the price equivalent of the loan.

Summary of the Loan Program

The government loan establishes for the farmer an alternate market to the commercial market. The loan, by absorbing the possible surpluses, tends to establish an artificial supply scarcity in the free market. Acreage allotments have proven ineffective as a method of reducing production, but marketing quotas have put some teeth into the program, as have direct subsidy payments for compliance. There is a high cash penalty that must be paid by farmers who overplant. The raising or lowering of the loan level on each successive crop has been an important price-making influence, particularly on the basic commodities. Also important as a price determining factor is the monthly report of loan entries and repossessions (weekly on cotton) issued by the government during the period of the year when loans can be obtained.

The Commodity Credit Corporation

The Commodity Credit Corporation, known as the CCC, is the instrument through which the Department of Agriculture carries out its loan and other support programs. It is authorized to perform the following functions:

1) Support prices through loans, purchases and payments,

2) Make loans to farmers for the construction of storage facilities,

3) Remove and dispose of surpluses,

4) Increase consumption of farm commodities by developing new markets,

5) Export or arrange for the export of agricultural commodities.

Purchase Agreements

As explained previously, the loan requires the storage of the commodity in government-approved storage facilities. Many farmers are not so equipped and, in the flush of the harvest movement, may not be able to find approved warehouse space. Or, if warehouse space is available, they may not wish to pay the costs involved in moving the commodity and storing it there. The net effect is that the producer is ineligible for the loan. However, the producer has an alternative. He can enter into a purchase agreement with the CCC. This is the second form of direct price support.

A purchase agreement is a document in which the farmer agrees to sell to the CCC a specified quantity of his commodity. The price the CCC is to pay is the same as the gross loan for that commodity. The delivery date of the commodity to the CCC will be approximately the same date as the maturity date for loans (last repossession day).

Again, as with the loan, the farmer has the right to default on that agreement if he wishes to do so. In other words, if the market price advances above the loan price the farmer would, in all likelihood sell his commodity on the open market, rather than deliver the commodity to the CCC against his purchase agreement. On the other hand, if open market prices remain below the loan, then the farmer can deliver any amount up to the quantity of the commodity specified in the agreement. For example, if the farmer had signed a purchase agreement to deliver 20,000 bushels of wheat to the CCC, he has the option of not delivering any grain at all or delivering any quantity up to 20,000 bushels. He cannot, however, decide to deliver more than that specified quantity.

The final decision by the farmer as to amount of the commodity he will deliver must be made within 30 days of the date specified as the final purchase date. Within that thirty day period, he will inform the county ASC of his intention to deliver and will receive delivery instructions. He will then receive his money.

Obtaining a purchase agreement is similar to obtaining a loan. He applies to the county ASC, and concludes an agreement. The commodity must still pass certain grade tests. There is a small service charge involved.

The primary differences between the loan and purchase agreements are that:

1) Under the purchase agreement, approved storage facilities are not required.

2) The farmer obtains his money as soon as he takes out the loan, which is probably shortly after the harvest. However, under the purchase agreement, the farmer cannot receive funds until the commodity is delivered, which is close to the end of the crop year.

Direct Purchases

Direct purchase is the third method of direct price supports. Actually, it takes two forms. Under one form, the Government announces its intention of purchasing either specified quantities or unlimited quantities of a commodity at given price levels. This type of support is usually limited to processed commodities, such as butter and cheese. Cottonseed, where the products (oil, meal, hulls and linters) can be stored more easily than the original form, has also been supported in this manner.

The cottonseed package support program of the recent past will serve as an example. While cottonseed cannot be stored more than a few months, its products can. The government, therefore, announced prices at which it would buy cottonseed by-products from crushing mills. These processors in turn had to pay the equivalent of a cottonseed support price to the farmers. The government price, of course, allowed a crushing margin of profit to the processor. By this means, the government assured the farmer of price support for his commodity (cottonseed), while still obtaining the commodity in storable form (oil, meal, etc.). Note that unlike other forms of direct price support, the government payments are not limited solely to the farmers, but are also made to processors.

The second form of direct purchase is merely the government's entering the open market to purchase specific commodities in an effort to bolster prices. This has been done in lard, eggs and meat. A public announcement is made several weeks in advance. This, in itself, usually has at least a temporary price firming influence on the market. Whether there is a more lasting effect depends upon the quantity and speed with which purchases are made. The commodities purchased are usually for school lunch programs or donations to institutions.

Incentive Payment Plans

This is the fourth method of direct price support. It is now used only to aid the producers of wool and mohair. Under this program, growers market their products through ordinary market channels and obtain a record of their sale called an "Account of Sale". The Agricultural Marketing Service is notified of the transaction and computes the average price received by all shorn wool producers at the end of the marketing year (March 31). The percentage increase needed to bring this average sales price up to a previously announced "incentive price" is then determined. Each grower is paid an amount equal to this computed percentage of the average sales price *he has received for wool during the year.* As a result, growers who have obtained higher prices for their wool receive larger incentive payments and vice-versa. To illustrate: Assume the government has announced an incentive price of 62¢ per lb. for wool, and that average prices received by all shorn wool growers must be raised 20% to bring the average up to the incentive level. All growers receive a payment of 20% of their own individual average sales price. A grower who has sold his wool for 50¢ per lb., receives 20% of this price, or a 10¢ per lb. incentive payment. Other growers who have sold their wool for 40¢ receive 20% of this price or only 8¢ per lb. Therefore, we can see that growers are offered an incentive to obtain as high a price as possible for their wool on the open market. The higher the price they receive, the larger will be the government check they receive.

Under the National Wool Act of 1964, the Secretary of Agriculture announces an incentive price which should induce domestic production of 300 million pounds to shorn wool. This is well above any production in recent times. The price is announced before the season begins.

From the consumers' and taxpayers' viewpoint, the incentive type of program has several advantages over the other forms of direct price support. First, the entire production goes to market so that the consumer at least has the benefit of the increased supply and, therefore, of lower market prices. While the taxpayer must still shoulder the cost of the program he does not also have to pay a high market price induced by the artificial scarcity created when the government takes much of the commodity off the market through loans and purchases. Such costs as the storing and shipping of the commodities acquired through loans and purchases are also saved, as are the salaries and expenses incidental to handling these accrued surpluses. Finally, under the incentive payment program, the government does not become a major agent for the crop. There have been years when over 90% of the wheat and cotton exported from the U.S. were government owned. The government stays out of the commodity business under the incentive payment plan, except insofar as the level of payments are determined. The total amount of money payable under the wool support program is limited to a percentage of the money received from the tariff on wool imports.

The Importance of Government Surplus Disposal Activities

The huge surplus accumulated, from time to time, by the government through the various support programs has made the disposal of these stocks an important market factor. At times, government sales have been the major source of supply in the domestic market. For years, they were the major source of export offers. The following are the most important surplus disposal regulations, along with some indication of their importance to specific commodities.

When CCC-Owned Surpluses Become Sources of Supply

Under the provisions of the Agricultural Act, the CCC cannot sell basic commodities and storable non-basic commodities *in the domestic market,* at less than a specified premium to the then existing support price, plus reasonable carrying charges, or the market price, whichever is higher. This premium now ranges from 5% to 15% depending on the commodity and is designed to prevent the paradox of the government supporting prices by absorbing quantities of the commodity through the loan and other programs, while simultaneously depressing prices by reoffering these commodities in the commercial market at low prices. Under this provision, in times of shortage (when prices skyrocket), the government stocks would be offered for sale, thus increasing the supply when needed, but at a price level which would first allow for loan repossessions and the sale of all private holdings.

For example, if wheat were being supported at a national average of $1.25 per bushel, the gross loan for #1 hard red winter wheat at Chicago would be approximately $1.47 per bushel. Thus the formula would be the Chicago loan ($1.47) plus the premium, which for wheat is 15% until 1973, plus a carrying charge or transportation figure of say 10½¢.

$$(\$1.47 + .222 + .105 = 1.797 = \$1.80)$$

The CCC selling price for #1 hard red winter wheat would be a minimum of $1.80 per bushel at Chicago. The government selling price, therefore, remains well above the loan, and usually well above the market price. However, when market conditions warrant, the price does rally to the government selling level, as it did on occasion in the 1970/71 season for wheat. *The government selling price becomes a ceiling above which prices cannot be maintained, as long as the CCC has substantial quantities available for sale.*

The Department of Agriculture publishes a CCC monthly sales list indicating the commodities available for sale and the prices at which they are offered.

There are, however, important exceptions to this rule of "premiums to the support price plus reasonable carrying charges" as the selling basis for CCC owned commodities.

1) Commodities that are non-storable, are deteriorating, or *in danger of deterioration,* can be offered for sale at the market price or at such levels as are established by the Department of Agriculture.

2) The restriction does not apply if the commodity is to be sold for other than primary uses, for new or by-products uses, for seed, or for feed, if these sales will not substantially impair any price support program. Sales under these provisions have at times been important, particularly for feed in drought areas.

3) Sales of peanuts and oilseeds for the extraction of oil are exempt. The government has many times been the sole domestic supplier of peanuts for crushing and, in recent years, has been a seller of soybeans. The government domestic selling price of soybeans has been the support price plus 1½¢ per month for each month after August of each year. In view of the rapid expansion of the soybean crop, government sales could become a more important factor in the market in future years. So far, the government has taken over only minor quantities of soybeans through loan defaults, and so has had relatively small quantities to sell.

4) Wool sales are exempt. Wool is now being supported by the "incentive payment plan," under which the government no longer accumulates any wool. The wool provision is, therefore, of no market conseqence.

5) Sales for export are also exempt. This has proven to be of major importance.

For years prior to September 4, 1956 when the present export program was instituted, practically all the wheat exported from the United States was CCC wheat. During the 1956/57 and 1957/58 years, practically every bale of cotton exported was from CCC stocks. In other words, since the CCC can sell in the world market at any price level, it can take the export market away from the commercial trade whenever it wishes.

The reason the CCC came to dominate the export market in wheat and cotton was, of course, price. Because of the loan program, the domestic price of these commodities was far above the world price levels. The only time U.S. exporters could sell in world markets would be after the foreign grown commodities had been absorbed. When world supplies were large, competition drove prices down to levels 25% or even more below those of the U. S., and thus stifled exports.

The CCC, however, found the foreign market an important outlet for U. S. surpluses. The CCC was pressed by the need to reduce the huge surpluses because of the mounting complaints of carrying costs, the depressing effect on loan levels and the shortage of storage space. Even the mothball fleet, anchored up and down the Hudson River and elsewhere, was loaded with surplus grains. Since the CCC could not sell in the domestic market (because prices were not at the minimum level) it concentrated offers in export channels.

Public Law 480

Another very important factor in the agricultural products price picture is the Agricultural Trade Development and Assistance Act of 1954, known as Public Law 480. This act authorizes the Department of Agriculture to carry out agreements with friendly nations for the sale of U. S. Agricultural commodities for foreign currencies (under Title I), and to transfer these commodities on a grant basis for relief purposes (under Title II), or for barter (Title III) or on a long term credit basis (Title IV).

The Title I provisions have been of particular importance since they have, in effect, given the Department of Agriculture *billions of dollars* (to use more or less as it sees fit) to dispose of surplus commodities. These "commodities" need not be owned by the CCC. The Secretary of Agriculture merely has to declare a commodity in eligible supply for it to be included for export under this program. Thus, cottonseed oil, soybean oil and lard have been placed on the eligible list. Over half of our exports of edible oils were made under P. L. 480 in each of several seasons, although the CCC did not own a pound of oil. By negotiating agreements for huge cottonseed and soybean oil exports, the prices of these products were raised. Lard prices also benefited as a consequence. This helped increase the price and demand for soybeans and cottonseed. Wheat and cotton have also figured prominently in P. L. 480 exports. The resulting increase in wheat, soybean and lard prices, affected both the demand and price of rye and corn. This led to a firmer price of hogs and therefore feed grains, etc. The effects of the program are felt in ever-widening circles.

One of the major post-war problems with regard to our exports had been the chronic dollar shortage of foreign nations. P. L. 480 circumvented this problem. The U. S. Government negotiates an agreement with, let us say, Brazil which needs wheat. That country agrees to credit the U. S. with a certain amount of its own currency, which the U. S. then uses for paying certain obligations within Brazil. This, however, utilizes only a small part of the foreign currency credit. The remainder, the U. S. lends on a forty year basis for various development programs in Brazil.

The U. S. Government, in turn, grants Brazil an equivalent amount of dollars to pay for purchases of U. S. wheat. The rate of exchange used to determine the dollar amount granted is determined by negotiation which, in many instances, is below the free market rate. Thus a large part of the dollars granted is pure gift. A specific period of time is established during which the dollars must be used to purchase the specified commodity.

The country receiving the purchase authorization then asks for bids from U. S. exporters and places the orders. The successful U. S. exporters then buy the commodity in the open market, if it is oils, wheat, etc., or possibly from the CCC.

This program has been successful in that it has produced a substantial increase in U. S. exports and higher prices for a large number of agricultural commodities.

It has also led, however, to vigorous protests from Canada, Australia and several other friendly nations. They argue that this is a policy of dumping U.S. commodities in export channels, and has resulted in a loss of their export markets.

The changing world situation has led to several revisions of P.L. 480. A new revision called the "Food for Freedom Act" (1966), basically keeps all the old provisions but changes the emphasis considerably—

1. It calls for eliminating the need for the commodity to be declared as "surplus" to be eligible as food aid. It calls for faster shipments as well.

2. Emphasizes long term dollar credit sales (Title IV P.L. 480) rather than foreign currency (Title I P.L. 480) sales. This recognizes the shift from the post World War II world dollar shortage to the U.S. balance of payment deficit that now exists.

3. Increases emphasis on "self-help" programs as a necessary part of food aid. Thus, there have been some unofficial suggestions for example that India shift acreage out of cotton and into wheat before additional long term aid be given in wheat shipments.

4. Emphasizes development of markets for American farm products. Sales for local currencies (Title I) are to be phased out by Dec. 31, 1971, except for special reasons such as actual U. S. need for that currency to pay for U. S. obligation in the recipient country.

The International Wheat Agreement
(The International Grains Agreement)

This program had some importance before P. L. 480 was utilized, and may become important again if P. L. 480 is ever discontinued. This agreement is designed to assure exports and imports oι wheat within specific price limits. The four exporting nations, the United States, Australia, Canada and France are obligated to sell specified quantities of wheat at a maximum fixed price. The more than 40 importing countries are obligated to buy specified quantities at a fixed minimum price. Between these two price levels, wheat export prices are free to move according to supply and demand.

The agreement covers about half the world trade in wheat. As far as the U. S. is concerned, exports under P. L. 480 and the wheat export program can be registered as IWA sales. Since we would, in all likelihood, have these exports anyway, IWA has little immediate significance.

The agreement in no way limits exports or imports above the quotas established. However, the export nations can request that all import nations signatory to the agreement accept deliveries of their quotas at prices equal to the minimum. There have been times when the importing nations have refused to fulfill their obligations under the agreement. If world wheat values should rise above the maximum levels specified in the agreement, the import nations can demand full quota shipment from the exporters at the specified ceiling price.

Under the 1967 Kennedy Round of Tariff Agreements, the name was changed to the International Grains Agreement. The changes were slight, raising the price ranges and pledging the developed nations to donate modest quantities of grain or its equivalent to needy nations as food aid or famine relief.

The Grains Agreement sets a minimum export price of $1.73 per bushel for hard red winter #2 wheat f.o.b. Gulf ports. The maximum price is set at $2.31 per bushel. Since the inception of these price ranges, however, each exporter has sought ways to undercut them when they have wheat surpluses.

The food aid contribution to underdeveloped countries is 4.5 million tons of grains or its cash equivalent per year for three years beginning July 1, 1968. Of this the U.S. is to supply 1.9 million tons per year.

"Section 32" Funds

Section 32 of Public Law 320 authorizes the Department of Agriculture to encourage exports and domestic consumption of agricultural products by diverting them from normal channels of trade. Later legislation provided that commodites may be purchased for donation to school lunch programs and for relief purposes. Although minor quantities have been exported under this program, the law has been used primarily to purchase commodities for school lunch programs, institutions and low income groups.

The Potato Diversion Program

In addition, a potato diversion program was put into effect. Under its terms, the government pays the grower to sell his potatoes to starch factories and for animal feed use.

For years, potatoes were subject to loan agreements. However, since they are perishable, literally mountains of potatoes had to be destroyed. Attempts at acreage controls failed and potatoes were finally eliminated from loan eligibility. Some other means of support were sought and "Section 32," allowing payment for diversion from ordinary use, was hit upon as an acceptable alternative.

Potato production at times is well above "normal" levels of consumption. The government has allowed each of the major producing states to establish its own Marketing Agreements under which growers cannot ship potatoes below a certain size and grade for table use. In addition to this limitation on shipments, the Department of Agriculture pays the grower a fixed subsidy for the tablestock potatoes they divert to starch factories or feed mills. The program has been moderately successful in diverting production and raising the price level. The CCC does not buy or stockpile the commodity.

The Food and Agriculture Act of 1970

As time progressed the various support schemes that evolved were altered by continuous amendments. Various pressure groups alternated in influence and various new emergency or political situations had to be met. The result became a patchwork of, at times contradictory, sections of a basic law that every few years needed a good overhaul. The various programs needed integration into a new law giving some semblance of meaningful order. This was the Food and Agriculture Act of 1965 which was modified in 1970. The aim of the program is still the same: to keep production on farms limited and to maintain high levels of farm income. The program encompasses most of the basic agricultural commodities and adds new variations to previous supports. It leaves much more to the discretionary power of the Secretary of Agriculture than had any law in the past. It is in effect for three years covering the crops produced during 1971 through 1973. It brings domestic market prices for grains and cotton down to world prices and largely eliminates payments to exporters.

The Agricultural Act of 1970 had one major innovation. While still limiting each crop to a specific acreage allotment per farm, it is no longer necessary to remain within the crop by crop planting restrictions. Instead, it works backwards. After determining the allotment on each farm for wheat, feed grains and cotton, the Secretary of Agriculture determines the number of acres on the entire farm that must be "set-aside" (not planted to these crops). The farmer, to participate in the various programs, must agree to set-aside this number of acres. He is then free to overplant on one allotment, say, for example wheat, and underplant on another, such as corn. It gives the farmer a little more flexibility in his planting pattern and rotation system. However, if necessary to prevent major surpluses, the Secretary of Agriculture can, in the final analysis, even eliminate this flexibility.

The 1970 Act also places a limit on the maximum payments each farmer can obtain under each of the commodity programs for wheat, feed grains and cotton. These three programs are the nucleus of the farm legislation. The limit is $55,000 annually on each. However, this limit is almost meaningless since it does not apply to loans or direct purchases which are unlimited. The limit is on payments for set-aside, diversion, price support, public access and marketing certificates. Each of these terms and their function will be explained in the specific crop discussions that follow.

The Wheat Support Program

The wheat support program combines the various individual programs tried over a series of years into a comprehensive whole. Acreage allotments, and land diversion payments are all part of the scheme.

Marketing quotas for wheat are suspended. Purchase agreements and export controls also are involved.

Wheat surpluses accumulated steadily during the years following World War II and government holdings filled all available storage space including the holds of the "mothball fleet" tied up in almost endless rows on the Hudson River. The changes in the support programs in the early 1960's however forced a reversal of the former pattern. Production had then been restricted deliberately to levels below total use, permitting continuous reduction of government surplus holdings. The level of government support prices and the level of govenment sales prices therefore when combined with the rate of government sales out of its surplus holdings determines the price level. To put it even more bluntly—the support program gives the Secretary of Agriculture the power to determine the market price for wheat. This power will continue at least for the years covered by the Food and Agriculture Act of 1970. It was designed that way. The crop failures in Russia and China and the potential famine in India and Pakistan during 1966 absorbed the bulk of the surplus wheat held in the entire world, including the United States. There are now loud proposals to prevent the sale of any additional supplies and to hold the remainder as a strategic reserve. Many feel a stockpile equal to at least one year's consumption is a necessary minimum in the event of a drought or similar disaster occurring in the U.S. or in the event of a major war.

Should another major crop failure occur in any major producing area there will no longer be any large world wheat carryover to be easily utilized.

Under the 1970 Act, the wheat farmer may receive as many as six different payments for one crop. These are 1) Domestic marketing certificates as a direct subsidy, 2) land diversion payments, 3) a possible wheat export payment, 4) Loans or direct purchase payments, 5) recreational access payment, 6) grazing payments on set-aside land for seven calendar months.

The Act specifies that a domestic use wheat acreage allotment be established. That will be the acreage necessary to produce a minimum of 535 million bushels annually. If wheat needed for domestic food consumption should be estimated at a higher level by the Secretary of Agriculture, then appropriately higher acreage may be announced. The 1971 figure is 19.7 million acres. Please note that this acreage figure is not a planting limit but merely a figure to be used for determining subsidy payments.

The national domestic use allotment is then broken down into state, county and individual farm domestic use allotments. This is done by projecting a yield per acre figure with due allowance for fertilizer, irrigation, normal weather, etc. Actual wheat planted on each farm will average probably twice this allotment. However, one of the government payments, the direct subsidy known as the Domestic Marketing Certificate payment, is based only on the domestic use acreage. Wheat farmers who participate in the program will receive 100% of parity (now about $2.85 per bushel) on the production of their full domestic allotment. The market price normally will be far below that level, say in the vicinity of $1.30 per bushel. The difference between the national average wheat price for the first five months of the marketing year and 100% parity on July 1, the beginning of the marketing year, will be the face value of the certificates. Thus, in our example, parity of $2.85 less $1.30 market price would mean a certificate of $1.55 per bushel face value. This $1.55 multiplied by the yield per acre and the number of acres on the farm use allotment determines the full certificate value. Of this, 75% will be paid to each farmer *IN ADVANCE*. That is, shortly after the beginning of the marketing year, on July 1, an estimate of the farm certificate value will be made and a payment of three-quarters of this amount will be sent each farmer by the government. The remainder, if any, will be paid in December. If the preliminary payment proves to be too high, the farmer keeps the extra funds. No refund is required. Thus, if a bull market develops and prices move sharply above government price forecasts, the farmer gets a windfall gain.

The wheat miller pays part of the domestic marketing certificate. For each bushel of wheat the miller buys to process into flour for domestic use he must buy a certificate from the government for 75¢ per bushel. Thus, out of the total subsidy which in our example came to $1.55 per bushel, the flour miller paid the government 75¢ while the remainder came out of general tax funds.

To participate in this program and receive other payments, the farmer must agree to set-aside a specified number of acres from his farm for soil "conserving" uses, such as grass, etc. In some years, the farmer has been paid for the unused set-aside acreage. For the 1971/72 marketing year, he will not be paid for this. It is mandatory. The set-aside percentage, however, must be limited so that no more than 13.3 million acres in 1971 and 15 million in 1972 or 1973 will be diverted. However, once the specified number of acres is set-aside, the farmer can plant the entire remainder of his farm to wheat if he wishes. Let us illustrate. For the 1971 season a minimum of 60% of the domestic acreage allotment must be set aside on the wheat farm. On a 100 acre farm, the domestic use allotment would be about 40 acres. If a 60% domestic use allotment is to be set-aside then 60% of 40 = 24 acres. Thus out of a 100 acre farm, 24 acres are to be set aside and wheat can be planted on the other 76 acres despite the fact that this is above the domestic use allotment.

Suppose further that there was a 200 acre farm that grew both wheat and corn. If there were a 24 acre set-aside required for wheat there would be, perhaps, a 20 acre set-aside required under the feed grain provisions of the act for corn. Thus, a total farm set-aside of 24 + 20 = 44 acres would be required for this farmer to be eligible for the wheat program. A farmer must set aside the *total* set-asides required for his farm to be eligible for the programs. However, once he has now set aside the 44 acres out of his 200, he is free to plant the remainder all with wheat if he wishes or all in corn for that matter. Because of the substitutability of one crop for another, the farmer need not actually plant his wheat allotment to receive his certificate payment. He can get it regardless of what he plants on that allotment. However, if he does not plant wheat, then under certain conditions his allotment would be reduced the following year. There is, however, also a provision in the act which does permit the Secretary of Agriculture to actually limit the wheat planted per farm.

What about the set-aside acreage? The Secretary may permit planting of any number of crops on that land such as sunflower, castor beans, flaxseed, safflower, etc. Except during the five month normal growing season, the land may also be used for grazing or planting sweet sorghum. This permits income on the set-aside lands while still qualifying the farmer for the certificates, etc.

Payments for diversion of acreage in addition to the minimum set-asides are also permissible. This will be done in the future, as in the past, to reduce possible surpluses. No diversion payments will be made in 1971/72 however, because of the desire for large new-planted acreage to overcome the effects of the small 1970 feed crop. In the past, diversion payments equalled the full rental value of the land according to a government formula. The wheat farmers must sign up to participate in the next season's program March 1-April 9 of the same year. This permits the Secretary of Agriculture to gauge the set-aside acreage.

Once the wheat farmer complies with his total set-aside acreage and any conservation acreage, he is entitled not only to the payments on domestic use allotments but also to loans and purchase agreements on the wheat crop planted on all acreage. Loans for wheat under the Act must be set at a minimum of $1.25 per bushel but may go as high as 100% of parity. The basic determining factors are the world wheat price, the feed grain loan level and the feed value relationship of wheat to feed grains. The national average loan for 1971/72 is $1.25 per bushel. County loan rates will vary from this national average according to their transportation costs from a major market. The more distant the county, the larger the transportation charge, the lower will be the county loan rate. This permits wheat coming in from diverse areas to one central market place such as Chicago to be priced competitively. Unlike other years, when marketing quotas were in effect, there is no penalty for any surplus wheat production during the 1971 through 1973 seasons.

Wheat taken over by the CCC by loan default may then be resold. Under the 1970 act, the minimum resale wheat price will be 115% of the then current national average loan rate, adjusted for location, grade, quality and reasonable carrying charges.

Finally, payments may be made to farmers who provide access to hunters and fishermen to their set-aside acreage or permit other free recreational use to this land.

Now for another possible payment. This is against the price of wheat exports. Prior to the act of 1965, farmers received an export certificate payment on that portion of their acreage allotment deemed necessary to meet export commitments. The new Act makes no provision for any such certificate. With the support price of wheat deliberately kept at around the world market price, there should be little need for subsidizing exports. Under previous plans, the U. S. wheat price was so far above the world price level that subsidies were necessary to exporters to permit them to compete in the world market. That is, if the wheat exporter had to pay $2.00 per bushel and sell it at the world price of $1.30, the government would make up the difference. A subsidy payment would be bid for by the exporter. An allowance for profit was always included.

The payments can go both ways. If the exporters must pay more for U. S. wheat than they can get for it in the export market they will still receive a subsidy payment. However, if the U. S. price is below the world price, the exporter must pay the difference to the U. S. Government. Thus the subsidy situation relative to the export market will change daily. It will be very complex. At the end of the year the Government will total up the receipts and disbursements. If the exporters paid in more money than they received, the surplus will go into a pool.

This pool will then be distributed to each farmer with a wheat acreage allotment on a prorata share basis. However, there will be no export marketing certificates for 1971/72.

The Corn and Feed Grain Program

As with wheat, feed grains will be eligible for both support loan and support payments on the crop produced as well as payments for diversion of acreage beyond the mandatory set-aside.

Feed grains included under the program are corn, grain sorghum and barley when designated by the Secretary of Agriculture, with wheat substitution permitted under certain conditions for planting on feed grain acreage. Corn is the basis for the program with other feeds supported at levels related to their feed value.

Corn

A Feed Grain Base is established by the Secretary of Agriculture and is allocated for each farm. As with wheat, a specified percentage of this feed base must be set-aside in order to be eligible for the various payments under the program. There is no minimum set-aside established under the Act but for the 1971/72 season it is 20%. That means only that an acreage equal to 20% of the feed base must be diverted but it does not limit the amount of corn that can be planted on the farm. In our earlier discussion of a 200 acre farm under the wheat program, 100 acres could have been a feed base. Only 20 acres would have to be diverted for corn and 24 for wheat. This left 200 –44 = 156 acres which he could plant all to corn, if he so desired.

Once the various set-asides have been complied with, the corn farmer is eligible for direct subsidies called support payments. The support payment will be made on the production of corn and grain sorghum (barley too, when permitted) on one-half the farm feed grain base. The payment rate for corn will be the difference between a) the market price and b) $1.35 per bushel or 70% of October 1 parity whichever is higher. The market price is to be the average of the first five months of the season. However, as with wheat a preliminary payment will be made shortly after the new season begins each October 1. Allowing for a 20% set-aside in 1971/72, the preliminary payment is 32¢ per bushel for corn. The direct subsidy support payment then is 32¢ × yield/per acre × ½ base acreage. If any additional payments are needed, they are made six months later. If any over-payment has been made, no refund to the government is necessary.

Sorghum grain payments are in relation to corn. If corn payments are 32¢ per bushel, sorghum is 29¢ per cwt. The sorghum crop year also is October 1. The barley crop year begins July 1. Barley payments are only permitted in special circumstances—not in 1971/72. As with wheat, corn payments can be received even if no corn is planted but all the set-asides are met. This permits wheat, and at times soybeans to be planted on corn base acreage with no penalty. Again, the idea is to permit farm crop flexibility. However, again as with wheat, the Secretary of Agriculture can, if he wishes, place a limit on acreage planted to feed grains.

Payments may also be authorized for diversion of land beyond the minimum set-asides (but this has not been done for 1971/72) when the supply-demand situation appears to deem it necessary.

Payments also are authorized for permitting access to and free public recreational use of the set-aside acreage.

Compliance with set-asides also makes the corn farmer eligible for loans on his crop. His entire corn production is eligible (if storable) not just that produced on his base acreage. The Act calls for a minimum loan rate of $1.00 per bushel but it may be raised to as high as 90% of parity. However, the world price level must be considered. For the 1971/72 crop year, the loan was set at $1.08 per bushel for #2 corn which is equivalent to the $1.05 for corn of average quality. This is the same loan rate as in 1970.

The emphasis for loan rates on other feeds has shifted heavily to their feeding value relative to corn rather than other criteria. Thus, for 1971/72 sorghum loans are at $1.73 per cwt., barley 81¢ per bushel, oats 54¢ per bushel and rye 89¢ per bushel.

The CCC can resell feed grains it owns but not below a minimum of 115% of the then current national average loan rate adjusted for grade, quality, location and reasonable carrying charges.

As with wheat, other crops may be planted on set-aside land or grazed when the Secretary permits.

The Cotton Program

The cotton program is similar in basic form to those of the grains with just a few modifications.

Marketing quotas and planted acreage restrictions are suspended for the crop years 1971, 1972 and 1973. Producers who can raise this crop competitively can expand output if they wish and still be eligible for loans and support payments.

A national production goal and a national base acreage are established. The base acreage is to be sufficient to produce enough cotton for domestic use plus 25% thereof. This has been set at 11,500,000 acres for 1971. The production goal, however, is to be large enough to include not only domestic use, but also exports and an allowance for a 5% market expansion. It is also to be sufficient to insure a carryover of 50% of total use. This production goal was established at 11,993,500 bales for the crop year beginning August 1, 1971.

To qualify as a participating farmer for loans and payments, the cotton farmer must set aside on his farm a number of acres to be determined by the Secretary of Agriculture. The set-aside, however, cannot exceed 28% of the base acreage. For the 1971/72 crop year, this was set at 20% of the farm cotton base acreage. In subsequent years, diverted acreage beyond the minimum may receive additional payments if set aside with the approval of the Secretary.

The support payments will be made on the full base acreage at a minimum rate of 15¢ per lb. This 15¢ is to be paid as soon as possible after July 1. It will allow for average yields of the three preceding years. An additional payment will be made if the difference between the average spot price for the August-December period and

(a) 65% of parity or

(b) 35¢ per lb. whichever is higher

exceeds the 15¢ per pound earlier payment. Certain small farmers will get a 30% bonus payment.

Loans will be available on all cotton produced on all acres of farmers who participate. The loan will be based on 90% of the average world price for the previous two years. However, if the carryover in subsequent years grows to exceed 7.2 million acres, the Secretary of Agriculture can limit the number of acres grown per farm and limit loan payments to cotton grown on that acreage.

The minimum resale price of CCC owned cotton will be 110% of the national average loan rate with adjustments for location, quality and reasonable carrying charges.

As with wheat and feed grains, other crops may be planted on the set-aside acreage or grazed with Agriculture Department permission and payments will be made for access to free public recreational use.

Additional Features of the Agriculture Act of 1970

The act extends PL 480 for the eighth time since its inception in 1954. This time the extension is through the 1973/74 crop year. It also continues the 10 year contracts for conservation reserve acreage, continues dairy and milk supports as well as the incentive payment plan for wool. The Act also permits the Agriculture Dept. to assist communities in purchasing farm lands to maintain open spaces (Greenspan) develop recreational facilities, etc. It also permits additional real estate loans to farmers and ranchers as well as rural development assistance to low population density areas.

Conclusion

This has covered the major programs under which the government helps determine the price level of commodities, whether or not it owns them directly. A knowledge of price support and surplus disposal methods is of major importance for those who would successfully trade in commodity futures. In varying instances, these programs determine maximum and minimum price levels for a crop year or the average about which prices will fluctuate. New programs that will evolve after the publication of this book should be studied to determine their ultimate effect on markets and prices.

CHAPTER 12.

THE THEORY OF HEDGING

We have now covered the development of commodity exchanges, the advantages of futures operations, the fundamentals of trading and some background information on each of the commodities. Let us now delve more thoroughly into the basic reason for the existence of futures markets. That is its use by members of the business community to protect their firms against extensive losses which could arise from adverse commodity price movements. This procedure, as we have noted, is known as "hedging."

The discussion of hedging has been divided into three parts, (1) hedging in theory, (2) hedging in practice, and (3) advanced hedging procedures.

Hedging In Theory

Hedging may be briefly defined as the establishment of a position in the futures market opposite from that held in the spot market. Thus, one who owns or buys commodities in the spot market would sell an equivalent quantity of futures as a hedge. He is then said to be long spots (or cash, or actuals) and short futures. This is the *selling hedge* (selling futures) designed to protect the value of inventories against possible price declines. If, after the commodities are purchased, the price of the commodity should decline, then there would be a substantial loss on inventory. However, because the price of the commodity declined in the spot market, the price of futures would have declined also. Thus, the loss on the cash value of the commodity would be recovered by the profit in futures. If prices rose after the hedge had been placed in the futures market, then there would be a loss on the short position in futures. This, however, would be compensated for by the rise in the value of the commodities owned (which could then be sold at the corresponding higher prices). In either case, there would be a loss on one side of the transaction (spot or futures) compensated for by a profit on the other. Some examples provided later will illustrate the entire procedure. The selling hedge is used by grain elevators, warehousemen, merchants, processors and manufacturers who own commodities. It is an operation which maintains the net cost of an inventory continuously valued close to the current market.

The *buying hedge* (a purchase of futures) is used to protect against possible price increases of the actual commodity. An exporter, for example, may receive an order for 900 short tons (thirty tank cars) of U. S. soybean oil for shipment four months later. The price at which he would have offered the oil would be the price prevailing on that particular day. However, since shipment is in four months, he has no idea what the price of oil will be at that time. He could, of course, immediately buy the cash oil and store it until shipping time. This, however, would involve his paying storage and insurance costs for four months and tie up his working capital for that period of time. He would probably have to borrow the money from a bank to finance the purchase, which would involve paying interest charges as well.

As one alternative, the exporter could simply not buy the oil and hope that the price would decline in that four month period. He would hope to buy the cash oil for export cheaper at the time of shipment and thereby make a speculative profit. However, if he did wait to buy his oil and the price rose sharply during that time, he could suffer a drastic financial loss. If the price rose only one cent a pound, his loss would be $18,000 on that shipment. What could have been an excellent and profitable transaction, could instead turn into a loss that could lead eventually to bankruptcy. Firms that wish to stay in business long cannot afford to speculate in this manner. They may be right the first time or the second, but eventually they will be wrong, with possibly disastrous results. Most firms, therefore, will not attempt to try for this added speculative profit. The risks are too great. Instead, they will attempt to eliminate price risks as much as possible, and concentrate their energies on providing the service for which they are fitted. For this service (in this case the function of filling the export order) they will attempt to obtain a normal business profit margin.

The alternative therefore is to buy the equivalent of the 900 tons in the soybean oil futures market. Then, if the price of cash oil goes up, the price of futures would go up also. When the exporter finally buys his cash oil for shipment at the higher price, he would sell out his futures at a profit, thus compensating for the loss on the cash sale. He still has a profitable transaction, but his profit is limited to his normal business margin.

On the other hand, suppose, after the buying hedge had been instituted, that prices did decline for the cash oil. Then the exporter would have a loss on his futures transaction. However, he would then be able to buy the cash oil for export at a cheaper price, thus offsetting his loss in futures. He would still export at the fixed price previously established, once again making his normal business profit.

A specific illustration of a selling and buying hedge will further tend to illustrate the theory of hedging. It will also serve to point out where the theory can be less effective under certain conditions and thereafter examples will be developed on a progressively more practical basis.

The Selling Hedge

There are thousands of grain elevators scattered throughout the farm areas of the United States. The farmers sell their grain to these country elevators, which in turn resell it either to terminal elevators (those situated at the major marketing centers such as Chicago) or to processors. The country elevator sells the grain either on a delivered basis or "track country station." In the first case, the price is based on that ruling at the point of destination. In the latter instance, the price is based on the point of origin, with transportation paid by the buyer.

If the country elevator operator buys 10,000 bushels of corn from a farmer and can immediately contract to resell it at a fixed price, let us say for shipment one week later, *then no hedge is needed.* By having immediately resold the grain, the elevator operator has passed on the risk of owning the commodity to the buyer.

Sometimes, however, the elevator operator cannot immediately resell the grain. He might have to wait quite some time to make a sale. To serve and maintain his source of supply, he must buy the grain when the farmer brings it to him. He can only resell it when the demand is there. The purchase and sales do not necessarily occur at the same time. The result is that the elevator operator may have to carry a substantial amount of unsold grain. This unsold inventory entails a risk of loss. To prevent that loss, he would hedge by selling futures.

Suppose that, on October 23rd, the farmer brings 10,000 bushels of corn to the country elevator. The operator will buy it from him at a price based on the price ruling at the nearest terminal market, say Chicago, which on that day is $1.50 per bushel. The elevator operator finds that he cannot resell the corn immediately. He therefore sells 10,000 bushels of December corn at Chicago at $1.50 per bushel. Two weeks later the elevator operator is able to sell the corn through a Chicago terminal commission merchant. In the interim, the price of corn has declined to $1.35 per bushel at Chicago. This means he has a 15¢ per bushel loss on 10,000 bushels for a total loss of $1,500.00. However, at the same time that he sells the corn, he rebuys his futures since he will no longer need the hedge. The spot price having declined

15¢ per bushel, the December futures will also presumably decline 15¢ per bushel. Consequently, he will rebuy the December futures at $1.35. Since he sold it at $1.50, the gain on futures offsets the loss on the cash sale.

The table below summarizes the results:

CASH MARKET	FUTURES MARKET
Buys: 10,000 bushels corn at Chicago basis $1.50	*Sells:* 10,000 bushels December corn at $1.50
Sells: 10,000 bushels basis Chicago at $1.35	*Buys:* 10,000 bushels Dec. corn at $1.35
LOSS $ .15/bu.	GAIN $ .15/bu.

(Less commissions for buying and selling futures.)

The table above indicates that the loss on the cash transaction is offset, but it seems to leave no room for the merchandising profit. However, this is not true. Remember that we said the elevator buys the corn from the farmer based on the price of $1.50 at Chicago. But in fact he does not pay the farmer this price. Certain deductions must be made. The price that he will pay to the farmer is arrived at as follows:

Take cash price at Chicago per bushel		$1.50
DEDUCT		
Freight to Chicago	$0.10	
Terminal Market Commission		
Merchant Charge	.01½	
Operating charge at elevator	.06	
	$0.17½	0.17½
	Price to farmer	$1.32½ per bu.

At this elevator therefore, the price to the farmer, based on corn selling at $1.50 at Chicago, is $1.32½. It is in the 6¢ per bushel operating charge that the elevator operator has the profit he wishes to protect by hedging. Of course, this is not all profit. This charge is for weighing the grain when received and again when shipped. The grain is also graded and stored. It might possibly have to be dried and cleaned. Finally, the elevator operator must also sell and ship the grain. These services, of course, involve expenses for building and managing the elevator, etc., so that the 6¢ per bushel is far from being all profit. After the expenses of the elevator are deducted, the residual is the elevator operator's profit. Competitive conditions; that is, the buying prices of other elevators in the vicinity, keep this operating charge to a minimum.

The other two deductions in the example are payments which the elevator operator must make. Both are fixed and known. First, the terminal commission merchant is paid for acting as a receiver of the grain from the country elevator. He checks the grade, finds a buyer for the grain, sees that the transaction is properly financed, and handles any damage claims against the railroad transporting the corn. He also provides the country elevator with general market information which the elevator, in turn, passes on to the farmers in its vicinity.

Second, the deduction of the freight charge to Chicago or any other terminal market is standard procedure, since this charge must be paid by the elevator operator. If he moves his grain for sale at Chicago through the commission merchants, the elevator operator pays the freight, If, instead, he sells it locally or to a nearby mill, his price would be quoted "track country station" which means at his elevator site. The price he will quote, however, is the Chicago price less the cost of transportation to that terminal. Therefore, even if he does not sell the grain to Chicago, the freight cost is deducted from the elevator's selling price, and likewise from the price paid to the farmer.

The Buying Hedge

Let us return to the exporter who, before he owned the oil, sold 900 tons (30 tank cars) of U. S. soybean oil for export at a fixed price (say based on a base oil price of 8¢ per pound) for shipment four months later. To protect himself against a possible price increase, he would have purchased soybean oil futures. In our example, if the price of soybean oil rose 1¢ a lb., the advance in futures would have compensated the exporter for the loss he would have had to entail in purchasing the cash oil at a higher price. The table below indicates how this result is brought about:

CASH MARKET	FUTURES MARKET

July 20th

Sells: 900 tons based on   *Buys:* 30 contracts Dec. SBO on
     cash oil at 8¢   Chicago Board of Trade at 8.50¢

Nov. 20th

Buys: 900 tons cash   *Sells:* 30 contracts Dec. SBO at 9.50¢
     oil at 9¢

LOSS 1¢/lb.   GAIN   1¢/lb.

(Less Commissions for Buying and Selling Futures)

The sale of the cash oil for export was based on a cash oil price of 8¢ per lb. To this would have been added the costs of preparing the oil for export, drumming, inspection, export documents, etc., as well as a profit mark-up for the exporter. The final price at which the cash oil was sold therefore included a profit margin which the futures transaction protected.

The Advantages of Hedging

The illustrations have pointed up the primary advantages of hedging; namely, the protection against possible major losses due to adverse price movements of the actual commodity. Hedging also provides some corollary advantages, several of which have been mentioned in passing. Others are an extension of previous discussions.

The buying hedge, through the purchase of distant futures, in many cases eliminates the need for the building or renting of additional storage facilities. This reduces the need for fixed capital investment and maintenance costs. It also avoids tying up working capital in stored commodities over extended periods, thus releasing these funds for productive use. It can help reduce total interest costs to the firm, since it may be possible to work with less borrowed capital.

The fact that futures can be purchased for delivery a year or more in advance is another advantage. Some commodities cannot be purchased in the cash markets that far in advance. In the United States spot copper, for example, is sold by primary producers for delivery only in the current and subsequent month. Even then, there is no guaranteed price. The sale is subject to price on "date of shipment." By purchasing futures, producers of processed or fabricated goods can obtain a fixed price for their raw materials and thus be fairly certain of their costs. In many cases where a finished product has an historically stable price which the manufacturer wishes to maintain, the purchase of futures at an appropriate time for "around the clock" delivery (each delivery month) may guarantee a raw material cost that will insure the normal operating margin of profit for the year. This is particularly so if an inverted futures market (distant months at discounts) exists Remember that delivery of the actual commodity on these futures purchases need not take place. They are only used as protection against a rise in the price of actuals. Should that occur, the profit in futures will offset the price increase in actuals, thus keeping the raw material cost low.

The selling hedge on the other hand can have other advantages. If a selling hedge is instituted in the distant deliveries when they are at sizable premiums to the near months and to the spot market, then the futures market in effect will pay all (or nearly all) of the storage and other costs for the hedger. How this is brought about will be illustrated in the next chapter.

The selling hedge also is a great help in obtaining credit from banks. Banks recognize the advantage of the hedge in reducing price risks. Consequently, they are willing to lend a considerably larger sum to firms who maintain a hedged position on their inventory. By keeping a hedged position and thus obtaining larger working capital from banks, the turnover of a firm's capital can be more rapid. Thus, profits can be increased substantially.

For example, without hedging, a bank may lend a commodity dealer $1.00 for every $1.00 to be invested by the dealer in unsold inventory. That is, the bank would lend 50% of the value of the inventory purchased or held. Commodity prices fluctuate over a wide range. Consequently, the risk involved is fairly large and hence the percentage to be lent must be restricted. There is no assurance that the commodity can be easily sold without a substantial price cut.

With a hedge as protection, however, banks are willing to lend 85%, 90%, or even more, on the value of inventory used as collateral. This increase, in terms of the amount of inventory a firm can carry with a specified amount of capital, is much larger than is generally realized. The table below indicates the difference in the amount of inventory that could be handled with an initial capital of $50,000, coupled with bank loans reflecting varying percentages of inventory value.

Inventory Value	Bank	Lends	Firm's Initial Capital	
$	%	$	$	
100,000	50	50,000	50,000	(No Hedge)
350,000	85.7	300,000	50,000	(Hedged)
500,000	90	450,000	50,000	(Hedged)

With $50,000 of its own capital, a firm that can use a hedge could handle half a million dollars worth of a commodity because a bank would lend 90% of value. Without a hedge, the bank would lend perhaps 50% of value. Hence the same firm, with the same initial capital but without a hedge, would be limited to handling $100,000 worth of the commodity. The effect on profits is illustrated below.

One Unit Capital	Gross Unit Capital Return	Net Profit	
1	1	1	(No Hedge)
1	5	4	(With Hedge)
		3	(Net Increase Due to Hedge)

During any particular period, a unit of capital can be turned into a certain unit of profit. With a hedge, the firm is able to do a much larger volume of business and thus make one unit of capital do the work of many more. In our illustration, a unit of the firm's capital with a hedge results in a gross return of five profit units. From this gross return, interest on the borrowed money and other costs must be deducted, leaving a net profit of four units. Profit was quadrupled and 75% of it, or three profit units, were due to the advantage obtained by hedging.

The above also illustrates why hedging may be worthwhile even if the hedge results in a loss in the futures market larger than the gain on inventory. In our example, the gross unit capital return was five. We said that the net profit was reduced to only four because of interest and other costs. Part of these "other costs" could be a loss on the hedge. This hedge loss however is the cost of the price insurance which allows the firm a greater use of capital. Despite the loss on the hedge, the firm is still left with a greater net profit. It still pays to hedge.

The Limitations Of The Theory

The examples given above serve to point out the broad outlines of the use of futures contracts as a hedge to offset major price risks. However, they are simplified to illustrate the major points without the added complexities involved in actual transactions. A hedge may not give complete protection against adverse price movements.

In both examples, the price of the cash commodity and the futures contract were assumed to rise and fall by *exactly* the same amount. There certainly is a tendency for spot and futures markets to move upward and downward together since the two markets must sell at the same price during the delivery period (as explained in a previous section). However, spot prices can change a little faster or a little slower than futures. The difference between spot and futures prices therefore will change.

Spot price fluctuations of a commodity in October need not be perfectly reflected in the fluctuations of a futures contract for delivery in December. There could be factors in the spot market such as the price pressure of the heavy harvest movement of corn which would be over, or at least lessened, by December. This could cause a larger decline in October spot prices than in the December future.

Conversely, there could be factors in the spot market that could cause the spot price to rise faster than a more distant futures delivery. In soybean oil, September represents the beginning of the new crop crushing season. If there were a shortage of old crop oil, the first run of new crop oil would probably meet a strong pent-up demand from consumers waiting to replace their diminished stocks. This could cause the spot price to advance fairly sharply in September. The December future however may not completely reflect this. It would be natural for many traders in futures to assume that by December, the weight of new crop crushings would have produced enough oil to satisfy the pent-up demand and possibly create some surplus oil. As a result, the buying of the December future may not be too aggressive. Or, it is even probable that those who were actively buying the cash oil in August and September were selling the December future as a hedge. This selling could have prevented the rise in the December future from fully reflecting spot prices.

The various futures months do not sell at the same price, but are at premiums or discounts to each other. They are therefore also at premiums or discounts to any specific grade of commodity in the spot market. For example, #2 Red Winter Wheat could be selling at $1.40 per bu. in the cash market while the December future could be $1.38 and the March future $1.41½ per bushel. What is more, we know that these price differences between futures months vary with conditions in the market and also reflect expectations of changes in market conditions. Simplified examples do not take premiums or discounts into consideration.

Another factor ignored by the simplified theory of hedging is that most futures contracts use one grade as the standard for the contract while allowing delivery of other grades at premiums and discounts. There are many grades of a commodity. Each meets different needs and each will sell at a slightly different price. Thus at any specific time a bushel of #1 soft red winter wheat may sell at a 3¢ premium to a bushel of #2 soft red winter wheat. However, because of the development of strong demand at some particular time, the discount for #2 wheat might narrow to only 1¢ under #1 wheat. The grade of the cash commodity which is used as the contract standard is called the "basis grade." However, the grade of the commodity that is being bought and which must be hedged can fluctuate in a somewhat different manner from the futures contract basis grade. Its relationship might change much as that of #1 and #2 wheat above. While the basis grade of corn might advance 10¢ per bushel, another grade may advance either 9¢ or 11¢. The changes in price differentials between various grades of a commodity are usually much smaller than the total upward and downward price movement of the whole commodity price structure. Nevertheless, they exist and must be considered when hedging is to take place.

The fact that the futures contract unit is not necessarily the same as the quantity handled in the spot market is another factor which prevents hedging from giving complete price protection. For example, a futures contract of cocoa involves 30,000 lbs. Assume that a cocoa dealer buys 75,000 lbs. He cannot hedge this exact amount. He can hedge by selling two contracts (60,000 lbs.) or three contracts (90,000 lbs.). His hedge will be either 15,000 lbs. too little or 15,000 lbs. too large. He does not have a perfect hedge even if the futures market fluctuates by exactly the same amount as the price of the grade he owns. Suppose he sold two contracts as his hedge, and suppose further that the price of both the futures he sold and the spot cocoa he owns declined by 3¢ a pound. The value of his inventory declined by $2,250. His sale of two futures recouped $1,800. He still has an inventory loss of $450. On the other hand, had the price of both spot cocoa and futures advanced 3¢ per lb. he would have had a speculative profit of $450 because he was under-hedged.

Before we close our discussion of the theory of hedging, it must be pointed out that hedging is most effective when the primary *commodity itself* is being bought, sold and hedged. As the commodity goes through various additional processing, for example: raw cotton into yarn, then into cloth, then into a dress or a jacket, the effectiveness of hedging tends to diminish. The fluctuations in prices of cotton jackets, for example, depends upon competitive conditions in the wholesale and retail field, brand name acceptance, labor costs, transportation charges, other materials that go into the jacket (such as zippers, buttons, etc.), in addition to the cost of cotton. Therefore, hedging of finished goods by manufacturers must be different than that of a raw cotton dealer. The greater the percentage of total cost of a finished item that is represented by the value of the raw commodity, the greater will be the similarity of price movements between the finished product and that commodity. Therefore, the greater will be the effectiveness of hedging. For example, hedging flour purchases in wheat futures is fairly effective since the cost of the wheat is a major part of the cost of flour. Both wheat prices and flour prices will generally move upward and downward together. However, prices of bread will not necessarily follow the price fluctuations in the price of wheat, since the many other ingredients which are used cause new market factors for the finished product to enter the picture. This does not mean that the large bakers cannot, or should not, hedge against price movements in flour (wheat futures) or shortening (cottonseed oil, soybean oil and lard futures). It does mean, however, that the hedging operation must be of a different type and must involve additional considerations.

In summary, hedging fails to give complete protection against adverse price movements for several reasons:

a) The spot price of the commodity and the price of various futures delivery months do not necessarily advance or decline together by exactly the same amount. There are premiums and discounts between the various futures months, and these tend to change over a period of time. Since the price differences between various futures months change, then some of these delivery months are not moving *exactly* as is the price of the spot commodity.

b) The prices of different grades in the spot market change at different rates. Sometimes one grade will sell at a smaller discount to another, sometimes at a wider discount. The futures market cannot *exactly* reflect the price changes of *all* the different grades because a futures contract is traded in terms of one basic grade. A person may be hedging a grade of the commodity that is moving up or down in the spot market a little faster or a little slower than the futures.

c) The size of the futures contract unit is fixed. A unit, or multiples thereof, may not precisely cover the quantity involved in a spot market transaction. Therefore, a price change in futures may not exactly reflect the change in value of the dealer's or processor's inventory.

d) A hedge may be against a product other than the commodity traded in futures. For example, flour inventories may be hedged in wheat futures, or cotton yarn in raw cotton futures. The price of futures therefore may fluctuate in a manner different from that of the product hedged.

The Basis

It becomes obvious from the above that the inability of the hedge to give complete protection against adverse price movements, arises from the fact that price changes of the futures delivery month in which the hedge is placed may not exactly coincide with the price fluctuations of the grade or variety of the cash commodity being hedged. *The difference between the cash and futures price is called "the basis."* For a hedge to be perfect the basis must remain unchanged. That is, if the cash price of the commodity is 2¢ above a specific futures month when the hedge is instituted, it should be 2¢ above futures when the hedge is lifted. For the reasons outlined above, this is not necessarily the case. The price fluctuations of the specific grade are a little different from the futures. Thus, the basis changes: The price difference between the spot and futures may widen somewhat or narrow somewhat.

Specifically, if the spot price of a particular grade of corn declines by 10¢ a bushel while the price of the December future declines by 9¢, the basis has changed by 1¢ on the particular grade. Those who owned that corn and hedged it by a sale of the December future received protection against 9¢ of the 10¢ decline. They were protected against the major portion of the adverse price movement. However, the hedge did not protect them against the basis change of 1¢ a bushel.

The basis change can also work to the advantage of the hedger. If as above, the price of a specific grade of corn declined 10¢ a bushel, but the December future declined by 11¢, the basis changed by 1¢. However, this time the owners of that corn received the benefit of the basis change. The value of their inventory declined 10¢ a bushel but their profit on futures was 11¢. They made a windfall gain of 1¢ a bushel.

What hedging does, when properly utilized, is to provide protection against *major* adverse price movements and *major* financial losses. The factors listed above are called the "basis risks" and hedging cannot protect against variations in "the basis."

The Choice Of The Market And Futures Month

Little attention is paid, when explaining the simplified theory of hedging, to the choice of the market and futures month in which to hedge. For some commodities, there is more than one exchange on which futures are traded. For example, wheat futures are traded in Chicago, Kansas City and Minneapolis. Other grain futures are also traded in Winnipeg, Canada. Active metal futures markets exist in London as well as in New York. When choosing the exchange on which to hedge, several factors must be considered. First, on which exchange is the basis grade the closest to the grade or type of the commodity to be hedged? For example, soft wheat is deliverable at Chicago but not at Minneapolis. If an inventory of soft wheat is to be hedged, Chicago futures prices would be more likely to fluctuate coincidentally with this cash wheat owned by the hedger than prices at Minneapolis. However, that is not the only consideration. The volume of trading on one exchange may be much greater than on another exchange. If a large number of futures contracts must be transacted to cover a hedge, it would be easier to place a hedge, and to lift the hedge later, in the market with the greatest volume of trading. The more active a market is, the easier it is to get market executions without having to make price concessions. The location of the market may also be important insofar as it may become necessary to make delivery. If it is near, then transportation and delivery costs may not be great. Moderate price differences may also exist between markets and these too must be taken into consideration.

The choice of the futures month in which to hedge is also of major importance. The hedge should be in a delivery month sufficiently distant to cover the entire period for which the hedge is likely to be needed. Yet, this consideration could become of secondary importance if another delivery month is selling at a more advantageous price. Remember that the various delivery months sell at different prices. It may be more advantageous to initially hedge in one delivery month and switch the hedge into another delivery month at a later time. The volume of trading is as important in the choice of a delivery month in which to hedge as it was in the selection of the market. Hedging in a delivery month in which little trading occurs could mean being forced to pay a higher price when purchasing as well as having to sell at a lower price than would be necessary in an actively traded month.

The choice of the market and month in which to place a hedge, therefore, will depend upon a variety of considerations. These must be carefully evaluated at the time the hedge is to be instituted. Which of the factors are to be given most weight in making the decision will vary with the circumstances of each case.

We have covered the theory of hedging and have pointed out some of the pitfalls to be guarded against, as well as some of the reasons why hedging does not give 100% protection against price changes. However, as we go on to a discussion of hedging in practice we shall see how advanced hedging techniques can mitigate some of these difficulties and improve the reliability and effectiveness of a hedge.

CHAPTER 13.

HEDGING IN PRACTICE

Practical hedging operations can take various forms. Starting with the more simple methods, this chapter will indicate under what conditions hedging will be fully successful, partially successful or actually questionable. The next chapter will consider the more complex types and point out how they overcome some of the uncertainties of the simpler procedures. These chapters are designed primarily for potential hedgers. Speculative traders may wish to skip them until the remainder of the text has been digested.

As was indicated previously, when a hedge is to be established in futures, it is possible for the futures contracts to be selling at either premiums or discounts to the spot market. Also, after the hedge has been established, prices can either rise or fall. We have, then, the following possible alternatives to consider in hedging, both when the distant futures are selling at premiums, and again when they are selling at discounts:

A selling hedge followed by either:

    a) A price decline for the spot commodity,

    b) A price advance for the spot commodity.

A buying hedge followed by either:

    a) A price decline for the spot commodity,

    b) A price advance for the spot commodity.

Each of these possible alternatives will be examined and the hedging results illustrated. It was previously pointed out that there is a maximum premium on distant months equal to the costs of carrying commodities for the intervening time. It will simplify matters if we assume that the premiums on the trading months remain at maximum carrying charges. This will allow us to give the examples arithmetic precision. The effects of this assumption will be examined at the conclusion of each case study.

Example 1 — A Selling Hedge In A Normal Market Followed By A Price Decline For The Spot Commodity

On December 1st, a Chicago terminal elevator operator buys 5,000 bushels of cash wheat (a basis grade) at Chicago for the going price of $1.40 per bushel. At the same time he hedges by selling a contract of March wheat at the full carrying charge premium. Since full carrying charges are about 2¾¢ per month, and since the grain could be delivered on March 1st, the carrying charges would have to cover December, January and February. The March premium therefore would be 2¾ x 3 months, or 8¼¢. The March future would therefore be sold at $1.48¼.

Suppose that two months later, on February 1st, he decides to sell his cash wheat. In the interim, cash prices have declined 10¢ per bushel to $1.30, at which price the sale is completed. Since the cash wheat is sold, the elevator operator no longer needs the hedge. He would therefore repurchase the March future he had previously sold. However, in all likelihood *the price of the March future would have declined more than 10¢.*

On February 1st, the grain covered by a futures contract is within one month's time of possible delivery on the March future. The carrying cost therefore is only 2¾¢, not the 8¼¢ as it was originally when the premium had to reflect three months' carrying charges. As time passes the carrying charge decreases. The March future therefore would be repurchased at a 2¾¢ premium over the Chicago cash price of $1.30 which is $1.32¾. Since it was sold at $1.48¼ and repurchased at $1.32¾, the gross profit on the futures transactions was 15½¢, which more than offsets the 10¢ decline in the cash price. The hedge not only fully protects the value of the inventory, but also results in a gain equivalent to the reduction in carrying charges. As the futures contract approaches maturity, the carrying charges accordingly decline each day. Thus the passage of time itself is a major factor in changing the value of the hedge.

The recapitulation below will bring the results into focus.

CASH MARKET	FUTURES MARKET
	Dec. 1st
Buys: 5,000 bus. at $1.40 in Chicago	*Sells:* 5,000 bus. Mar. Wheat at $1.48¼
	Feb. 1st
Sells: 5,000 bus. at $1.30	*Buys:* 5,000 bus. Mar. Wheat at $1.32¾
LOSS .10	GAIN .15½

Result—Full price protection, Plus 5½¢ gain (derived from the carrying cost differential).

Now, suppose that the March future had not declined as much as shown in the example. In that case, on February 1st, the March delivery would be selling at *a premium exceeding full carrying charges.* This establishes the automatic profit possibility discussed in an earlier chapter. Many firms would buy the cash wheat, sell March futures and deliver the cash wheat against it. They would have to pay the carrying charges only from February 1st to delivery time but, since the March premium exceeds these costs, they would be guaranteed a profit.

Obviously such a situation could not last long. Too many firms in the grain business would be ready to grasp just such an opportunity. The only way this situation could endure (and it has occasionally happened) would be if all the storage space at the delivery point, in this case Chicago, was filled. The resulting inability to put wheat into deliverable position would temporarily prevent traders from capitalizing on this opportunity. However, this situation would last only until the actual delivery period. Once deliveries against March contract could be made, those who owned the grain would obviously deliver it at the higher futures market price rather than sell it in the spot market. This could alleviate the scarcity of storage space. Many individuals who accept delivery would move the grain to their own locations or to those of their customers. In addition, toward the end of the delivery period, grains (and other commodities) can be delivered against futures while loaded on railroad cars. Thus the storage space difficulty may be circumvented. The heavy selling of futures to make deliveries, and the heavy deliveries that would ensue, would force down the price of futures until they were in line with spot prices.

The other alternative is that futures could decline still more than shown by our example. That is, the March premium could go down to less than fully carrying charges. It might, for example, go down to only 1¢ over the spot price. In that case, when the hedger sold his cash wheat and lifted his hedge, he would still have a loss of 10¢ on his cash transaction. However, he would now have a profit of 17¼¢ on his futures transaction, for a net gain of 7¼¢. This, of course, would make the hedge even more profitable. Such a situation occurs quite frequently.

The other assumption made in this example was that the hedge was against a basis grade of wheat. That is, wheat that is the standard upon which the futures contract is based and which is deliverable against futures at the contract price (without a premium or discount). The hedge might have been instituted to protect the value of a grade of wheat other than a contract grade.

Actually, while all wheat prices go up and down together, some grades can go up or down a little more than others. The price relationships between the different grades change a little. Sometimes a given grade can sell at a 1¢ discount to another, sometimes more. This will affect the hedging result. While the whole wheat price structure went down 10¢ in our original example, some grades might have declined only 8¢, others as much as 12¢. The relationship of each grade to the price of futures would therefore also change. To put it in trade parlance, the basis changes and one cannot hedge against these changes in the basis. Hedging will afford protection against the major price swing of the whole commodity price structure. It cannot guarantee 100% protection however, since the price of a specific grade may decline more than the average.

When a person buys spot commodities and sells futures as a hedge he is said to be "long the basis." That is, he is long spot commodities and short futures. A strengthening of the basis will give him a profit. This can occur either by spot prices rising more than futures, or futures prices declining more than spot prices.

The opposite position, the buying hedge, where futures are bought against the short sale of actuals, is referred to as taking a "short the basis" position. In this case, if futures are stronger than the spot price there is an added profit on the hedge. If futures advance more than spot prices, the purchase of futures means an added profit on the futures side of the transaction. If spot prices decline, but futures decline by a lesser amount, then the added gain would be on the short sale of actuals.

How these basis changes are used as part of hedging procedure will be demonstrated after we complete this series of examples.

Example 2 — A Selling Hedge In A Normal Market Followed By A Price Increase For The Spot Commodity

Let us assume the same set of circumstances used in Example 1. The elevator operator buys 5,000 bushels of cash wheat (basis grade) on December 1st at Chicago, for the going price of $1.40 per bushel. He hedges in the March futures (at full carrying charges) at $1.48¼. This time, however, when he decides to sell the cash commodity two months later, he finds that the spot has advanced by 10¢ per bushel. He sells the cash wheat at the higher price of $1.50 and lifts his hedge by purchasing the March future. Since it is now only one month to March 1st, the full carrying charge premium is only 2¾¢. The March future would therefore be purchased at $1.52¾. The result would be as follows:

CASH MARKET	FUTURES MARKET

Dec. 1st

Buys: 5,000 bus. at $1.40   *Sells:* 5,000 bus. Mar. Wheat at $1.48¼

Feb. 1st

Sells: 5,000 bus. at $1.50   *Buys:* 5,000 bus. Mar. wheat at $1.52¾

GAIN   .10   LOSS   .04½

Result—A net gain of 5½¢ per bushel. (less commissions)

The cash grain was purchased at a basis of 8¼¢ off March. It was sold at 2¾¢ off March. The difference of 5½¢ is the basis gain. The basis gain developed out of the fact that futures could not rise as fast as spot prices. As delivery time approaches, futures must begin to reflect spot prices. Had the March future advanced more than shown in our table, it would have been at a greater premium than full carrying charges, again setting up the automatic profit possibility of buying spots and selling futures. The resultant selling keeps the March future from remaining above full carrying charges, except under extraordinary circumstances as mentioned in Example 1.

The hedge resulted in a gain, but fell short of the full 10¢ rise in spot prices which could have been realized had no hedge been instituted. It must be remembered, however, that the elevator operator had no way of knowing whether prices would rise or fall following his purchase of the cash grain. As explained at the outset of this book, most firms do not wish to speculate that prices will rise rather than fall. They are willing to give up the possibility of speculative gains for the price protection offered by the hedging process. Still, these two examples clearly demonstrate that a selling hedge in a premium market will not only usually provide virtually full price protection, but may also lead to gains which will be equivalent to part or all of the costs of carrying the commodity.

We have assumed, in both instances, that the firm sells the cash wheat while the futures are at full carrying charges. However, since fluctuations in cash and futures prices are usually not exactly parallel, the probability is great that at some time during the period in which the hedge is carried, futures prices will be quoted at a premium *less* than full carrying charges. The firm having the grain would in all likelihood choose this time to sell the cash grain, making an extra profit.

In Example 2, for instance, on February 1st the March future instead of being at a full 2¾¢ premium to the cash price might have been at only a 1¢ premium. The elevator operator would then have sold the grain at 1.50, but bought back the March future at 1.51, instead of the 1.52¾ as shown in the table. He originally bought the cash grain at 8¼¢ off March. In this instance, he would now sell at only 1¢ off March, for a profit of 7¼¢ rather than the 5½¢ shown on the table. The hedge, in addition to affording price protection, allows the firm to take advantage of basis changes for extra profits.

These two examples illustrate that the *selling hedge* at a full carrying charge premium is almost always worthwhile. It gives either partial or full price protection regardless of whether cash prices subsequently rise or fall. They also illustrate another important tendency of a normal market. While prices are rising, spots usually rise more than futures. They also decline less than futures in a bear market. The reason, of course, is that the cash grain is deliverable against futures contracts. Therefore, futures prices must adjust to spot prices as delivery time approaches or is underway. The carrying charge premium must get smaller and smaller as time goes on and delivery (maturity of the contract) approaches.

The excellent results obtained in our examples of the selling hedge in a normal market stem in large measure from the fact that we assumed the sale of futures was made at a full carrying charge premium to the cash market. Actually premiums large enough to cover all carrying charges are not available too often. More often than not the premium on futures will be less than the full cost of storage, interest, insurance and commissions. Our assumption was made so that the examples could be arithmetically precise. We were able to show how the carrying charge and the passage of time automatically worked to the advantage of the selling hedge.

The smaller the futures premium is over the cash price, the less likely it is that the selling hedge will give full price protection over the long run. The costs of carrying the physical commodity must still be paid. If the sale of futures is made at a smaller premium than this, there would be the possibility of not recouping these full costs. An evaluation of new considerations would have to be made before the hedge would be placed. First, what are the possibilities of the basis changing sufficiently to make the hedge profitable even if full carrying charges are not initially obtainable? In the previous chapter and in the discussion above it was pointed out that the fluctuations in the cash price of a specific grade of a commodity and the futures price will not necessarily coincide perfectly. Thus, as illustrated above, if it is likely that the basis will firm, the hedge at less than full carrying charges would still be instituted. Second, what are the probabilities of a major decline in price? If they are great, then the hedge, even at less than full carrying charges, is an important element of price protection. Even should the decline not occur, any possible loss on the hedge would be the cost of the necessary insurance obtained. Third, the effect on the amount of working capital the firm can borrow must be considered. We have previously pointed out that a firm with a hedged position could obtain a considerably larger loan and handle a considerably larger volume of business than one who was not hedged. In all probability it would pay to keep a hedged position and, consequently, the larger volume of business. If the hedge does not prove completely effective, it is, again, a necessary business expense more than compensated for by the profits on the increased business volume.

The smaller the futures market premium is over the cash price, the more important these considerations become. The smaller the hedging premium, the less is the selling hedge likely to give full price protection. As the premium gets smaller, the less attractive becomes the institution of a selling hedge; at discounts, the selling hedge may not be attractive at all. We will treat hedging in a discount market later.

The Buying Hedge

Let us now turn to the buying hedge—the purchase of futures as protection against a price advance where the actual commodity has been sold short. As a case in point, a foreign importer could have accepted bids submitted by an American exporter for 500,000 bushels of wheat, to be shipped two months later. The American exporter may not have the actual grain. Since he has sold at a fixed price, any upward price move that develops before he can purchase the grain would lead to a loss. The exporter would therefore buy futures as a hedge until he could cover his requirements of the actual grain. Since we are assuming that futures are at full carrying charges, he immediately runs into a major problem. When he buys futures for a hedge, he is paying a higher price for futures than the current spot price. As shown in our previous examples, if spot prices subsequently rise, then futures would not rise as much over the longer term. Therefore he could receive, at best, only partial protection against a price advance. Should spot prices decline, then futures would decline more than spot prices and he would be worse off than if he had no hedge at all. However, these futures versus spot price adjustments take time to work out. Over a period of only a few days, it is probable that the futures versus spot price relationship will remain fairly stable. The exporter therefore would buy futures as a hedge only for the few days that it might take him to purchase his cash grain at a favorable location for his export order. During these few days, if spot prices rise, futures would probably rise as much (or nearly so). The same would tend to be true of a price decline. Let us see what the results could be if he depended upon a buying hedge for protection against a sharp spot price advance in a premium market for the entire two month period.

Example 3 — A Buying Hedge In A Premium Market Followed By A Price Advance For The Actual Commodity

CASH MARKET		FUTURES MARKET	
	Dec. 1st		
Sells: 500,000 bus. cash wheat basis at Chicago	$1.40	*Buys:* 500,000 bus. March wheat at	$1.48¼
	Feb. 1st		
Buys: 500,000 bus. cash wheat at	$1.50	*Sells:* 500,000 bus. March wheat at	$1.52¾
LOSS	.10	GAIN	.04½

The exporter must originally buy futures at 8¼¢ over the spot price. However, over the long pull, futures cannot remain at more than full carrying charges over spot prices. Therefore, when he buys his cash wheat two months later, the March future will be at a smaller premium to the spot price. On February 1st, the futures are only 2¾¢ over spot prices. While spot prices rose 10¢, futures could only rise by 4½¢. He bought futures as protection against the possibility of just such a rise in spot prices, yet at best this move gave him only partial protection. That is, it recouped only 4½¢ of the 10¢ adverse price movement.

Suppose the spot price had declined during this two month period. The results would be as shown in the following table.

Example 4 — A Buying Hedge In A Premium Market Followed By A Price Decline

CASH MARKET	FUTURES MARKET
Dec. 1st	
Sells: 500,000 bus. cash wheat	*Buys:* 500,000 bus. March
basis $1.40	wheat at $1.48¼
Feb. 1st	
Buys: 500,000 bus. cash wheat	*Sells:* 500,000 bus. March
at $1.30	wheat at $1.32¾
GAIN .10	LOSS .15½

The buying hedge results in a loss greater than the gain resulting from buying the cash commodity at a cheaper price than was originally possible.

The previous examples demonstrate why a buying hedge in a full carrying charge premium market is not common practice where it is needed for more than just a few days. At best, it gives only partial protection; at worst, it can result in a greater loss than if no hedge were used. Since we assumed full carrying charges, there would be little to be gained from a long term buying hedge. The exporter would be better off buying the cash grain either for shipment in two months, or for storage under his own name. In this way, he could locate grain that was either at his port of export, or near enough to it so that he could save on transportation charges. In all likelihood, he would not have made the offer for export unless he had previously made certain that he could buy cash grain at a favorable basis and freight point.

The unfavorable results in the above example are due to the fact that the futures are originally being bought at 8¼¢ higher than the spot price. If the premium was at less than full carrying charges then the results would not be so poor. The lower the premium on futures, the more favorable a buying hedge can become. Thus, for example, if the March future were originally selling at only 1¢ over the spot price, the buying hedge would become much more attractive.

If prices advanced, then the loss on the purchase of the cash grain could be made up completely (or almost so) by the gain in futures. If the futures went to full carrying charges, the hedge would be lifted with the March future at $1.52¾ for a profit in futures of 11¾¢. This would more than offset the loss in cash grain. If futures remained at a 1¢ premium, then a 10¢ gain in futures would just offset the loss on the cash side of the transaction. It is also possible that a sharp advance of spot prices might be accompanied by a less rapid rise in futures. In this case, futures could actually move from a premium to a discount in relation to spot prices. Thus, if the March future advanced to only $1.49, or went from a 1¢ premium to a 1¢ discount to spot prices (the cash basis went from "one off March" to "one on March"), the advance in futures would still give 80% protection against a price advance.

In Summary

As shown by our specific examples, the selling hedge in a full carrying charge premium market is usually very advantageous, whether spot prices subsequently advance or decline. This is due to the fact that the hedger has the advantage of the high premiums over spots at which he sells futures, and the fact that the spot and futures markets tend to come together as the maturity date for futures approaches.

On the other hand, the buying hedge in a full carrying charge premium market is at best likely to prove only partially successful if held for any length of time. At worst, it can lead to losses greater than if no hedge were utilized. This is due to the fact that the futures must be purchased at such a high premium to the spot market. Yet as time passes, the two prices tend to come together. However, if the buying hedge is needed for just a few days, it may be highly successful. The time element (which forces the fluctuations in futures prices to be less advantageous) does not come into play, and futures prices have a good chance of moving up as much as spot prices, or nearly so.

Finally, to the extent that the premium is less than full carrying charges over spot prices at the time the hedge is instituted, the less advantageous is the selling hedge likely to be, and the more advantageous is the buying hedge likely to be. In fact, if the futures are at discounts to spot prices when the hedge is instituted, the situation becomes completely reversed. In this event, the buying hedge becomes the most advantageous while the selling hedge tends to be less profitable.

Hedging In A Discount Market (Inverted Market)

In Chapter 4 we pointed out that unlike the situation in a carrying charge market, in an inverted market there is no limit to the premium of spot or near month prices over the more distant months. That is, the discounts of distant futures to near months can be small or large, as can the discount of near months to spot prices. If a short squeeze develops, then near months can go to very large premiums over the more distant deliveries.

This prevents us from setting up the precise arithmetical examples we used when discussing a premium market which has a carrying charge limit. Nevertheless, with the information furnished by the discussion of the previous examples, we can arrive at several significant (albeit general) relationships.

1) *Futures prices will tend to be stronger than spot prices over the longer term.* Futures and spot prices must come together at maturity of the futures. Since futures are originally at a discount, then either spot prices must decline to the price of futures, or futures must rise to meet the spot price. If spot prices are rising, futures will be forced to advance more than spot prices, over a period of time. If spot prices are declining, then futures will decline less, or even advance. For example, assume the spot price of coffee (basis grade) is 60¢ per lb. on December 1st and the March future is at 10¢ discount (or 50¢). On March 15th, spot coffee prices have declined to 57¢. The March futures price by that time would in all probability have advanced from the former 50¢ level to reflect the full 57¢ value of spot prices (or nearly so).

	December 1	March 15
Spot	60¢	57¢
March Future	50¢	57¢

Last trading day (maturity) of the March contract would only be a few days away.

Buying of futures would develop from short covering. Those who sold March coffee could either deliver actual coffee or buy back their short contracts. If the spot prices of coffee remain above futures, shorts would lose money by purchasing the more expensive spot commodity to deliver against the lower-priced futures. They would instead buy back their futures thus, in effect, adding to the strength of futures and forcing it up to the spot price.

2) *Distant months will ordinarily fluctuate more slowly than near months.* There is a definite tendency, when distant months are at discounts, for them to have a narrower price fluctuation. That is, they will tend to be more stable (move up and down less) than the nearer months. They are selling at discounts because, for any of a variety of reasons, the general concensus among traders is that prices can (or will) be lower at a later date. If spot prices move higher, or stay firm, the near months rise to meet the spot price as the maturity of the contract ap-

proaches. There is no time left in the near month, for the expectation of lower prices to be fulfilled. The short covering and new buying which develop (as explained above) bring up the price of the near months. The distant months do not rise as fast, since the expectations of lower prices in the future still have time to be fulfilled. This will tend to limit new buying of the distant months. In fact, the more limited advances which do occur may lead to new selling.

If spot prices began to decline, the near months tend to move down rapidly. The distant months, already reflecting the possibility of lower prices, move down more slowly. If distant months (as shown above) begin at a 10¢ discount, then of course spot prices must decline by that full amount just to meet the distant month futures at maturity. The distant months may actually trade within a very narrow range until spot prices actually come down to an area which is close to the price of distant futures. If the decline in spot prices continues long enough, the discounts on the distant months will disappear and may even develop into premiums. The "inverted" market thus turns into a "normal" market.

For an inverted market to become a normal market, one of two things must happen; the near months would have to decline more than the distant months or the distant months could advance more than the near months. The latter is very rare. This illustrates another important fact. When prices are rising in an inverted market, the near months will ordinarily advance faster than the more distant positions. When prices are falling, near months will decline faster. Taking into account the above considerations, as well as the examples given for hedging in the normal carrying charge market, we can say:

3) *Over a period of time, the buying hedge in a discount market will be partially or fully effective.*

4) *As a corollary, the selling hedge in a discount market can be partially effective, or ineffective, as a means of price protection.* Points 3 and 4 above are just the reverse of what is to be expected in a carrying charge market. The buying hedge has the advantage since futures will be purchased at a discount. *Even if spot prices merely remain steady,* the buying hedge will be profitable since the futures must advance to meet the spot price. *If spot prices rise,* the contingency against which the buying hedge was established, futures will have to rise faster to catch up. They began at a discount. The gain on the long futures position would be larger than the loss incurred by having to purchase the spot commodity at a higher price. Again, the buying hedge is useful and profitable. *Should spot prices decline* after the buying hedge

was established, then futures will decline less than spot prices. The gain in being able to buy the spot commodity cheaper would exceed the loss on the decline in futures. The buying hedge in a discount market appears worthwhile under virtually all conditions.

This cannot be said of the selling hedge in a discount market. *If prices remain steady* following the establishment of a selling hedge at a discount, then futures rising to meet the spot price will result in an uncompensated loss on the hedge. *If spot prices rise,* the faster rise in futures will mean a hedge loss that is greater than the inventory gain. *If spot prices fall,* the hedge can be at least partially effective.

If spot prices fall very sharply, then the selling hedge (even when established at a discount) will recoup most of the loss on inventory. This is the situation in which the selling hedge at discounts can be effective. For example, assume that a selling hedge was established in cocoa at a 300 point discount when spot cocoa was selling at 65¢. Assume also that prices subsequently declined sharply. The results would be as follows:

SPOT MARKET	FUTURES MARKET
Sept. 1st	
Buys: Cocoa at 65¢	*Sells:* March at 62¢
Feb. 1st	
Sells: Cocoa at 45¢	*Buys:* March at 45.30¢
LOSS 20¢/lb.	GAIN 16.70¢/lb.
or on one contract	or on one contract (30,000 lbs)
LOSS $6,000	GAIN $5,010

The hedge, although established at a discount, recovered over 80% of the loss on inventory. Notice that this result occurred even when we allowed the futures to go from a beginning discount of 300 points to a full carrying charge premium over spot prices at the time the hedge is finally lifted. The decline in futures then is the minimum that could have occurred in relation to the spot price. The March future could not have declined less, since the futures price would then be at more than a full carrying charge premium; a situation which, we have seen, could not last. Had futures remained at a discount, the gain on the hedge would have been even greater.

Hedging in a discount market, then, leads to results diametrically opposite to the results obtained from hedging in a carrying charge market. In the latter case, the selling hedge is to be highly recommended. In the discount market, the buying hedge is generally advantageous. In the other cases, much greater caution must be used, with great consideration given to the possible trend of spot prices to be expected after the hedge is to be established.

These conclusions apply to a hedge that will be held over a considerable period of time. If the hedge is to be needed only for a few days, it can usually be relied upon to give price protection against any major adverse price movements.

Over the shorter run, the fluctuations in futures will usually be relatively close to those of spot prices, whether futures are at a premium or discount. There will of course be some differences, but the lack of any extended intervening time period will usually mean that the basis between spot prices and futures will not change very much. This is particularly true for the nearer months in futures. There simply will not be time for this to occur.

Many market reports, in discussing discount markets, will frequently contain the sentence, "Belated hedge selling appeared on the rally." Firms that buy and hold commodities will not always hedge automatically. When the futures market has a rallying period, many firms may temporarily withhold hedging until the market appears to have reached a top. In that event hedging gives them price protection at a better level. The hedge would usually be placed in delivery positions other than the near month, and, as explained previously, this is one factor that helps keep the distant months rallying more slowly than near months. It is frequently necessary for firms to hedge at discounts anyway, because many banks demand a hedged position as a prerequisite for working capital loans when the commodity inventory is used as collateral, as was previously explained. It should also be remembered from the earlier discussion that a carrying charge market develops when supplies are large, and that an inverted market develops when supplies are small compared to anticipated needs. In practice, then, we can expect to find hedge selling relatively heavy in carrying charge markets and somewhat lighter in discount markets.

Most firms who can do so, sell off their inventory in the cash markets when futures are at discounts and frequently sell short in the actual market for forward delivery. They simultaneously purchase futures at the existing lower prices. This does several things. It allows the firm to take advantage of the higher prices ruling in the cash market by profitable sales. Should cash prices continue to rise the purchase of futures will protect them against losses on their short sales. As previously pointed out in our examples, the futures would rise faster than cash prices since the two must sell at the same price during the delivery period. On the other hand, should cash prices break after their forward sale of actuals, the decline in cash prices would be greater than that of futures for the same reason. When the time arrives that the physical commodity is needed to fulfill the forward sale, the firm can either demand delivery on their long futures position, or buy the actual commodity and liquidate their futures position. The choice depends upon the grade and delivery point specified in the cash sale. We can therefore expect a greater use of the buying hedge when distant futures are at sizeable discounts to the cash market than when they are at carrying charges.

This even holds true for the major grain elevator firms which own tremendous storage capacity. At some point it becomes profitable for them to own futures rather than spot commodities, even though they still have the fixed expenses involved in owning the storage facilities. At these times, special efforts are made to rent out this storage space to others who may be willing, or forced, to carry commodities.

This chapter has illustrated some of the practical problems which must be faced in hedging under various conditions. It has indicated that while automatic hedging is desirable at times, an unhedged or only partially hedged position may be necessary at other times. Hedging results can be considerably improved if greater cognizance is taken of basis changes. This, and "on-call" trading, which uses the futures market as an automatic hedge, will be discussed in the next chapter.

CHAPTER 14.

ADVANCED HEDGING PROCEDURES

Buying And Selling By The Use Of The Basis, On Call And Ex-Pit Transactions

A practice which has been prevalent in the cash grain business is spreading to other spot commodity markets. That is the use of futures market quotations to buy and sell spot commodities. Rather than quote a fixed price for a spot commodity, prices are quoted only in their relationship to futures. Thus a commodity might be offered for sale at "six over March," or "five under September." This, of course, is nothing more than quoting "the basis" — something we have touched on previously. It immediately ties in the futures market to the spot market, and makes it easier to obtain an automatic hedge at the desired basis.

Basis Variations

In discussing "the basis" previously it was pointed out that while futures tend to go up and down with the spot market, there are variations in the price differential between specific grades of a commodity, as well as between specific grades of spot commodities and futures.

Anyone dealing in physical commodities who automatically hedges will find that his profit or loss depends upon changes in his buying and selling basis. If a wool dealer buys wool at a fixed price and sells December futures as a hedge, he may find that he has bought his wool at 5¢ under the December future — his "buying basis" was 5¢ off December. To make a profit he would have to sell at a basis that was better than 5¢ off December — let's say at 1¢ off December — and simultaneously lift his hedge. If he bought and hedged at 5¢ off December and sold at 1¢ off December, he would have a 4¢ per lb. profit regardless of whether the spot and futures prices collapsed or advanced to astronomical heights. Suppose spot prices broke sharply after the wool dealer had bought his actual wool. After the break, the dealer finds a buyer at 1¢ off December, at which price he sells. In terms of fixed prices, he might have bought the wool at $2.00 and sold it at $1.50 per lb. Nevertheless, since he was hedged, he still made his profit because he bought at five off December and sold at one off December. This is illustrated below:

CASH MARKET	FUTURES MARKET
Buys: Wool at 5¢ off December which is $2.00/lb.	*Sells:* December futures at $2.05/lb.
Sells: Wool at 1¢ off December which is $1.50/lb.	*Buys:* December futures at $1.51/lb.
Loss on cash .50/lb.	Profit on futures .54/lb.

Profit — 4¢/lb.

Through buying at one basis and selling at another fixed basis, the dealer can obtain his desired operating margin. Note, however, that this is only true if the dealer has established a position in the futures market. In our example above, had the dealer not sold futures, he would have had a 50¢ per lb. loss on his wool despite his selling at a better basis. It is only because he is hedged that the dealer can concentrate his energies on obtaining a better selling basis, and need not worry about whether prices are going up or down. In other words, when trading on the basis, it is more important to try to forecast the changes in the basis than the changes in price trends.

Just as most commodity prices follow a seasonal pattern of price changes, so do basis changes. Each year there will be a period when prices are lower than the average for the year. There will be another period when prices will be higher than the average. This same pattern of price movement is found to be repeated each year.

Most commodities also show a seasonal pattern with regard to the basis variations. That is, there are certain months during each year when one grade of a commodity is low-priced relative to futures. There are also certain months when these same grades are high-priced relative to futures prices. These changes tend to occur year after year because of the peculiarities of the production and marketing of the commodity. One segment of an industry, using only specific grades of a commodity, may have peak demand at a different time than another — thus causing (for a time) a firmer price for those particular grades than for others.

For example, a recent study by the author found that the basis variation of cocoa butter prices relative to cocoa futures prices, on the New York Cocoa Exchange displayed a very marked seasonal pattern.

The premium of cocoa butter prices relative to futures was lowest in August. It firmed sharply thereafter, reaching its highest point in November and then proceeded to narrow down slowly but steadily to the subsequent August. The pattern, graphically shown below, appeared to hold true whether the trend of cocoa prices was rising or falling.

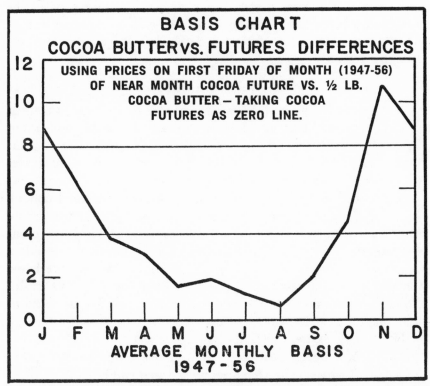

BASIS CHART
COCOA BUTTER vs. FUTURES DIFFERENCES

USING PRICES ON FIRST FRIDAY OF MONTH (1947-56)
OF NEAR MONTH COCOA FUTURE VS. ½ LB.
COCOA BUTTER — TAKING COCOA
FUTURES AS ZERO LINE.

AVERAGE MONTHLY BASIS
1947-56

The reason why this pattern of basis changes is repeated, year after year, is related to the uses of cocoa. When cocoa beans are ground, two products are obtained — cocoa powder and cocoa butter (fat). This is much like obtaining soybean meal and oil from the crushing of soybeans. During the summer, cocoa powder is used for syrups, etc., but little cocoa butter is used. The butter therefore tends to accumulate as surplus, and its price stays low relative to cocoa futures. In the autumn, however, when solid chocolate production (bars and candies) begins to run full steam, the demand for butter (used in producing solid chocolate) increases sharply and its price increases relative to futures.

Knowing the seasonal pattern of basis changes, a cocoa butter dealer increases his profit making potential. Since butter prices are lowest relative to futures in July-August, the butter dealer will attempt to buy butter and accumulate inventory during those months, selling futures immediately as a hedge. Toward the end of the year when the basis has improved, he will attempt to sell off his inventory and make com-mitments for forward deliveries. At the same time that he sells his inventory he, of course, lifts his hedges. The dealer thus buys at a low basis, sells at a high basis, and obtains his merchandising profit. If he can sell at a better basis than he bought, he will make money even if the actual price of cocoa butter has declined in the interim. It is the basis that counts.

"On Call" Transactions

Buying and selling on the basis allows a further change in market-ing procedure which is advantageous to both the buyer and seller. That is the practice of selling "on call". Once a dealer has sold his commodity at a specified basis (on or off futures) it does not matter to him what the actual selling price of his commodity is.

If he is hedged and has sold at a better basis than he purchased, he has a profit. This is true even if his actual selling price is 50¢ per lb. below his buying price, as in our wool example. The hedging profit makes up the difference. The final fixed selling price is of secondary importance to him. It does matter to the buyer however; the buyer wants to get the lowest fixed price. In selling "on call", the dealer allows the buyer to choose the day, and even time of day, at which to determine the final fixed price of the sale.

First, let us examine the process step by step.

1) A wool dealer owns spot wool at five off December and is hedged at that basis. The December future was sold at $2.05.

2) A mill operator who is the wool dealer's customer telephones him and says he needs wool to keep production going, but doesn't want to buy it today because he thinks the price will break.

3) The wool dealer says he has the wool and is willing to sell it at 1¢ off December "buyer's call."

4) He explains that if the mill operator will agree to pay him 1¢ per lb. less than the December future, the mill operator can have up to thirty days (or ten days, sixty days, or whatever time period is agreed upon) to determine when he wishes to "fix the price" of the actual sale. The mill operator agrees. The dealer has now sold his wool at "one off December buyer's call."

5) Two weeks later the price of wool has declined sharply and the December future is selling at $1.51. The mill operator decides the

price has reacted enough, and he wishes to have his wool bought at today's price.

6) The mill operator will phone the wool dealer's futures market broker and order the broker to buy December wool *for the wool dealer's account*. Permission to do this will previously have been given by the wool dealer. The futures broker buys December wool at $1.51. The mill operator or the futures broker telephones the wool dealer and confirms the price.

7) The December future was bought at $1.51, and the mill operator agreed to pay "one off December" for the actual wool. The mill operator will therefore be billed at $1.50 per lb. for the wool he purchased.

8) As far as the wool dealer is concerned, we are left with the exact figures given in the example a few pages back. The dealer bought wool at five off December, which was $2.00 per lb. He sold at one off December, which proved to be $1.50 per lb. However, instead of losing 50¢ on the transaction which would have happened were he not hedged, the dealer made a profit of 4¢ — the improvement in the basis. The ostensible loss in the cash transaction is offset by the profit in futures.

A few points need repetition and amplification for clarity. The mill operator obtained his wool when it was needed. However, he retained the right to price-fix at his own discretion. The wool dealer satisfied his customer and guaranteed himself a profit by merely fixing his selling basis. The actual price at which he would finally sell was of secondary importance to him. This actual selling price is fixed by having his customer buy a December future for the dealer's account. In this way the customer has the choice of picking the day (and time of day) when he feels prices are lowest. Since the dealer was previously hedged by a sale of December, this purchase of a December future for his account *automatically covers in the dealer's hedge*. It not only covers the hedge, but automatically establishes the actual selling price of the wool at the same time.

The illustration above was of a *sale on buyer's call*, where the buyer determines the final price. A similar procedure is involved in a *purchase on seller's call*. In that case the *seller determines the price* through selling futures for the buyer's account. This is just the opposite of the illustration we have just given. For example, a wool grower believes that prices will rise. Yet the dealer to whom he regularly sells his wool might need a specific quantity for a commitment. The grower agrees to sell his wool at a specified basis, but with the stipulation that he can fix the actual price at any time within thirty days. Two weeks later the price goes up sharply. The grower sells a futures contract for the account of the dealer. This does two things. First, it fixes the final price at which the grower has sold his wool. That price is the price of the futures contract plus the basis previously agreed upon. The grower now knows exactly how much money he will get for his wool. Secondly, the sale of futures for the account of the dealer automatically gives the dealer a hedge against the purchase of the wool.

Finally, it is possible to combine both procedures and have a dealer both buy and sell on seller's and buyer's call. His supplier sells futures for his account, his customer buys futures for his account. The dealer, once he has established his buying and selling basis, can unconcernedly wait for the prices to be made known. This is the most complex use of futures as a hedge, and sounds very intricate. However, in following the process step by step, it will become clear that it is quite logical and straightforward once the jargon involved is mastered. This method establishes only the buying and selling basis with the fixed prices on both the purchase and sale determined later. Let us take a strictly hypothetical instance involving very wide price swings as an illustration. It will point up the fact that, as long as the basis is properly established, what happens to prices subsequently does not matter. We will show a cotton dealer can buy at 57.80¢/lb., sell at 18.15¢/lb. and still make a profit; a) if he is hedged; b) if he has established a proper buying and selling basis.

Suppose a cotton merchant buys 100 bales at "20 points off October *seller's call"* when October is at 30¢. He does nothing about hedging. Some time later he finds a customer who will pay him 15 on October on *buyer's call,* at which basis he agrees to sell. He has now bought at 20 points under October and sold cotton at 15 points on, a basis which gives him a 35 point (35/100 of 1¢) profit per lb. on 100 bales (50,-000 lbs.). He does not know his actual buying or selling price, nor has he as yet any position in futures.

Now suppose there is a tremendous rise in prices and the October future advances to 58¢/lb. The merchant's cotton supplier phones the merchant's futures broker and *sells October cotton for the merchant's account at 58¢.* The merchant is then notified that he is now short October cotton at 58¢ and, since he agreed to pay 20 points under October for the actual cotton, please send a check based on the price of 57.80¢ per lb. The merchant is now short futures and has bought the actual cotton at 57.80¢.

Suddenly, a new factor enters the picture and cotton prices collapse.

When the price falls to 18¢, the merchant's customer calls up the merchant's broker and buys October cotton at 18¢. Since he agreed to pay the merchant 15 points over October, he has fixed the price at 18.15¢ per lb. He sends a check to the merchant based on this price.

The merchant therefore has bought cotton at 57.80¢ per lb. and sold at 18.15¢ per lb. Nevertheless, he has a profit. When the supplier fixed the price, he sold an October cotton at 58¢. When the customer fixed his price he bought an October cotton at 18¢. Both the sale and purchase of futures were made for the merchant's account. The result as far as the merchant is concerned is:

CASH MARKET	FUTURES MARKET
Bought: at 20 off October or 57.80	*Sold:* October at 58.00
Sold: at 15 over October or 18.15	*Bought:* October at 18.00
LOSS 39.65¢/lb. on 50,000 lbs. or $19,825	GAIN 40.00¢/lb. on 50,000 lbs. or $20,000

NET GAIN: $175 or 35 points per lb.

Notice that once the merchant fixed his buying and selling basis, his profit was secure, regardless of when and at what level prices were finally established. The supplier, by selling a future for him, *automatically* establishes the merchant's hedge at the moment the price is determined. The customer price-fixes through buying futures for the merchant's account thus *automatically* cancelling the hedge and establishing the profit on the hedge. The difference of 35 points profit is locked into the transaction. It doesn't matter if the customer or the supplier price-fixes first. The results are the same.

The Ex-Pit Transaction (Exchange For Physicals)

The price-fixing method previously illustrated is the standard procedure in the cotton trade. A somewhat different procedure is followed in the grain trade, cocoa trade, and a few others. This is commonly known as the "ex-pit transaction" in grains, the "exchange for physicals" in cocoa, and "against actuals" in coffee and sugar.

The ex-pit transaction works in a manner somewhat similar to price-fixing in cotton. That is, the basis is established first and then a futures transaction is made which determines the actual dollar and cents price for the cash commodity. However, in this case, the futures transaction is not made by open outcry in the ring or pit, but is completed by the floor brokers privately, outside the ring — hence the designation "ex-pit transactions." The exchanges, as well as the Commodity Exchange Authority allow this exception to the general rule that all trades must be made by open outcry within the ring. An ex-pit transaction is legitimate only if it involves the settlement of a cash transaction between the two participating parties (see Regulation 1866, 1809, 1809A of "Rules and Regulations, Board of Trade of the City of Chicago").

Again, it will be easier to explain the procedure by an example. A wheat exporter consummates a sale for 100,000 bushels, let us say, for July delivery to Holland. The exporter does not own the actual wheat, and buys the July future as a hedge against a possible price rise in the interim. As July approaches, the exporter finds an elevator operator who will sell him 100,000 bushels of the desired grade of wheat at "five over July." This basis is one which allows the exporter to make his profit margin, and he accepts.

1) The futures broker of the exporter and elevator operator are told to get together *outside the ring* and transact 100,000 bushels of July futures at either the market price or a price previously agreed upon.

2) The exporter who was long 100,000 bushels of July sells his futures to the elevator operator at the agreed upon price or at the market. This sale automatically liquidates his buying hedge. (Remember, he had previously bought July as a hedge; he is now selling July.)

3) The elevator operator buys the 100,000 bushels of July from the exporter, let us say, at $1.40 per bushel. The futures price plus the 5¢ over July, which was the basis previously established, is the price at which the elevator operator has sold the cash wheat. The final price of the cash wheat has been fixed at $1.45 per bushel.

4) If the elevator operator who had owned the wheat had been hedged (as he probably was) by a sale of 100,000 bushels of July futures, the purchase of futures from the exporter would also have automatically covered that hedge. (He sold July before as a hedge and he has now bought July.) If the elevator operator had not been short July as a hedge, then his ex-pit purchase of futures from the exporter would now make him long futures.

5) The exporter has exchanged his 100,000 bushels of July futures

(plus 5¢ per bushel) for 100,000 bushels of cash wheat. The elevator operator has exchanged his 100,000 bushels of cash wheat for 100,000 bushels of July futures plus 5¢ per bushel.

The ex-pit transaction is registered on the books of the exchange just as if it were consummated in the ring.

This procedure differs from the cotton price-fixing method described in our previous example. In the cotton method, the price is fixed by the cash commodity buyer purchasing futures for the account of the cash commodity seller, thus establishing a price to which the agreed basis is added. Tradition appears to be the only reason why one method is used in cotton, and another in grains.

There is, however, a good reason for the transaction to take place "ex-pit" (out of the ring) rather than through the normal procedure of open bids and offers in the ring. Under the normal procedure, if the exporter offered 100,000 July in the ring, chances are that at least part, if not all, of these offers would be absorbed by someone other than the elevator operator. When the elevator operator wants to buy 100,000 July, he might very well receive a different price than the exporter. We would then have a situation in which the exporter sold his futures (and covered his hedge) at one price, while the elevator operator bought futures at another price. To which price should the 5¢ basis be added in order to arrive at the fixed selling price of the cash commodity? One would prefer the higher price, the other the lower price, and an average would not satisfy either. By completing the transaction ex-pit, this problem is avoided. The buying and selling prices are the same. The hedges are covered at the same price, and there can be no dispute concerning the final price of the cash wheat.

CHAPTER 15.

PRICE CHART METHODS USED FOR FORECASTING

In an earlier section, it was stated that the commonly used methods of price forecasting fell into two principal categories; trading on the fundamentals, and chart trading. The former was then covered in detail and a checklist of items to watch was presented. We now come to the second method.

Price charts are now extensively used by speculative traders, as well as by many trade firms. While some firms follow a policy of automatically hedging their inventories for price protection, some restrict their hedging only to periods when prices are declining or appear ready to decline. They are willing to take a speculative position on inventory, but need some means of following price trends closely enough to quickly forecast an impending price decline. Price charts fill that need.

The Theory Of Chart Trading

A true chartist will reject the use of any statistical compilation of supply and demand data and its analysis. Similarly, he would reject the seeking out and interpretation of news events as a basis for commodity speculation. His whole thinking is oriented towards the idea that market action (i.e., the price swings) will indicate whether prices are going higher or lower.

The chartists' reasoning is along the following lines. Supply and demand data are subject to individual interpretation and the interpretation of the same series of data has time and again led to diametrically opposite conclusions as to the probable course of prices. Furthermore, the figures usually are not current, but indicate a situation that existed in the past. In some cases, the statistics are projected into the future, but the projection itself is a forecast and, hence, will have a bullish or bearish bias.

The same objections can be made to the evaluation of news events as a basis on which to trade, says the chartist. First of all, many people probably have heard the news item well before it became generally known. Therefore, part or most of its price effect may have been felt. Trading on the news would mean entering the market after the price adjustment to the news has already occurred. Another difficulty would be in the interpretation of the news. One might easily bullishly interpret news which the remainder of the traders feel is bearish. Thus, the wrong position would be taken in the market with a consequential loss resulting.

All of these difficulties can be avoided, says the chartist, by the simple procedure of refusing to interpret news or statistics, but waiting "for the market to tell you" when to trade and whether to buy or sell. All known factors in the supply and demand picture (as well as those that are not yet public knowledge), and all news events that are acted upon by traders, will be recorded in the market place through price changes. That is, if most of the traders believe on the basis of their own knowledge that prices will move higher, buying will be more aggressive than selling, and the price level will rise. The reverse is true if most traders feel the situation is bearish.

Each trader acting individually affects price. The direction of the resultant price movement will indicate whether the sum of all these individual trades will be bullish or bearish. Thus, by refusing to interpret statistics or news events, but merely by watching the direction and amplitude of price movements in the market, one can know how others are thinking and acting, and, hence, how to trade. All statistics and news events are meaningless unless acted upon by traders. Once they are acted upon, they will affect price. Therefore, merely watch prices and you will know how to trade. You need not fear misinterpreting statistics or news events, nor missing major news events or statistical items which may change the entire picture.

How Charts Mirror Changes In Psychology

Furthermore, says the chartist, trading on the statistical supply and demand situation alone ignores one of the fundamental and most unpredictable price making influences; namely, the psychology or mood of the trading public. Time and again, when a strong upward trend was underway, the market has failed to respond to specific news events of a bearish nature. The public either chose to ignore the news because of their overwhelming confidence, or rationalized it away as of piddling moment. Innumerable similar experiences could be cited when a downward trend was in progress. At times, the public is just not receptive to any rational statistical appraisal.

There are equally numerous examples of a market suddenly reversing an established upward trend, with prices breaking sharply, for no apparent reason. No major news event has occurred, no change in the statistical picture is apparent but the public confidence in the price level and in the trend has unexpectedly changed. Wave after wave of liquidation develops with the consequent adverse effect on price.

These examples indicate that trading only on statistical data or news events could lead to costly errors. If, instead, trades are instituted on the basis of past and current market action, as illustrated by past and current price movements, these errors can be avoided.

Having arrived at this decision the chartist then proceeds to keep a record of price movements, in a variety of ways, in the expectation of discovering certain patterns called "chart pictures." These patterns, through historical precedent, indicate that a price movement is underway or that the trend of price is turning (say from an upward movement to a decline). The chartist also believes, in many cases, that he can foretell the extent of the coming price movement, as well as its direction. Let us see just how this is done.

The Different Charting Methods

There are many different methods of charting, that is, of keeping pictures of price movements. The most popular are:

(a) The daily high-low-close bar chart
(b) The point and figure method
(c) Moving averages of closing prices.

Each of these chart methods has its own merits and serves a slightly different purpose. Those chartists who have the time, may keep a series of each. However, this takes a great deal of time and, in most instances, employing just one method will be sufficient to indicate most of the things for which a chart is useful. A description of how to make each type of chart will be given later.

The daily bar chart has the advantages of being the simplest to make, the easiest to interpret, and takes only seconds a day to keep current. It gives a clear picture of price movements from one day to the next. The chart picture is clearly discernible and remains current up to each day's trade.

Some chartists, however, feel that knowing the range and closing price is insufficient. They believe that it is important to know at which prices *within* the day's trading range most of the activity took place. The prices at which most of the buying and selling took place would indicate more accurately the critical values which must be watched to forecast price trends. The "point and figure" chart is then used. This type of chart records the minor price movements that occur within the trading day, as opposed to the bar chart which just indicates the range. Those chartists who have the time to watch the trading tape all day long can keep these charts current. Most of us, of course, cannot spend the day watching a commodity board. Therefore, to keep up point and figure charts would require purchasing a service (whose bulletin is mailed out each night) to record these price changes for us. This can become expensive. The prices needed for a daily bar chart, however, are available in the daily newspapers which most would read anyway, and would not, therefore, involve any extra expense. Keeping point and figure charts naturally means that much more time must be spent in charting, since rather than merely a single bar, all the small intra-day movements must also be recorded on the chart. Because of the different method of constructing a point and figure chart, the chart pictures which develop are sometimes different from those which develop by the bar chart system. Thus, many chartists keep both types. Whether the added time and expense involved in keeping point and figure charts is worthwhile, depends upon the individual trader. Many traders also feel that the point and figure chart is much more difficult to interpret, and is confusing compared to the simple straightforward bar chart.

A very complete up-to-date commodity chart service can be obtained on a weekly basis from Commodity Research Bureau, Inc., One Liberty Plaza, New York, N. Y. 10006. This organization issues approximately 130 vertical line charts each Friday evening which show the daily, high, low and closing prices of every active commodity contract in the U.S. and Canada for the life-of-contract through the date of issue. The service also provides a professional analysis of chart trends weekly, and periodic mailings of complete long range continuation charts. Individual charts and chart collections can be obtained from this same firm.

Diametrically opposed to the thinking of the chartist who uses either bar or point and figure charts, is the one who depends primarily upon "moving averages." Unlike the point and figure chartist, he does not want to know the little jiggles in price which occur during the day, nor even the daily fluctuations. These, he believes, are minor fluctuations around a major trend. By misinterpreting these minor fluctuations, the major trend and major price movement will be missed. Therefore, says the advocate of moving averages, we must take a broad perspective on price movements which can be obtained by moving averages, rather than the narrow perspective given by point and figure work, or even daily bar charts. By plotting the average of closing prices over a specified time period, we can obtain a very clear picture of the real price trend, eliminating the minor movements which can cause us to misinterpret the true situation. Or, as a refinement, by plotting the daily closing price against the moving average price, we can obtain a picture of the trend and an indication of when it is turning.

The moving average method undoubtedly indicates the trend in which commodity prices are moving. However, because it *is* an *averaging* method, there is a delay in the indication of the turn in the price trend. Many times, the delay is much greater than would be the case utilizing either of the first two methods. Therefore, market action may come too late. Thus, if a price trend has been upward, and prices suddenly begin to decline, the average would not turn downward until several days later. This can result in short sales being made well after the movement has begun, or even when the move is ready to reverse.

While protagonists of the moving average method concede this possibility, they point out that the same danger exists with any chart trading regardless of the system used. As with any chart trading method, the procedure is designed not to be 100% correct, for this cannot be achieved. It is designed to limit losses, in those instances where one is on the wrong side of the market, but to allow profits to accumulate by staying with the market when one has accurately forecast the trend. Thus, one can have losses on 50% of his trades, or more, and still make money on balance. (The latter statement is quite true and will be expanded upon later.)

Any further discussion of chart trading would require that the reader possess a more exact knowledge of just what these various types of charts look like, and how they are constructed. They are illustrated and described in detail below:

Bar Charts

The daily high low close bar chart is practically self-explanatory. Along the vertical side of a sheet of graph paper, a scale of prices is marked at evenly spaced intervals. Along the horizontal side, the lines are marked with each trading date. To keep uninterrupted continuity, holidays and weekends may be omitted. On this graph, a single line is drawn connecting the high and low prices for a day's trading in one contract of a specific commodity. A horizontal bar is placed across this line at the closing price. If there is a split price close (that is, at the final second of trading a particular contract was traded by various brokers at somewhat different prices, such as 32.55¢ and 32.65¢ per lb.), then two lines may be drawn horizontally, showing both prices. Most chartists merely show the lower figure or in the case of a bid and ask price, just the bid is recorded as a horizontal line. On each successive day a new line is drawn, resulting in a graph such as Figure 1. The bar chart thus pictures the trading pattern from one day to another.

FIGURE 1   VERTICAL BAR CHART

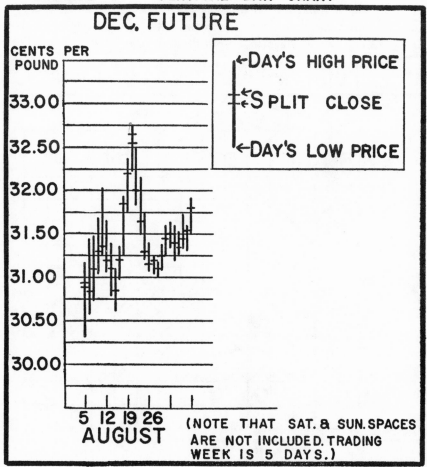

DEC. FUTURE

CENTS PER POUND

DAY'S HIGH PRICE
SPLIT CLOSE
DAY'S LOW PRICE

5 12 19 26
AUGUST

(NOTE THAT SAT. & SUN. SPACES ARE NOT INCLUDED. TRADING WEEK IS 5 DAYS.)

A bar chart need not be limited to daily ranges. The same high-low-close bar might be used to represent a full week's trading, or even a full month. In all cases, the method is the same. The highest and lowest prices for the period to be included (a day, week or month) are connected by a vertical line, and the closing price by a horizontal line.

Point & Figure Charts

Construction of the point and figure chart at first seems somewhat complicated, but in practice it proves to be relatively straightforward. A special type of graph paper is sometimes used, but is not actually necessary. Along the vertical side of the paper, the prices are again marked. This time, however, instead of the *lines* being marked, each space or box now represents a certain price. Point and figure charts are made by filling in these boxes by cross marks as shown in figure 2A. Since all the ups and downs of each day's trading are to be charted, there is no indication of dates along the bottom as there is in the bar chart. Instead, some chartists simply black in the final square of the

POINT & FIGURE vs. BAR CHART

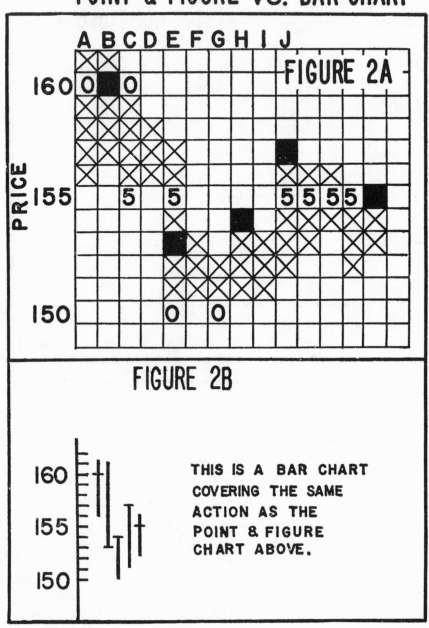

FIGURE 2A

FIGURE 2B

THIS IS A BAR CHART
COVERING THE SAME
ACTION AS THE
POINT & FIGURE
CHART ABOVE.

day to distinguish each day's trading. Furthermore, to allow easier chart inspection, sometimes the digit "5" is used, instead of an "x" to mark every space whose value ends in five (such as 155 in figure 2A). A zero is used to designate the spaces whose value ends in zero, such as 150 and 160 on the chart. This is just done for faster sight reading of prices from the chart, and has no special significance. Figure 2A has been drawn to the scale of each box = 1¢. The scale can vary according to individual preference. Some traders prefer to chart each ⅛ or 1 point change in price. If a market is one in which price swings are wide and trading is active, this would lead to a jumble of small price swings which would be difficult to keep, and would not add to the chart's meaning. For the more active and volatile commodities, each box should be made to represent a larger figure, say ½¢ or a full cent in grains, or 20 to as much as 50 points in other markets. In our hypothetical chart in Fig. 2A, we have chosen full 1¢ units for each box. Therefore, we would fill in a space on our chart only when this commodity sells at full 1¢ levels.

For example, suppose Figure 2A was a grain chart. Each box in Figure 2A is one cent, but grains actually trade in ⅛¢ units. Our chart begins with the 161 space filled in. That means that the grain traded at 161. Subsequently, it may have declined to 160⅛, then rallied to 161⅞, but we would not mark anything down on our chart until the commodity actually trades at another full 1¢ unit. According to our chart, that occurred when the commodity traded at 160. Therefore, directly below the first x, another x is made in the 160 space. As is shown in our chart, the market declined from 161 to 156. Each box down to 156 is, therefore, filled in by an x in the same vertical column, which we have labelled column "A."

After the market has traded down to 156, it rallies and trades back up a full cent to 157. We, therefore, have to fill in the 157 box, but this has already been filled in on the way down. We must, therefore, start a new column and fill in the 157 space in column "B." Now, if the market moves up or down we have room to fill in the spaces. As shown by column "B," the market moved up to 160 at the close without having fluctuated downward by one full digit in the interim. Since the market closed at 160, we have blacked in that space. The next day, the market opened around the same level and, after trading within fractions of a cent of 160, traded up to 161. Since this space is still empty in column "B" we mark it in the same column. We do not start a new column simply because it is a new day as we would do in a daily bar chart.

After it has traded at 161, the price declines again to 160. Again,

— 175 —

when we go to mark down this price on our chart, we find it has been filled previously. We therefore move to the next column (column "C"), and fill in the 160 space there. After that we can fill the prices in column "C," whether the market goes up or down. The procedure for the rest of the chart is the same. Each column is used until a space that has already been marked must be filled in. Then we move to another column. Simply because of the method of construction, each column will have at least two spaces filled.

Below Figure 2A, we have constructed a daily bar chart as Figure 2B, covering the same trading shown in the point and figure chart. The two methods can now be compared. We began our bar chart at a high of $161\frac{7}{8}$ just to show how it can vary slightly from the P & F (point and figure) chart. Remember that since our P & F chart is in full 1¢ units, that chart had to begin with 161. The rest of the bar chart, however, was made to correspond exactly with the P & F.

It becomes immediately apparent that the P & F chart shows what has occurred within each day's trading in much greater detail than the daily bar chart. Whether the P & F is more difficult to interpret than the bar chart, you will have to judge for yourself. Defer judgment, however, until you have finished reading this section.

The chart, as drawn, gives the P & F a slight advantage because of the wide price swings deliberately chosen for clarity. The range of each day's trading is much wider than would ordinarily occur. The second day's trade would, for example, be more than the maximum decline allowed for oats. Rather than the wide price swings shown, a range of 1¢ to 2¢ per day would be closer to normal. A narrower price range would perhaps make the bar chart show up to somewhat better advantage. Nevertheless, in most instances, the P & F will display much greater detail.

Reversal Charts

As pointed out above, although the P & F chart shows great detail in active wide-swinging markets, this can lead to too many small variations which can fool the trader into a series of trades and small losses. What appears to be the beginning of a certain price move turns out to be nothing more than a chance fluctuation. All these false moves are acted upon; first, the chart may indicate a "buy" in anticipation of an upward move, only to have the chartist quickly reverse himself and sell out at a small loss. Then the chart indicates a "sale" through a certain chart formation which also proves to be just a jiggle on the chart. Again there is a small loss plus commissions to be paid. This process is known as "being whip-sawed." To prevent this from occurring too often, two preventative methods are used. First, a scale larger than the minimum fluctuation of the commodity can be employed. Thus, in Figure 2A of the hypothetical grain chart, each box was made to represent a full 1¢ fluctuation, rather than the ⅛¢ which is the minimum trading unit for grains. While this eliminates some of the detail for which P & F charts are desired, it still leaves more detail than the bar chart, as can be seen by comparing Figure 2A with 2B.

The second method for eliminating the minor erratic fluctuations from the chart (they are assumed to be meaningless and due to chance) is to draw "reversal charts." Figure 2A was also deliberately drawn to illustrate this. A reversal chart is one in which a price trend must be reversed by a predetermined amount before it is marked on the chart, and that amount must be at least three times the magnitude of the units picked for each box. Thus, our chart is constructed in 1¢ units, but prices must reverse 3¢ before it will be recorded as a meaningful change in trend. This sounds more complicated than it actually is in practice.

Notice in Figure 2A that each column has at least three boxes filled in. Columns D, F, G, I, etc., each have three squares marked off. Thus, the price declined to 155 in column C. When keeping a regular 1¢ chart, as the price then rallied to 156 we would begin column D, by filling in the 156 square. If, however, we were keeping a "3¢ reversal chart," the market would have to rally 3¢ to 158 before we would chart it. If the market rallied to only 157⅞ (a rally of only 2⅞¢), then declined once again, we would not mark it down. Column d would not yet be started. However, the market did rally a full 3¢ and traded at 158. The three boxes 156, 157 and 158 would then be filled. Notice that not just the 158 square was marked. To keep the continuity of the chart, all three spaces are filled. Remember, however, that the market first had to rally the full 3¢ before this was done.

Once the market has rallied or declined by the minimum reversal amount, and a new column is started, each additional individual 1¢ move is subsequently added. Thus, after the market had rallied to 158 (column D), prices began to decline again. As the market sold off to 155 (a full 3¢), column E was started, with the filling in of the three spaces; 157, 156 and 155. The market then sold off another cent to 154, filling that space. It sold off another cent to 153, filling that space. As shown by that space being blacked out, the market closed at that price. The next day the market continued to decline without a 3¢ rally occurring. Each time it sold off by another full cent, another square was filled in until finally the price had declined to 150. Only then did a 3¢

rally occur and so only then did we begin column F. The rally did not extend further. It backed down a full 3¢ again, and so we had to start the next column, etc., etc.

Just by looking at Figure 2A, one cannot know whether this is an ordinary 1¢ chart showing all 1¢ movements, or whether it is a 3¢ reversal chart in 1¢ units which would not show any price reversals of less than 3¢. It is, therefore, necessary to label each reversal chart as such, in the margin, for purposes of clarity.

It becomes clear now that the P & F chart offers great flexibility in determining just how much trading detail is to be shown. First, there is the choice of the scale to be used for the chart. This can be anything from the minimum fluctuation of ⅛¢ or one point, upward. Secondly, a reversal chart can also be used to eliminate more of the minor swings. Only by varying the scale, can the fluctuations in the bar type chart be made larger or smaller. Even then, however, the fluctuations still show exactly the same details, namely the high, low and close.

A very popular form of chart is the "minimum reversal chart." In grains, this is called the "⅜¢ reversal chart," and in other commodities is the "three points (3/100¢) reversal chart." The chart scale is kept at the minimum of ⅛¢ in grains and one point in other commodities. However, prices must reverse by ⅜¢ (or 3 points for the one point charts) before they are indicated by starting another column. This has an added advantage. Remember that after the minimum reversal occurs, each trade in the same direction is subsequently marked on the chart. If the scale is the lowest it can be; i.e. ⅛¢ in grains, one point in others, then the highest and lowest points at which the market traded will be shown. Remember that in Figure 2A, the high in column A is shown as 161. Yet when we look at the bar chart Figure 2B, we can see on the first bar that the high was actually 161⅞. Our P & F chart does not show this because the scale was in full 1¢ units. If the scale were ⅛¢, the true high would be shown. Keeping the scale at the minimum, however, would mean showing all the minor up and down price fluctuations which are assumed to be meaningless. Therefore, to eliminate these little chance variations in price, the chart is made into a ⅜¢ reversal type. Only those fluctuations of ⅜¢ or more are shown. Thus, we can have a record of the actual highs and lows and, at the same time, eliminate the insignificantly small price fluctuations. It goes without saying that the reversal chart need not be ⅜¢. It could also be ½¢, ⅝¢, or any other figure one would like. It all depends upon how closely one wishes to follow price variations.

The Moving Average Method

Moving average charts are rather easy to create. By plotting averages only, the market fluctuations appear to be automatically reduced. For example, suppose a market closed at 2, 4 and 6 cents on three successive days. We plot the three day average 4 (see figure 3), and have one point on the chart. Suppose the next day the market jumped to 11. Now if we take an average of the last three days, we add up 4, 6 and 11, divide by 3, and reach an average of 7. We now have a second point for our chart, and we connect these two. Notice that although the market advanced 5¢ in one day (from 6 to 11) our average advanced only 3¢. Suppose that on the next day the market sold down to 10, a 1¢ decline. Our average of the last three closing prices would now be 6 plus 11 plus 10, divided by 3 equals 9, which we plot as the third point on our average price chart. Notice that while the actual daily close was lower, our average continues to advance. The next day the market declines further to 9. Now our average will be 11 plus 10 plus 9 divided by 3 equals 10. The average is

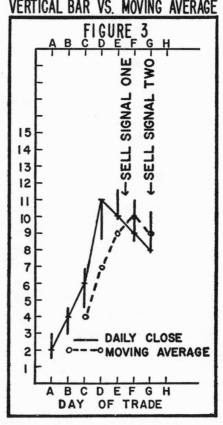

VERTICAL BAR VS. MOVING AVERAGE

FIGURE 3

still advancing and has not shown the downward fluctuation which has actually occurred in the daily trading. The next day the market sold off still further to 8. The average of the closing prices of the last three days is, therefore, 10 plus 9 plus 8 divided by 3 equals 9. The reaction by now is sustained enough to cause the average to turn down also. In other words, on both the upside and the downside, the average lags behind the daily market.

The method of construction should now be clear. To construct a moving average, first determine how long a period you wish to use. In Figure 3, a period of three days was used. The closing prices of the first three days (A, B and C) were averaged and the point marked on the chart on the third day (day C). When the fourth day of trading was completed, the average of days B, C and D was taken and plotted on "D." In other words, on each ensuing day, the closing prices of the most recent three days is taken, added together and divided by 3 to get the average.

Any period may be chosen. Thus, five-day, ten-day, twenty-day and even ten-week moving averages are kept by some traders. The longer the period chosen, however, the greater could be the time-lag between a change in the trend of prices and the illustration of this change by the moving average.

Utilizing Moving Averages

There are several ways in which moving averages can be used. First, *the average can be used by itself*. When plotted alone, a long position in the commodity is taken and held so long as the moving average continues to increase in value. When the average turns downward as it did in day "G" of Figure 3, the long position would be liquidated and a short position established. Since we would not know that the moving average has turned downward until after the close of day G and the inclusion of its price in the average (E plus F plus G divided by 3), the actual liquidation of any long position could not take place until the subsequent day, day H.

Note that the lag in the average indicating a reversal of the price trend means that liquidation or short sales would not occur until well after the price has begun to decline. This, however, is true of any chart trading method. The value of a chart is not in picking the top or the bottom of a move but in trying to determine long term trends and, by trading with these long term swings, to make substantial profits.

When only a three-day moving average is used the delay before actually liquidating a position or selling short is not too great, but when a ten-day, twenty-day, or other average is used, the market may already have had a substantial move before the chart would indicate to the trader that action should be taken.

A method subsequently used to reduce the delay before a trader places orders in the market, is the plotting of the daily closing prices or the daily bar chart on the same graph as the moving average, both of which we have done in Figure 3. Now, when the line connecting the daily closing prices crosses the moving average, a trader will take action. Thus, in Figure 3, the daily closing price line crosses the moving average on day "F." While the moving average is still on the uptrend, the daily closing prices, by going below the average, have indicated that the market is weak enough to at least indicate the liquidation of long positions.

That is the first selling signal. Some traders, however, while liquidating long positions on this type of market action, would not establish short positions in the market until the downtrend is confirmed by the moving average turning downward as well.

Subsequently, as shown on the chart, the moving average did turn down also. This would be taken as confirmation of the reversal of the trend, and become selling signal #2. Short positions would be established by those who did not do so when the closing price line went below the average (the first selling signal). Those who had sold short on signal #1 would increase their short positions on signal #2.

Using The Bar Chart With The Moving Average

Using the bar chart in conjunction with the moving average, that is taking into account the daily high and low in addition to the daily close, sometimes causes some minor problems which can, however, be corrected. In figure 3 on day "F," when the moving average still is advancing, the daily range went below the average for the first time, indicating a possible reversal of trend. The next day, however, the daily range—while closing below the average—had once again gone above it. Thus, a trader who had gone short, based on the action of the previous session, might well be tempted to get out of that position. He might even go long the market during the trading session, only to liquidate based on the lower close. In other words, the trader could have been whip-sawed back and forth, or at best remained quite confused. Because of this, those traders who use bar charts in conjunction with a moving average will usually do one of two things. They will set an arbitrary amount below and/or above which the daily range must go before they will take action, or they will use the bar chart to find certain specific chart pictures, such as those discussed in the next chapter, before taking action. The latter course is by far the most prevalent.

It is, of course, no longer merely a moving average method but is a combination of the bar chart technique and the moving average method, with one supplementing the other. Based upon this combined technique, the trader would have remained short. Why this is so, can be determined after the discussion of chart pictures in chapter 18.

Before we turn to these, however, there are several other methods of using moving averages that should be discussed. One uses another combination of the bar chart and moving average. A moving average (either 3-day, 5-day, 10-day or 20-day) is made of the daily high and another moving average (using the same time interval) is made of the daily low. This results in a wide band running across the chart around which all daily ranges should tend to fluctuate. When the daily prices move outside of this band, a new price trend may be developing. Thus, a buying signal would be given if a commodity trades or closes (depending upon the method chosen) by a previously determined amount above the moving average of the highs. A sale would be indicated if the market trades or closes at a specified amount below the moving average of the lows.

The trick appears to be to determine just what that arbitrary level should be—25 points, 40 points, ½¢ or what? There is no set rule. Before using this method it is necessary to inspect previous daily bar charts for the commodity to determine whether price fluctuations are wide or narrow. If daily price ranges tend to be small, as in oats or corn, the arbitrary variations above or below the average which constitute buy or sell signals would be small. If, on the other hand, daily price fluctuations tend to be wide, as in rye or soybeans, the limit must be set at a higher level. By plotting the two moving averages on daily bar charts of already expired contracts, and inspecting the variations above and below these averages, the limit to be used for each commodity can be established.

Variations Of The Moving Average Technique

The last method to be discussed is merely a representative sample of many possible combinations. It is a chart using two moving averages of different time periods. Figure 4 is a representation of the 5-day and 10-day moving averages used to forecast price trends.

The chart shows two lines. The solid line is a 10-day moving average of closing prices of October hides. The dotted line is the 5-day moving average. You will notice that the shorter time-period average fluctuates markedly more than the longer one. This is always true. One method of trading, which uses the two averages, is to sell each time the shorter time-period average moves below the longer average, and to buy each time it moves above. Remember, however, that an average will have a time lag compared to daily prices. Therefore, when the average turns down, the daily price will usually be lower. When the average turns up, the daily price will usually be higher. Two things must, therefore, be remembered.

1) When the averages cross on the downside and a sale is indicated, the actual price at which the sale will be made will be below the price at which the averages cross.

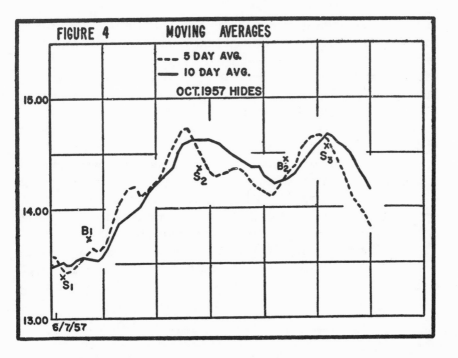

FIGURE 4   MOVING AVERAGES

--- 5 DAY AVG.
— 10 DAY AVG.
OCT.1957 HIDES

15.00

14.00

13.00 6/7/57

2) Since the moving averages are of closing prices, we cannot be sure the averages will cross until after the close. That means the actual sale cannot be made until *the next day*, which also usually means it will be made at a lower price than the point at which the two averages cross. The exact reverse is, of course, true when the longer average is crossed on the upside and a purchase is indicated. It will usually be at a higher price than the point at which the averages cross.

Figure 4 indicates the exact buying and selling points, and gives an indication of the possible results of each trade. A selling signal is given on the third day with the actual selling point (s_1) proving to be near the low for the move. The sale at (s_1), of course, occurs the day after the averages crossed. As the market reverses and establishes an upward trend, a buying signal results (B_1). The previously established short position is covered with a loss, and a long position is now established. The trend continues upward. At one point, the two averages come together, but do not quite cross. The long position is still held. Finally the market again turns downward, and the decline is apparently both fast and sharp. This is shown by the fact that the actual selling point (s_2) proved to be considerably below the point at which the two averages crossed. Nevertheless, when the long position is liquidated, the profit is enough to cancel the previous loss and leave a net gain. A short position is also established on this selling signal. The market then traded within a relatively narrow range until the upward trend was apparently re-established. The short position had to be covered again at point (B2) with a slight loss, and a long position re-established. The upward trend proves to be a failure and at point (s3), the long position is liquidated with a slight gain, and a short position established. As the chart ends, the downward trend is still intact and the short position gives promise of leading to substantial gains.

All of these trades illustrate both the strength and weaknesses of this method of trading. When prices trade within a narrow range, the chances are that a series of trades with small losses will result. However, once a trend is established and moves for a considerable distance in the same direction, the chances for profit are good.

Moving averages are widely used by many of the advisory services which sell trading advice to clients. To be sure, they have developed their own variations of the technique but they are basically moving average methods.

CHAPTER 16.

FINDING CHART OBJECTIVES

Once commodity prices appear to have established a definite trend either up or down, just how far can the move be expected to carry? This becomes a very important question, since the answer will probably determine whether or not a trader will merely seek to take a quick profit (a "trading turn"), or hold onto a position despite a "temporary" reversal in the expectation that the trend will continue for a long time.

All chart-trading methods avoid the possibility of trying to pick the exact top or bottom of a price move. A chartist will wait for a trend to get underway and be confirmed by certain chart pictures before he is willing to accept the fact that the trend has turned, and that taking a position in the market is warranted. The profitability of the trade depends upon the primary assumption that prices will continue to move in the same direction for a considerable length of time. "The count" is the method employed by those who use the point and figure technique to determine just how far a move will carry. It has been adapted for use with bar charts as well. The technique, at best, gives only an approximation since its basic assumption is far from scientific. Nevertheless, in practice, it is used to determine whether or not a subsequent price move will be small or large.

The basic assumption of the count technique is that there is a definite one-to-one relationship between the horizontal extent of a movement on a point and figure chart and the subsequent vertical price movement, either up or down.

Suppose that prices for a certain commodity have declined for a considerable length of time. Prices then begin to display resistance to any further decline; they stabilize and trade within a relatively narrow range. It does not take too much imagination to realize what is happening. Those who feel that the lower prices have fully discounted the supply and demand factors or news events which caused the initial downward trend to develop, begin to cover their short positions in the market. Others, who feel the market has over-discounted the original events or that some new piece of information should alter the original picture, begin to establish long positions in the market. Should this feeling be prevalent in spot market circles, demand for the actual commodity would probably show improvement and lead to lifting of hedges in futures. All of these factors tend to bring support into the futures

— 185 —

market in the form of the buying of futures contracts.

On the other side of the market are those traders who have watched this downtrend get underway but have previously failed to act. They have been waiting for some sort of rally in the downtrend to sell short. You will always find some traders in the market anticipating a "technical rally" which will allow them to sell short at a little better price than exists at any moment. The pause in the downtrend (which we are now assuming to have occurred) affords the opportunity for these traders to sell short on the initial rally, in the expectation that the downward trend will resume. Certain firms that have established inventories, but who delayed establishing hedges because the market "got away from them", also take this as an opportunity to establish some price protection, albeit somewhat late. Thus "belated hedge selling" enters the market.

New buying of actual commodities seems to develop in waves. There will be a period of strong demand when many firms appear anxious to cover their forward requirements, followed by periods when virtually nobody wishes to take on new supplies and add to inventory. Such a pause in the downward price move of a commodity as was just described, is usually a signal for one of these buying waves to develop, if it is not actually the originating cause for the halt to the downward drift of prices. Few firms will take on new supplies while prices are declining, unless they are forced into it by production requirements, because they assume they can obtain them cheaper the next day or next week. However, to meet production schedules, a time comes when these can no longer be postponed. The developing demand from these firms may be sufficient to halt the progressive deterioration of prices. Other firms which are not yet being forced into the necessary purchaser category would, on seeing the end of the price decline, be induced to purchase some additional supplies anyway. While prices were declining they would not purchase. But, now that a price reversal might develop, they would buy at least part of their forward requirements in the hope of having "cheap supplies" in the event this does prove to be the beginning of an upward trend. However, many of these purchases would also be at least temporarily hedged in futures, as insurance against inventory losses in the event that prices do not reverse their downward course. All of the above would lead to selling of futures.

The Congestion Area

We are, therefore, left with a situation in which rallies are met with heavy sales, and declines with good buying. The market, in other words, has established a temporary equilibrium around a certain price level.

The price chart will, therefore, indicate a sideways price movement called a "congestion area" as shown in Figure 5.

The longer this sideways movement lasts, the more we can assume that old positions are being liquidated and new positions established within the constricted price range. Therefore, when prices finally do break out of the congestion area and establish a new price trend, those who are on the wrong side of the market will be anxious to get out of their positions. The longer the congestion area, the greater should be the number of traders with new positions who have losses, the greater should be the number of orders placed in the market to cover, and the greater should be the impetus to the new price move.

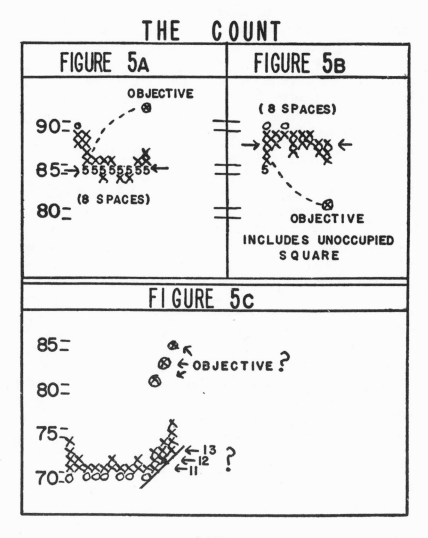

Notice that those orders to liquidate losing positions would be a spur to prices in the same direction as the new price trend. For example, suppose that prices advanced out of the congestion area. Those who had sold short would have losses. To liquidate their losing positions, they would have to *buy* futures. This added buying power in the market helps push prices higher. The longer the congestion area has been in effect, the more of these buying orders that should materialize. In addition, a large number of new buyers who have no previous position would enter the market if the congestion area lasted for a considerable period of time. The decreased likelihood of misinterpreting the chart picture would be a spur to new buyers.

The above considerations have been used to justify the basic assumption of the chartists that the longer a congestion area persists, the more extensive will be the ensuing move. There is logic in this statement, but not necessarily in the "one-to-one" relationship. Such a relationship implies that the vertical movement will precisely equal the horizontal movement. There is nothing in the reasoning to make such an *exact* relationship hold true, particularly since new factors are always entering the commodity price picture. However, for want of a better method of approximating the exact extent of the new price movement, it continues to be used.

The Count

Figure 5A indicates just such a pattern. The downward price move gave way to a congestion area, out of which prices finally advanced. How high should this advance carry prices? In this instance, you will notice that the decline was in a straight line, as was the advance out of the congestion area. In other words, the congestion area was bracketed by two vertical "walls". *The count is taken across the line which connects the two walls.* In Figure 5A this is 8 spaces across. Consequently, the advance should be approximately 8 spaces high. If the scale of the chart is one space = 1¢, then the advance should be 8¢. If the scale on the chart were one space = 2¢, then an 8 space advance would mean that prices should rise by approximately 16¢.

Figure 5B is a chart picture of a price advance reaching a top, developing into a congestion area, and finally reversing its trend and breaking out of the congestion range on the downside. Again, to determine the objective of the price decline, the horizontal number of spaces on the line connecting the two vertical walls are counted. Notice, however, that in Figure 5B, this line has one space that is not filled in, the third from the left. That doesn't matter. It is still counted as if it were filled in. The count, therefore, remains at 8 spaces.

Figure 5C indicates one of the problems which may arise in attempting to determine the count. It is all quite simple when the congestion range is bracketed by two vertical walls. But what happens when one or both of the walls is not vertical? From what point is the count taken? The right wall in Figure 5C is slanted. There are three possible points from which various chartists would prefer to take the count. The first is the line having 11 spaces across because this is the most solid line, the one that has the greatest number of filled-in spaces. Second, the line above it with 12 spaces would be the one from which the first advance out of the congestion area was maintained. Finally, the line above, with 13 spaces, which confirmed the breakout by prices having first reacted back to the slanting trend line and then advancing sharply away from it. Any of these choices could be logically supported.

Another important method of determining the count is by watching for the completion of the chart pictures discussed and illustrated in the next chapter. Once these chart pictures have been completed, the number of spaces along their widest point is taken as the count. Remember, however, that the chart is primarily used for its trend-determining technique value. The count is a useful subsidiary tool which, at best, will give an expected approximation of the extent of a move. Should the chart picture indicate a trend reversal, even if the count objective has not been reached, the chart picture should take precedence, not the mechanical objective given by the count.

Support And Resistance Areas

Along somewhat more empirical lines, but also based upon some logical assumptions, are the objectives obtained by the use of support and resistance areas.

A congestion area has previously been described as an area in which prices move in a sideways direction. That is, prices will fluctuate for a considerable time within a limited range. It is not unusual that several such congestion areas will interrupt a trend before it is resumed. When a trend turns downward these congestion areas which were "resistance areas" during the initial uptrend now become "support areas." That is, the reaction tends to be halted at the price level of the old congestion area.

In Figure 6, we have illustrated two of these possible situations. In Figue 6A, breaking out of a congestion area (1) into an upward trend, prices rapidly move higher until a point is reached where some profit taking and hedge selling develop. The price advance is consolidated as prices churn about within a narrow range creating a second congestion

CONGESTION AREAS

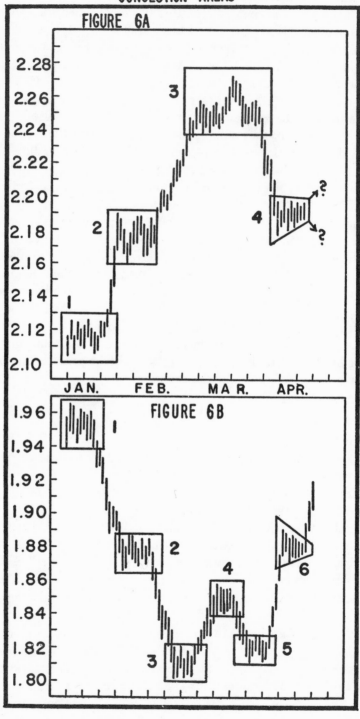

FIGURE 6A

FIGURE 6B

area. Again, prices advance sharply and form a third congestion area. This time, however, after trading within a narrow range, prices try to advance further and fail. They trade again in the congestion area, but this time break out on the downside. The upward trend now appears to have been reversed. How far down can prices be expected to move? One way to determine this would be "the count" across the width of the congestion area, if a point and figure chart were used. A second way would be to look for the previous congestion range which had developed when the trend was still upward (congestion area 2). The reaction could be expected to reach the *upper level* of that congestion area. Resistance to further price declines can be expected to develop at that point.

There are several reasons for this. First, traders who had originally sold short in area 2 may have held onto their positions despite their losses. As prices approach their original selling points, they begin to buy back their short commitments. After having watched considerable losses develop, they are happy and anxious to cover now with only a minor loss. Second, many traders who had bought futures in congestion area 2 would have taken profits on the upward move which appeared to be ending near the point where the top finally developed. In fact, their selling may well have contributed to the change of trend. Now that prices have reacted back to approximately their original buying price, they again buy futures and go long the market. Third, many traders who for one reason or another had failed to go long during the original upward trend, now see this reaction as an opportunity to get into the market. This may just be a sharp price correction in a basically upward trend. Fourth, presumably some belated hedge selling might have entered the market after the sharp price advance. The reaction in futures may have widened the basis to the point where the hedgers would be anxious to sell actual commodities and then buy back their hedges. Or, seeing a good-sized price reaction after a long upward trend, many commodity buyers might feel this is an advantageous time to buy needed supplies. This too, would lead to hedge lifting; i.e., buying back hedges by the sellers of actuals. Finally, after prices have reacted for a considerable distance, a general feeling develops that "prices have gone down far enough." Call this a psychological quirk of traders if you will, but this type of thinking becomes an important market factor, with short covering and new buying developing only on this assumption. The result of all these factors (and probably some others which you might think of yourself) leads to a general buying of futures which halts the price decline and many times creates a new congestion area

(4) out of which prices may move in either direction.

All of the above is particularly true if the reaction has carried approximately 50% of the previous upward move. If the price advance from area 1 to area 3 were 20¢ per bushel, then strong resistance to the decline develops when prices have reacted 10¢ per bushel. Short covering, hedge lifting, new buying, etc., enters the market. Again, the initiating factor may be the general feeling that "prices have reacted far enough", but it leads also to the other factors which have been listed above.

We have mentioned the fact (and illustrated it in Figure 6A) that the resistance area develops just above the old congestion area. This is usually true when the market still has basic strength. The bottom of the new congestion area will be just about on a par with the top of the old, with perhaps a small overlap.

Of course, the new congestion area (4) may develop around the lows of the old one (area 2), or even slightly below. This is usually a sign that the market is still basically weak. Chances are that prices will break out of the congestion area on the downside. Area 4 may prove to be merely a pause in the downward trend with the next objective the price level just above congestion area. (1) In either event, the old congestion area is usually a price level at which resistance to the decline will occur.

In Figure 6B, we have illustrated a reversal from a downtrend to an uptrend. After a prolonged decline, the market congests and then breaks out on the upside with what appears to be a reversal of trend. The rally carries up to the *lower level* of the previous congestion range (area 2) where the advance runs into resistance (belated hedge selling, long liquidation, new short sales, etc.). After possibly some congestion, the market sells down to the *top* of, or into, the low range of prices. After some further milling around (area 5), but staying always above the extreme low point of the former downtrend (the lowest point in area 3), prices rally once more and go up past area 4, confirming the uptrend. The next objective is the price range just below area 1, at we called the old congestion levels, "resistance areas."

Notice that in our discussion of Figure 6A, where a downtrend had developed, we spoke of the previous congestion ranges as "support areas". In the discussion of Figure 6B where an uptrend was evolving, we called the old congestion levels, "resistance areas".

Figures 6A and 6B are two of the most important chart pictures that traders look for. We shall have more to say about these and other formations in a subsequent section.

CHAPTER 17.

THE STOP-LOSS ORDER AND
ITS USE IN CHART TRADING

Before describing those chart formations which are most often sought as aids in forecasting commodity price trends, the use of the stop-loss order must be understood.

In the event that a chart interpretation does prove wrong, the chartist wants to liquidate his position quickly. The whole philosophy of trading is to trade with the trend, let profits accumulate and limit losses. By "let profits accumulate" is meant leaving a profitable position in the market until such time as the market demonstrates, through its price action, that the trend is reversing. This is the opposite of what most traders do. Most traders take a position, for example, buy futures, and if prices rally two or three cents, they happily liquidate and take their profit. Prices may rally an additional 20¢ to 30¢ thereafter. Once they liquidated at the lower level, few speculators would re-establish their long position at a higher price. They consequently miss the major part of the move. They are limiting their profits, rather than letting them accumulate.

On the other hand, once a chart trader has established a profitable position, he would not limit his profit this way. He would maintain his long position until his chart picture indicated a change of trend. Thus, if a rally of 30¢ were to develop, the chartist would not get out with a 2¢-3¢ profit, but would probably be able to make a 20¢ profit out of the 30¢ price move.

The average trader, while limiting his gains by taking quick profits, will probably let *his losses accumulate.* The same trader, who was happy to take a 3¢ profit would not liquidate if the market went against him by that amount. Instead, he would hold onto his position, hoping that the market would rally. As prices keep declining, he is apt to get more obstinate, until finally he is forced to liquidate with a much larger loss and very possibly at a time when the market is finally getting ready to reverse.

The chart trader, on the other hand, when establishing his position would calculate in advance just how far the market would have to move against him to prove him wrong. Thus, if a chartist believes the trend is turning upward on the basis of his chart interpretation, he would buy futures. However, if prices instead were thereafter to react downward by say 3¢, his chart picture would indicate the trend was not turned upward. The chartist would then liquidate his position, taking his small loss.

Thus we see that the chartist will try to capitalize on trends to take large profits and small losses. Notice that this implies a willingness on the part of chart traders to take losses. It also means that they can have losses on half of their trades (or even more), and still come out ahead at the end of the year. For example, a hypothetical trader can have a series of trades resulting in the following returns:

— 3

— 3½

+ 6   Out of the eight trades, half showed profits and half

+ 9   were losses. However, the losses were limited to rela-

— 3½   tively small amounts, while the profits were allowed

+ 8   to accumulate. Thus, the final result was a sizeable

— 3¾   net gain.

+ 7

———

+16¼

Limiting Potential Losses

In order to limit their losses to the predetermined amount, many traders (non-chartists as well) use the "stop-loss order". A "stop-loss order" is an order to buy or sell at the market when the market reaches a specific price—but under certain unique circumstances. A "stop-buy" order is placed at a price *above* the market. A "stop-sell" order is placed at a price *below* the market. For example, suppose that May wheat is trading at $1.30 per bushel and a person buys wheat in the expectation of a price rise. The trader wishes to limit his possible loss to 3¢. Thus, after he has gone long, the trader might place an order with his broker to "sell May wheat at $1.27 stop." This means that if May wheat declines and trades at $1.27, the trader wishes to sell May wheat "at the market." Under ordinary circumstances, if someone wishes to sell a commodity they wish to do it at as high a price as possible. However, with a stop-loss, the sell order becomes effective only after the market has declined. At first, this might sound illogical but remember the circumstances under which a stop order is placed.

Additional Uses Of The Stop-Loss Order

These include:

a) A stop-loss is used *to liquidate and limit losses if the market has gone against a trader's established position.* Thus, if a long position were held, the market would have to sell lower before the trader would be convinced that he was wrong. He would then liquidate only after the market had first declined.

b) A stop-loss is used *to protect profits on a previously established position.* In line with the attempt to maximize profits, many traders would use "stop-loss" orders to protect profits on a previously established position. Thus, if a trader had bought May wheat at $1.30 and it advanced to $1.33, rather than liquidate and take his 3¢ profit, the trader might decide to hold onto his position as long as the trend appears headed higher. His chart picture might indicate that, if the market sold down 3¢ to $1.30 again, the upward trend would no longer be intact and he should liquidate. Thus, he would place an order to "sell May wheat at $1.30 stop, good-'til-cancelled." Now let us assume the market continues to rise. The stop-loss order was, therefore, not executed, and the trader is still long the market. His stop-loss order is still in effect, since the words "good-'til cancelled" were added. This means that the order to liquidate if May wheat sells down to $1.30 will be in effect every day without new instructions being issued by the trader. When May wheat reaches $1.40, the trader might cancel his old order and raise his stop-loss order to $1.36. If the market keeps rallying, the trader could follow the rise by continuously increasing his stop-loss selling point, first $1.40, then $1.43, then to $1.45, etc. The trader is, therefore, able to take advantage of the continued rise in price, protecting his increasing profit by moving his stop-loss point higher each day or week. At one point, say after the market has reached $1.50, it might begin to react and the stop-loss order at $1.45 is touched off. Thus, out of a possible 20¢ gain ($1.30 to $1.50) the trader obtained 15¢ profit, instead of taking the first 3¢ and then missing the major part of the move.

c) A stop-loss is used *to initiate new positions.* One of the major uses of chart pictures is to determine at which price the market must sell to confirm the indication of a new trend. How this is done will be discussed later. However, once the trend is confirmed, chartists and other traders are anxious to get into the market quickly. Thus, suppose October cotton is selling at 33.45 and the chart picture indicates that an upward trend is confirmed if the market can rally 20 points to 33.65. A chartist would place orders to "buy October cotton at 33.65 stop". The chartist does not want to go long and the market until he has confirmation that the trend is up. Therefore, he does not buy cotton while the price is down at 33.45, but he is willing to pay 20 points more for the cotton if that is necessary to confirm the new trend. He feels that in the long run he will be safer and make more money by waiting for the trend to be underway before establishing his position, than by trying to anticipate a trend which may never develop.

Bids or Offers May Set Off Stop Orders

"Stop" orders may be executed on some exchanges notably the Chicago Board of Trade although previous sales were not made at the stop price. If there were merely an *offer* at or below the "sell stop" price, or a bid at or above a "buy stop" the order may be filled. Rule 40 reads:

"Stop Order or Stop Loss Order. An order to buy or sell when the market reaches a specified point. A stop order to buy becomes a market order when the commodity or security sells (or is bid) at or above the stop price. A stop order to sell becomes a market order when the commodity or security sells (or is offered) at or below the stop price."

One should also note that a stop order does not guarantee that the price named in the stop will be obtained even though the market sells or is bid at said price. If the market moves through the stop-price, it will then become an order to be executed at the market, at whatever price the market is selling at, which could be higher, lower or the same as the stop-price.

CHAPTER 18

THE DIFFERENT CHART FORMATIONS — HOW THEY DEVELOP AND GIVE "BUY" OR "SELL" SIGNALS

We turn now to the chart pictures or chart formations sought by the chartists. Whether one uses the vertical bar technique or point and figure charts the patterns to be identified are similar. These are the keys to chart trading. By recognizing these formations, or variations of them, the chartist hopes to recognize the major trend and by trading with that trend, to make money. When you see these chart pictures, you will probably agree that when the chart patterns are clearly defined, determining the trend is merely a matter of common sense. The patterns, when completed, are representations of the trend as it exists at that time. Since they are a record of prices as they occurred, they cannot be wrong. What may lead traders into difficulty is attempting to read more meaning into them than is actually warranted. Chart formations are not always as neat and clear as we will represent them, and at times there are as many different interpretations of the same "pictures" as there are people looking at them. Consequently, over and over again, the lament is heard, "My charts were right, but I interpreted them wrong." The most important chart formations are included in this chapter. There are others which are primarily variations of the ones we will discuss, but an ability to recognize and classify those which are listed should serve as a sound basis for chart trading. For illustrative purposes vertical bar charts will be used in the following discussion.

The Trend Line

Figure 7 represents two basic forms of the trend line. It has been found that for some unknown reason, once a price trend gets underway, the limits of the price fluctuations in that trend tend to remain along a straight line. More precisely, in an *uptrend*, the *lower* limits of the fluctuations tend to form a straight line (figure 7A), and in a *downward* trend (figure 7B), the *upper* limits conform to a straight line.

To draw an uptrend line (figure 7A) wait for what appears to be the beginning of a new price trend. Watch its fluctuations, and draw a line connecting the low points (A) and (B). As long as the uptrend is intact, the extension of that line should not be violated. That is, the low points of each successive minor fluctuation should approach or just reach that line, as at points (C) and (D), but the market should not trade below it. Should prices go below that line, and particularly should the market close at a price below that line, it can be taken as the first indication of a coming price reversal and the possible development of a downtrend.

To draw a downtrend line (figure 7B) connect the points of the successive minor fluctuations that form a straight line along the top of the pattern, points (A_1) and (B_1). As long as the downtrend remains intact, that line should not be penetrated. Rallies in the downtrend should carry no higher than the points at which they just touch that line.

How does one trade in the market on the basis of the trend line? Once an uptrend appears established (figure 7A) it must be confirmed

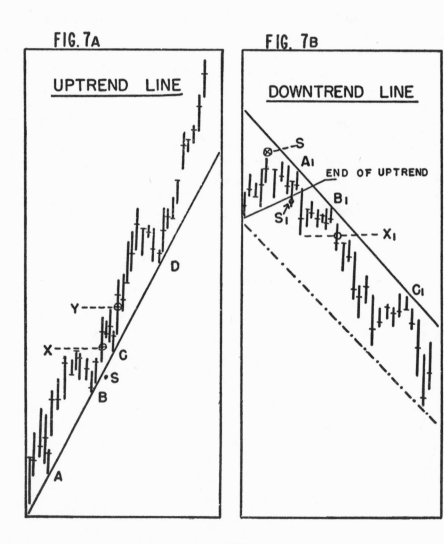

FIG. 7A

UPTREND LINE

FIG. 7B

DOWNTREND LINE

END OF UPTREND

by trading at a price above the high point of the previous rally. Thus, after the reaction to the trend line at (B) the market rallies into new high ground at (x). At this point a long position could be established with a stop-loss selling order placed just below point (B), the low of the previous minor price dip. As an alternative, the stop-loss point could be placed slightly below the trend line vertically below the purchase point, at (s). Some traders prefer not to put the stop loss order immediately below the trend line but slightly lower so that a chance fluctuation would not touch it off. Placing the stop-loss order below the low of the previous minor price dip, at (B), gives that added measure of leeway.

As the upward trend continues, another minor dip can be expected. It occurs with the price approaching the trend line at point (C), then rallying again to continue the upward trend by trading at a new high, at point (Y). A trader could add to his position at point (Y), which is the new confirmation of the upward trend, or he could have purchased additional contracts as the price dipped toward the trend line at point (C). Since the upward trend had previously been confirmed by having traded at (x), buying on a subsequent dip is perfectly acceptable chart procedure. As the price movement continues upward, trading at price (Y) and higher, the stop-loss selling order is raised; first to point (C), then to point (D), etc. Thus, instead of being satisfied with arbitrarily accepting a 3¢ or 4¢ profit when it becomes available, full advantage is taken of the upward trend as long as it continues. Profits, therefore, are not arbitrarily limited to a pre-determined, hoped-for amount. Instead, they tend to accumulate as long as the trend continues and the stop-loss order is not touched off.

At the top of the figure 7B, the upward trend line is broken by a moderate amount. Long positions would then be liquidated automatically by the stop loss orders at (S₁) being touched off. Some of the more aggressive chart traders would not only take profits on long positions here, but would also sell short at this point, placing a stop-loss order just above the previous high at (S). In the event that this first penetration of the upward trend line proved to be a false move, and the upward trend was re-established, they would have only a small limited loss. More conservative traders would await the confirmation of the change in trend before establishing short positions.

As shown in figure 7B, the subsequent rally failed to get very far. A congestion area then developed out of which prices broke on the downside. Once this occurs, the price break can no longer be viewed as merely a rather large technical reaction in an upward trend. It must be considered as the beginning of a new downward trend. As the congestion area was formed, stop-loss selling orders would have been placed by chart traders at price (X_1), just below the low point of the congestion range. As the market sold down through that point, short positions would have automatically been established.

The downward trend line is then drawn connecting points (A_1) and (B_1), which are the outside points of the price chart. Once short positions are established at price (X_1), stop-loss buying orders would be placed either just above the trend line, or just above the previous congestion range at price (B_1). In the event the market reversed itself again, the losses which the chart trader would sustain would be limited to the small amount between the selling point at (X_1) and the stop-loss point at (B_1).

As shown, however, the trend continued downward. As prices declined, the stop-loss buying orders would be moved lower along the trend line, or above the next congestion range at (C_1).

Again, notice that a chart trader will not try to guess the top of a trend. He will liquidate his long position only after the chart picture indicates the upward trend is over. He will sell short only after the chart picture appears to indicate the trend has turned downward. Therefore, the chart trader will never sell at the exact high of a move or buy at the exact low. Only after a trend appears underway, will he enter the market; always trading *with the trend, never against it.* If the chart picture indicates the trend is down, he will only trade from the short side of the market. If the chart picture indicates the trend is upward, he will always initiate trades from the buying side of the market. We all realize that there will be moderate rallies in a downtrend, and moderate reactions in an uptrend. However, trying to catch these counter-trend moves usually leads to losses, not profits.

In figure 7B, we have also drawn a dot and dash line parallel to the downtrend line and below the lower limits of the various price fluctuations. This line and the downtrend line combine to define the outer limits of a trading channel. Some traders prefer to trade for quick turns. Thus, they would buy as the lower limit of the trading channel is approached, and sell as the upper line is approached. Most traders would agree, however, that this is not a particularly good method of trading because half the time you would be trading against the trend. For example, should a wave of liquidation develop after the downtrend has been confirmed, prices could easily break sharply, going well below the lower limit of the indicated trading channel. Thus the trader would be long in a downtrend market. Of course, stop-loss protection could have been used immediately below the channel line to limit the

FIGURE 8 A

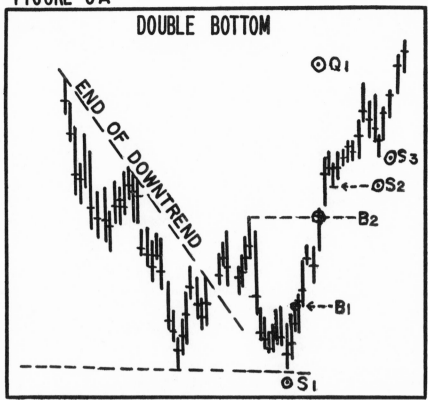

DOUBLE BOTTOM

loss. However, this still would mean that the trader could not have taken advantage of the major part of the price decline.

The Double Top Or Bottom

The double top or bottom, or the M or W formation, or the fulcrum are all different names used by various chart traders and advisory services as a description of the same chart picture which we have labelled as figure 8. Figure 8A is a representation of a "bottom formation." That is, a reversal of a downward price trend into an upward trend. Figure 8B is a representation of a top being formed, and a reversal into a downward price trend.

Looking at figure 8A, we see a downward trendline penetrated on the upside after a rather sharp final downward thrust. The rally carries to the level of the former congestion area, where renewed heavy selling and liquidation force another sharp decline. However, as the old low is approached, resistance to the decline becomes obvious. The market fails to penetrate the old low. The decline was checked before it established a new low. The subsequent rally then carries through until it approaches the high point of the first big rally which had initially broken the downtrend line. This first rally has now become the center of a "W" and is also known as a "fulcrum." Instead of meeting resistance at the high point of the fulcrum, however, the buying is strong enough to carry prices upward through this level (B2). The "double bottom" formation is complete, the upward trend confirmed and chartists would now buy futures. Stop-loss protection would be established just below the old low at (S1).

Some of the more aggressive chart traders may not wait for the completion of this broad "W" formation before establishing a part of their expected total long position. On the secondary reaction, when the decline was checked, a small congestion area was formed. As prices rallied out of this formation, penetrating the high point at (B1) some traders would buy futures with a stop just below the old low at (S1). Their possible loss would, therefore, be much smaller than if they first purchased at (B2). However, the fact that the double bottom formation had not really been completed also meant that they risked this not being a true reversal of the downward trend.

How far can we expect this new upward trend to carry? On a point and figure chart, the "count" for the objective would be taken along the horizontal line just above the high of the fulcrum. On the vertical bar chart, which we are using, the count is taken vertically. The vertical distance between the high point of the fulcrum and the old low is measured. This same distance is then added vertically from point (B2) to give the first objective, which we have marked on our chart as "O_1." Thus, if the distance from the fulcrum to the old low represented $5\cent$ on the chart, the move above point (B2) might also be $5\cent$. This, of course, is again a purely mechanical type of objective which we could not expect to hold as rigorously true. Nevertheless, as chart trading has grown in popularity, more and more people use these mechanical objectives. Therefore, more and more selling actually develops at these points. This, in effect, forces resistance to actually occur at these levels.

If this "double bottom" formation developed after a rather long decline, the second objective of the rally would be a retracement of approximately 50% of the entire decline, or to the level of a congestion area in the vicinity of this 50% retracement. The third objective would be the congestion area above the 50% retracement; and the final objective, a retracement of the entire downtrend back to the price levels from which the price decline originally began.

Another way of following the advance is to draw in the new upward trend line, and keep a stop-loss sell order below the trend line and/or below the low of the previous minor dip. As prices move upward, the stop-loss order is raised from (S1) to (S2), to (S3), etc., until eventually the new upward trend line is broken and the long position is liquidated.

Inverting figure 8A, we have the "double top" formation of figure 8B. The logic and trading policies to be followed are similar to the discussion above. The market is in an established uptrend. As it reaches a new high, heavy selling develops and a reaction occurs. The market rallies again, but additional heavy selling develops on the rally and the market fails to make a new high. This time prices dip below the low of the previous reaction which was at price (X₁). This confirms the reversal of trend, and short sales are called for at that point (X₃). Additional short sales could be made on any subsequent rally to the

FIGURE 8B

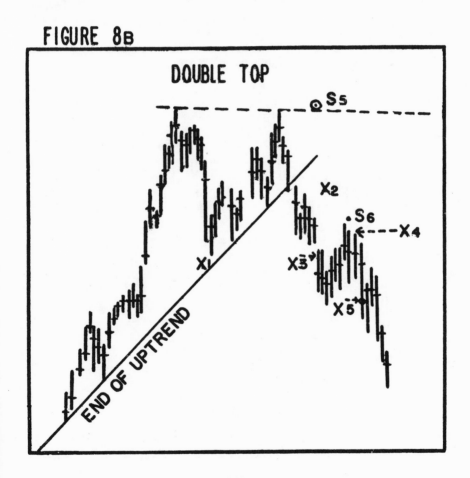

fulcrum area (X_4), and on the reaction which penetrates the low point of any secondary rally which may have developed, at (X_5). Again, the more aggressive traders might not have waited for the pattern to have been confirmed by breaking through the low of the fulcrum. Many traders would not only have liquidated long positions, but would have established short positions when the initial upward trend line was broken at point (X_2). Stop-loss protection would first be placed at $(S5)$, then moved down to $(S6)$, etc. A new downward trend line would be drawn, along which the stop-loss position would be lowered as the market declined. We have refrained from drawing in this trend, since our diagram has already become quite complex.

The Head And Shoulders Formation

The chart picture illustrated in figure 9A is the "head and shoulders" top. It indicates a reversal from an uptrend to a downtrend. When inverted, it illustrates the "head and shoulders" bottom (figure 9B), which is one of the key patterns formed as a downtrend ends and

FIGURE 9A

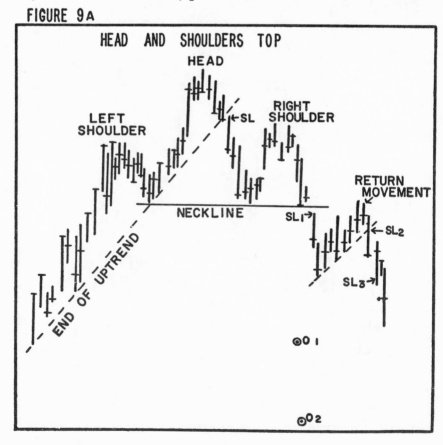

HEAD AND SHOULDERS TOP

reverses into an uptrend.

The "head and shoulders" top is formed as follows. After an uptrend has been underway for some length of time, a moderate reaction develops. This is normal and is awaited, as all such reactions are, by traders who wish to establish or add to their long positions. The market rallies again under the impetus of buying, and goes into new high ground. Once again profit taking and other selling enters the market, and a reaction occurs. This time, however, the selling pressure is sufficiently strong to break the upward trend line. At this point, chartists would at least liquidate long positions, probably automatically through stop-loss orders at price (SL). This, and possibly new short selling and belated hedging, forces prices still lower, until the low range of the previous congestion area is reached. At that point, some traders, who have them, would take quick profits on short positions. Others, also not yet convinced this is a change in the upward trend, buy to establish new long positions. Again the market rallies, but this time buying power is insufficient to bring the market up into new high ground. Instead, heavy selling develops before the old high is reached. Prices react not only to the price level at which support developed twice before, but continue right through that point, absorbing any support buying that might occur. The chart picture is complete. The trend reversal is now confirmed, because both a lower "high" and a lower "low" have been recorded on the latest price swing, as compared with the previous one. A line connecting the low points of these last two support areas is called "the neckline." The first rally in the chart picture is called the "left shoulder." The price swing that proved to be the high for the move is called "the head," and the final rally from the neckline is called the "right shoulder." After the neckline is broken, a return movement sometimes develops which brings prices back to the area of the neckline before the price reaction continues.

There are several places at which short positions could be established on this type of formation. The first point, of course, is at (SL), where the uptrend line is initially broken. While this is anticipating the formation of a downtrend, selling short here usually allows a rather small stop-loss limit. The stop-loss would be placed just above the old high. If this proves to be the beginning of a downtrend (rather than just an exceptionally sharp technical reaction in an uptrend), the trader has established his initial position at a very favorable price. The rally which eventually forms the right shoulder could be a second point for instituting a short position. Again, going short here *anticipates* the formation of a downtrend. The stop loss limit would again be above the old high. When the neckline is finally broken, we have the first real confirmation of the downtrend. Stop-loss sell orders at price (SL1) would have been placed by many chartists to establish short positions. The protective stop-loss, to limit losses in the event the market reverses itself once again, would now be placed above the high price of the right shoulder. Some traders would add to short positions on any return movement to the vicinity of the neckline, or where the minor uptrend line formed by this return movement is broken at (SL2). Finally, short positions could be increased as the low point of the return movement is penetrated at price (SL3).

How far down could prices be expected to carry? If this pattern were formed on the point and figure chart, the objective would be given by a count horizontally across the neckline. On the bar chart, the count is the vertical distance from the top of the head to the neckline. This distance is then measured downward from the neckline to give us the first objective at price (01). The second objective is then obtained by measuring downward from (01) a distance equal to that from the top of the right shoulder to the neckline. This would make the second price objective (02). The third objective would be a congestion area in the

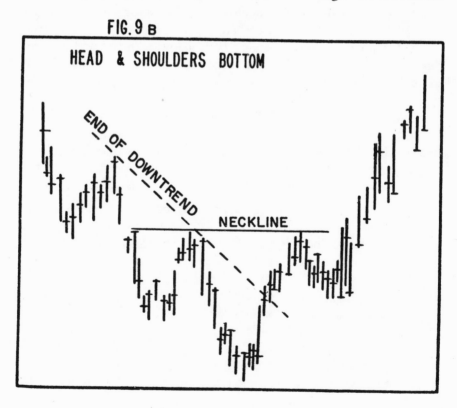

FIG. 9 B

HEAD & SHOULDERS BOTTOM

END OF DOWNTREND

NECKLINE

vicinity of a 50% retracement of the entire previous advance. Thereafter, each successively lower congestion area becomes an objective, until the entire initial upward trend has been retraced.

The "head and shoulders" bottom formation (figure 9B), indicates a reversal from a downtrend to an uptrend confirmed when the neckline is broken. Probable buying points would be: first, cover short positions when the downtrend line is broken; second, buy on the dip which eventually forms the shoulder, with stop-loss protection just below the low; third, add to long positions when the neckline is broken, with stop-loss protection raised to just below the shoulder.

Triangles, Coils, Flags And Pennants

These formations are all similar, with a flag being a more rectangular version of the others. Figure 10 illustrates three forms of the triangle or pennant. These represent specific types of congestion areas. They are usually formed after a trend has been underway for some time. They occur as interruptions to the trend, in which buying and selling forces appear fairly evenly balanced.

Figure 10A is a picture of an "ascending triangle." That is, the side of the triangle which slopes does so in an upward direction. As pictured, an upward trend is underway, but runs into liquidating and selling pressure which causes a fairly sharp reaction. The market rallies again but, at around the level of the previous high, runs into renewed selling which forces prices to react again. The low point of this reaction (2), however, proves to be higher than that of reaction (1). In other words, buying has become more aggressive. Again, prices rally under the stimulation of this new buying, only to be met by heavy sales in the vicinity of the old high. The selling pressure is great enough to cause a setback once more. The reaction is even more limited this time, with aggressive new buying coming into the market at a higher price than before. The low point of this reaction (3) is again higher than the previous one (2). Each time the market rallies, it runs into resistance at around the old high. A line across the top of these points, therefore, would be horizontal. However, on each subsequent reaction buying comes into the market at a little higher level, so that the low points get higher and higher (points 1, 2, 3, and 4). A line connecting these points slopes upward. This forms the ascending triangle and, as shown, indicates that a breakout of the pattern will usually be on the upside. Once this occurs, the price will generally move rapidly higher. Many times the triangle proves to be the mid-point of the entire price move, particularly if the formation has been preceded by a sharp upward thrust.

In that case, the triangle is called "pennant on a pole," or simply a "pennant." If prices advanced 10¢ before the triangle or pennant was formed, the price objective of the move after the breakout from the triangle will be another 10¢.

Sometimes, the ascending triangle is formed, but instead of the anticipated resumption of the upward trend which this pattern usually portends, prices break on the downside. In this case, the reaction will

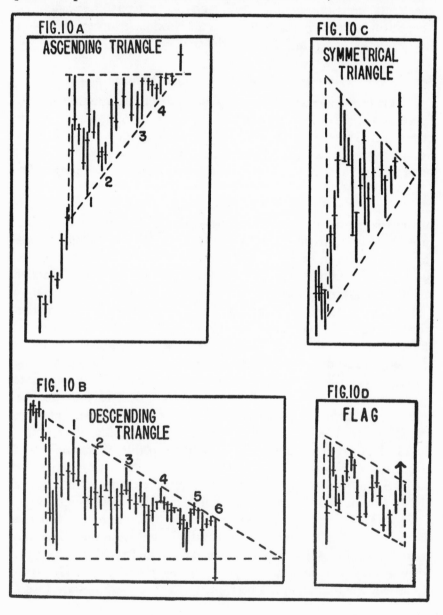

FIG. 10 A
ASCENDING TRIANGLE

FIG. 10 C
SYMMETRICAL TRIANGLE

FIG. 10 B
DESCENDING TRIANGLE

FIG. 10 D
FLAG

be expected to carry first to the low point of the triangle (point 1). Then, after a moderate recovery, the market would be expected to retrace the entire advance, ending back at the starting point of the upward trend. Therefore, it is usually prudent to wait until the pattern is complete before establishing new positions, rather than anticipating the pattern or the direction of the breakout.

While the ascending triangle is in process of formation, the pattern might well just be mistaken for a double top. In that case, some short positions might have been established; but an "open" (another way of saying "Good-'til-Cancelled") stop-buy, order should have been placed above the high point, thus limiting the loss when prices finally do move higher.

To establish new positions, futures should be bought once the market's move into new high ground confirms the continuation of the upward trend; that is, when the horizontal line in figure 10A is broken. As protection, stop-loss orders could then be placed just below the horizontal line from which the breakout occurred. This is somewhat risky, since the market could sell back to that level in a normal "return movement."

Figure 10B represents the "descending triangle." It is formed by price swings similar to the ascending triangle. In this case, each swing ends with a lower high point, while support continues to develop at the same approximate price on each reaction. Since the high of each move continuously moves lower, it is an indication that selling is becoming more aggressive and that prices will eventually break out of the formation on the downslide. When this occurs, short sales are recommended, with stop-loss protection just above price (6). Again the triangle would probably prove to be around the midpoint of a downward trend.

Figure 10C is a "symmetrical triangle," in which the highs are moving lower on each price swing and the lows are moving higher. Thus, there is no prior indication as to the probable direction of the breakout from this formation.

Figure 10D is a "flag." It differs from the other formations shown in that both the highs and lows of the price swings do not tend to come to a point as in a triangle. Instead, lines connecting the highs and lows remain parallel. That is, both the highs and lows move lower or higher together, so that the figure when completed looks like an unfurled flag. The slope of the flag will be in an opposite direction from that of the main trend. Thus, if the trend has been upward, the flag will slope downward. Nevertheless, it is usually an indication, as with the pennant and triangle, that a major part of the price move is still to come. The flag is merely an interruption of the trend, in which a temporary equilibrium is reached, while the forces are gathered for a second thrust.

Buying and selling procedure is the same as for other chart formations. Wait for the completion of the pattern and the breakout. Buy (or sell) on the breakout, with the assumption that the price will continue in the same direction as the breakout. Place protective stops at some logical point, such as just below (or above, if you have sold short) the last minor price swing of the pattern.

The Round Top, Saucer Top, Scallop Top

This formation, as the names suggest and as shown in figure 11, is a gradual reversal of trend. The chart picture indicates an upward price movement gradually reversing as selling pressure overcomes new buying. Prices slowly work into a downward trend. When figure 11 is inverted, it is a picture of a "round bottom" formation; that is, a gradual reversal from a downtrend to an uptrend. This type of formation is occasionally accompanied by minor price swings creating a scalloped effect shown by the dotted line on the diagram.

The "round top" ("bottom") becomes obvious before the pattern is quite complete. This allows the establishment of new positions close enough to the high point of the move (price S1) to utilize it as a stop-loss point. The round top is usually formed by a commodity whose daily range is rather restricted. The first selling point is, therefore, taken to be the *low* of the minor price movement (price x) following

FIG.II

ROUND TOP

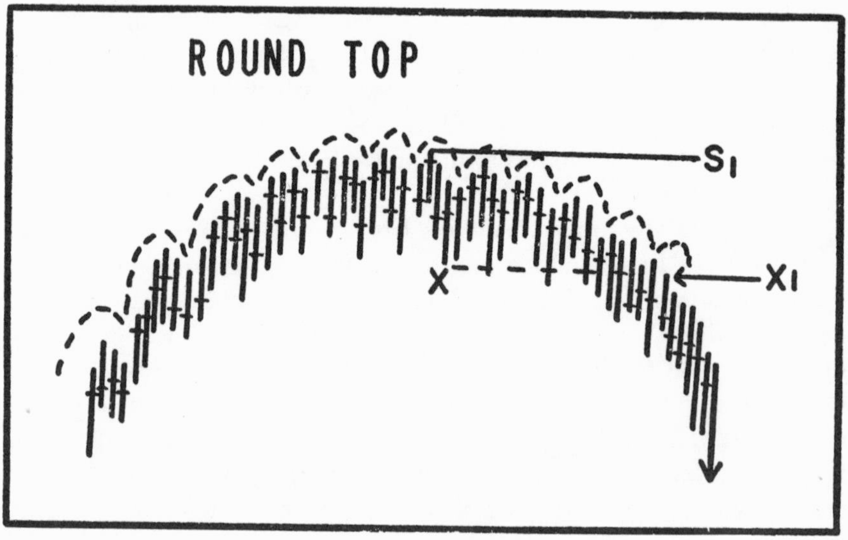

the high (price S1). The round top becomes recognizable as a pattern after it has sold lower than this level but, usually on one of the minor return movements, that price will be reached again. A short sale could then be established at X1, with stop-loss protection immediately above the old high at price S1.

It is difficult to obtain an objective from this type of chart picture. It is usually followed by a major move, but its approximate extent can only be judged by the areas of congestion established previously, when the trend was still upward. Price resistance can be expected at each of these former congestion areas. Stop-loss orders should be lowered accordingly.

Gaps

A gap is a space on the chart between the high of one day and the low of the subsequent day, or vice versa. In an upward gap, the market is strong enough to open at a price which is higher than the high of the last trading session. If the buying is aggressive enough to bid prices up to a level that creates a gap, then presumably it should be aggressive enough to keep prices moving upward for some time to come. This, however, is not strictly true. There are various types of gaps, as shown in figure 12, which have various significance. In a downward gap, the market opens lower than the low of the previous day, again leaving a space on the chart in which no trading occurred.

The "common gap" is usually formed in a market with very small volume. When the number of actual sales during any trading session is small, the bids and offers change many times before an actual trade is consummated. Since the chart only registers the actual sales, the chart picture will show many gaps. As prices fluctuate over a period of several days, these gaps will be formed and subsequently filled in. By "filled in," we mean that prices will eventually trade in the price level which was originally skipped and left blank on the chart. The common gap has no particular significance, and is marked as (1) on figure 12.

The "breakaway gap" (#2 on figure 12) proves to be the beginning of a major price movement. It is usually accompanied by a sharp increase in the volume of trading and a large price movement. It generally occurs after a chart pattern has been completed, and induces new traders to enter the market. This creates the momentum necessary for a gap to develop. It can also result when an unexpected news event, which alters the price prospects for commodities, materializes. The Korean war, for example, caused a wave of buying which created gaps in many commodities. The news event can be more specific, and affect only one commodity. An unexpectedly large (or small) crop estimate can be responsible for altering traders' opinions enough to create a gap in the chart picture.

Once a breakaway gap occurs, prices should move rapidly in the new direction, up or down, depending upon which way the breakaway developed. The space on the chart should not be filled in by trading during subsequent days, if the move is to be of major proportions. If the gap is subsequently filled (gap #3 on figure 12), it may still prove to be significant, although somewhat more caution is necessary in attempting to evaluate the prospective size of the anticipated price movement.

When a gap occurs, many traders who are on the wrong side of the market fail to take their losses immediately. Instead, they wait and hope for a reaction, during which they can cover. Others, who are on the profitable side of the market, may not believe the news event which

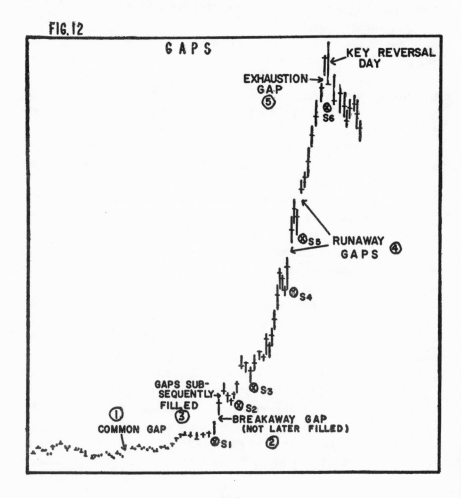

FIG. 12

GAPS

caused the gap to be of major significance. Hence they will tend to use the sudden rise or fall in price to take profits. The result is that prices may return to the starting point; that is, the gap is filled in. This becomes a test of the market. Once the gap is filled, those who initially failed to establish positions hasten to do so. If whatever caused the gap is really of major importance, this return movement should just about fill in the gap and then resume the new trend. Notice, however, that this return movement occurs only when the factors creating the gap are subject to interpretation or doubt. If the factors causing the initial gap are clear-cut, the gap will not be filled.

Once the return movement has occurred, and new buying enters on confirmation of the factors initially causing the breakaway gap, new highs for the move will be established. The trend tends to accelerate. Those who doubted the significance of the initial events, or hoped for a further reaction, are then convinced that they were wrong and begin to buy in their shorts. Other traders who failed to establish long positions earlier, now also jump into the market. A second wave of buying develops which, in turn, causes new gaps to develop. These are called "runaway gaps," and are marked as (4) on our chart. Runaway gaps many times prove to be approximately the midway point of the advance (or of the decline if the new trend was down).

As prices continue to move upward, many traders begin to feel the advance is being overdone and hence some, anticipating a reaction, begin to establish short positions. As these short positions accumulate against the trend, losses mount. A third wave of short covering may develop, which can lead to new gaps. Once this short covering is out of the way, however, the resulting buying power disappears. New selling (hedging or otherwise) finds support missing and prices suddenly give way. Traders with long positions showing good profits have been watching the market closely for a sign of weakness. This is their signal to begin taking profits. Suddenly selling orders appear from all directions, and the trend turns downward. This type of action will usually result in what is called a "key reversal day." Prices on that day will begin by moving higher, and appear to continue the upward trend. As the selling suddenly finds no support, prices begin to sag, and that is when the liquidation begins. Prices, which originally were higher, now move lower. They close with a loss for the day, at or near the bottom of the day's price range, accompanied by very heavy volume. The upward trend is over. The final gap has proven to be an "exhaustion gap" (#5).

From the foregoing discussion it can be seen that the common gap and the breakaway gap are fairly easy to recognize. What is more difficult, however, is to differentiate between a runaway gap and an exhaustion gap. It is only after the market has broken, that an exhaustion gap can be confirmed. Waiting for this type of confirmation could result in the dissipation of a major part of the accumulated profits before long positions are liquidated. Therefore, two types of action could be taken. First, if a key reversal day appears to have developed, liquidate. Secondly, if no key reversal has developed after the third series of gaps (#5 on figure 12) has occurred, place a stop-loss order below the low of the day before the gap developed. If it is not an exhaustion gap, it should not be set off. Placing the stop below the low of the previous day also allows for any minor return movement which might just fill the gap before the trend is removed.

Trading on the type of action illustrated in figure 12 would consist of something akin to the following. First, a long position could be established after the breakaway gap occurs. (On our chart picture, a long position would actually have been justified on the day before the gap appeared, since the market broke out on the upside of what had been a trading range). A stop-loss order should be placed below the low of the previous trading range or, if that is too far down, below the low of the previous day at (S_1). On the return movement, as Gap #3 is filled, another purchase is warranted to add to long positions, keeping the stop at (S1). As the market moves into new high ground, a third purchase could be made, moving the stop-loss up to just under the low of the previous return movement at (S2). After new highs and a possible further purchase were made, the stop-loss would be raised to (S3). The market, after this point, begins to run away. When the runaway gaps are formed, the stops should be moved up to below the low of the previous dip, at (S4) and (S5). The price advance, thereafter, is so steep that it is difficult to know how high to raise the stop-loss orders. One procedure acceptable to many would be to raise the stop each day to a point below the low of the previous day, or the low of two days before. When gap #5 is created, the stop would be placed at (S6), which is again below the low of the previous day. This stop could have been the last, and would have been touched off as the market broke. All the long positions previously announced would have been liquidated with excellent profits. As previously mentioned, when the key reversal day appears to develop, some (if not all) of the long positions justifiably have been sold out.

You will notice that a trend line was not drawn on figure 12. That was because the price movement became successively stronger, resulting in a parabolic (curved) trend line. A straight trend line would have been kept far below the levels at which actual trading took place.

Appraisal Of The Use Of Price Charts

The use of price charts appears to have a definite place in commodity trading as an aid to both the hedger and the speculator. They present a picture of where prices have been and thus allow comparisons to be made with other periods of the past, providing some *tentative* conclusions about where prices *may* be headed in the future. Thus, for example, they may reveal patterns of price movements, an indication of whether or not price movements are normally wide or narrow, whether prices have tended to go much below Government loan levels, etc.

Whether or not the use of the chart should be given priority in trading, over the analysis of fundamental price making influences in the market (crops, exports, etc.) remains an unresolved dispute.

The pure chartist's view that he does not want to know anything about the fundamentals of supply and demand before trading in the market, relying solely on the chart formations, appears too extreme for acceptance. It appears more logical to first determine, through an appraisal of the fundamental supply and demand conditions, the probable course of prices. If, after studying the fundamentals, a trader arrives at the conclusion that prices are too low and should move higher, then an examination of the chart picture should prove extremely useful. It will help determine the time and place to establish his long position, and also where to limit his loss if his appraisal of the situation is wrong.

If the chart picture indicates prices are still moving lower, the potential trader should wait before instituting his long position. When the price charts indicate that the market is stabilizing, the long position could be established. If his analysis of the fundamentals is correct, then his long position will be established well below the point at which the pure chartist would enter the market. Remember that the trend must be well established and confirmed before the pure chartist will establish a position.

Once the trader, who has depended primarily on the fundamentals, has established his long position, the chart would also indicate the logical point at which to place a stop-loss order, admit that he is wrong, and liquidate his position. The loss involved would be much smaller than if he had waited until the chart picture confirmed an upward trend before establishing his long position, and was proven wrong.

This is so because the stop-loss order would be much closer to his original buying point.

Using the charts alone can also lead to buying and selling at illogical points. For example, there are certain price levels at which the huge government surpluses can be sold in the domestic market. In the chapter on price supports, it was pointed out that the surplus basic crops could be sold in the domestic market at 105% (cotton at 110%) of the support price plus reasonable carrying charges. The government announces these prices monthly in its monthly sales list. There were times when the chart picture indicated that long positions should be established (or added to) at prices which were at, or close to, the government selling level. Losses could have resulted, had this been done. Other similar situations could be pointed out where the chart picture may have been misleading.

The chartist answers these arguments in the following manner. Most people do not, and cannot, know all the important supply and demand elements in the market; nor can they follow changes in these conditions fast enough to trade on them. Therefore, establising market positions solely on fundamentals will put them into (and take them out of) the market either too soon or too late. Even if they wait for the market to appear to have stabilized, the chances are equally good that the old trend will be resumed, as they are that the trend will reverse. They will, therefore, have more numerous trades with losses, although those losses will admittedly be small if stop-loss orders are used.

Market prices, on the other hand, will reflect all changes in supply and demand prospects even before these are generally known. Therefore, ignoring the news and waiting for a confirmation of trend on the chart before establishing positions still gives the greatest chance of profits. The chartist will admit that the charts, at times, cause purchases at "illogical points." However, he contends that once the market reverses, the chart picture will indicate the change, and the position will be liquidated with only minor inroads into capital.

These arguments have been debated for years and will apparently continue. The tentative conclusion one comes to is that knowing the fundamentals is important. It can prevent some trades which could lead to losses, and help increase profits on other trades. On the other hand, keeping charts and watching them is also very important. It is rare that establishing a position contrary to the trend indicated by the chart will prove profitable. Money is made by trading with the trend, not against it. Experience has demonstrated that the general trader cannot successfully fight a market and win.

For those traders not in a position to keep in touch with market conditions in the actual commodity, charts do offer a means by which price trends can be forecast with reasonable accuracy. Chart trading has in the past, and can in the future, prove highly profitable.

In an earlier chapter, a method of price forecasting based on the analysis of fundamentals was presented. Use of this technique, in conjunction with chart analysis, should increase the probabilities of profitable trading.

CHAPTER 19.

"OPEN INTEREST" AND "VOLUME OF TRADING" STATISTICS — SUBSIDIARY TOOLS FOR THE CHART TRADER

When the breakaway gap and key reversal day were discussed, it was mentioned that they would be accompanied by an increase in the volume of trading. Two subsidiary tools are used along with chart pictures to help forecast price movements. The volume of trading is one, and changes in the "open interest" is the other.

The "open interest" is the number of contracts that remain to be settled in the futures market. During any single trading day, some traders liquidate their positions while other people establish new positions. For example, if someone has previously bought a March future and now sells a March future, he liquidates his position. By virtue of this liquidation, the number of contracts in the March delivery still remaining to be settled is reduced by one. The open interest has been reduced by one. Someone else, however, may have decided to establish a new position in futures, and buys a May future. This creates a new contract, which must be settled at a later date either by selling out the position or taking delivery. The open interest has been increased by one. The open interest, therefore, is a measure of the number of contracts still on the market. It takes two people, a buyer and a seller, to establish one contract. Since the open interest is the number of contracts outstanding, it is also both the number of long positions still in the market and the number of shorts. If the open interest is 100, it means there are 100 longs and 100 shorts in the market.

Significance Of Open Interest Changes

By watching changes in the open interest in conjunction with price changes, a clue can be obtained as to whether or not the market has been strengthened or weakened by recent trading, and whether one can, therefore, expect subsequent price improvement or easiness. Only changes in the total open interest figures reflecting all the trading months combined, are significant and used in the analysis.

The diagram below, originated by a well-known commodity futures broker, indicates this in simple form:

	(	Price Up = New buying
OPEN INTEREST UP	{	(Technically strong)
		Price Down = Hedging or short selling
	(	(Technically weak)

	(	Price Up = Short covering
OPEN INTEREST DOWN	{	(Technically weak)
		Price Down = Long liquidation
	(	(Technically strong)

When the open interest is increasing, it means that new positions are being established. Some traders are going long, some short. When the *increase in open interest is accompanied by higher prices,* it means that the buyers are more aggressive. They are still willing to keep paying higher prices for the commodity, and hence continued strength is still to be expected. The market is said to be "technically strong." As prices continue to advance, however, many individuals who have sold short will realize they are wrong and begin to cover in their short positions (either voluntarily or because they have received a margin call and do not want to put up more money). They are, therefore, forced to buy back their short futures. This buying will, at first, add strength to the market. Since they are liquidating previously established positions, however, they are tending to reduce the open interest. When *prices are still advancing but the open interest begins to go down,* it means that *new* buying has stopped and that the buying being done is only short covering. New buyers no longer have confidence that prices will continue to advance. This means that the market is becoming "technically weak." Once the short covering is out of the way, there will be no buying to offset sales at current prices. The declining open interest also means that the traders who are long are liquidating and taking profits. They too, lack confidence in the market's ability to keep advancing. Therefore, *prices advancing but open interest declining* is a signal that the price trend may be getting ready to reverse.

The same reasoning applies when *prices are declining.* If lower prices are being *accompanied by an increase in the open interest,* it means that the new sellers are being more aggressive than new buyers (otherwise prices would not be going down). New traders are willing to keep selling, even though prices have already declined. Somewhere along the line, however, those who have long positions will realize they are wrong and begin liquidating their old positions, thus tending to reduce the open interest. When the open interest actually begins to decline, it is a signal that:

1) New sellers are no longer willing to enter the market at these lower prices.

2) The selling which is taking place is primarily long liquidation, either voluntary or due to margin calls. Once the bulk of it is completed, there will be little new selling power in the market to meet new buying, and prices will recover.

3) The decline in open interest also means that those who had previously established short positions are now taking profits. They also believe the market will not go down much further. In other words, *a price downturn accompanied by declining open interest* is an indication that the downward price movement may be coming to an end. The market is becoming "technically strong."

In summary, therefore, when prices and open interest both move in the same direction (both going up, or both going down), it is indicative of coming or continuing price improvement. When the open interest and prices are moving in opposite directions (one going up, the other down), it is a symptom of possible price weakness ahead.

The use of open interest analysis is complicated by several factors. The first is that the open interest follows a seasonal pattern which must be taken into account. The open interest rises sharply during and just after the harvest period when supplies and, therefore, hedging are the heaviest. Thereafter, as the commodity is consumed during the remainder of the season, and the supplies which must be hedged diminish, the open interest tends to decline steadily. In watching for changes in open interest figures, therefore, these trend factors must first be eliminated. Only a fairly sharp, or fairly quick, change in the open interest will show up as significant. Then too, while the changes in open interest will definitely indicate technical strength or weakness, it is not a precise indication of the timing of any potential change in price trend; and timing is of major importance in commodity trading. One can be correct in his analysis, but still lose money by entering the market too soon. The open interest, therefore, has rarely been successfully used *alone* as a means of price forecasting. However, when used in conjunction with chart pictures, it could considerably improve the forecasting results of the latter.

The phrases "technically weak," "technically strong," "technical rally," "technical reaction" will frequently be heard or read in any discussion of commodity futures markets and price trends. The use of the word "technical" in this context, however, is rarely explained. It refers to the factors in the market which are exclusively and directly related to the trading in commodity futures. These are the open interest; the volume of trading; how far prices have advanced or declined; how quickly this advance or decline has occurred; the source of buying and selling; whether it is hedging, hedge lifting, or speculative.

These factors give the full picture of market action and are sufficient to cause some traders to buy or sell, regardless of any "outside" factor. "Outside" factors are those which affect commodity prices but are not exclusively related to the futures market. Examples would be a change in general business trends, weather conditions, political unrest, war news, election results, a new crop forecast, etc.

When, for example, a futures contract has advanced sharply over a relatively short period of time, one may expect a "technical reaction." That is because (and only because) prices have so quickly advanced so far, some traders are going to take a quick profit on their long positions. This selling should cause prices to react temporarily. The outside factors of supply and demand remain exactly the same. The price reaction is brought about purely by "technical" factors.

The same is true when prices have declined quickly and sharply. Many traders who are short will feel the market has gone down too quickly and, hence, will buy in their short positions for a "quick profit." This type of buying may be enough to cause the market to rally temporarily. It is a "technical rally." None of the outside factors affecting supply and demand have changed. The rally occurred only because of the way the futures market behaved and the action it induced traders to take.

Another important example of a market trend changed primarily by technical considerations is associated with the open interest. It occurs frequently and should be watched for. After an uptrend has been underway for some time, the open interest tends to expand rather rapidly. This is indicative of increased public participation. The larger the open interest, the more vulnerable the price structure becomes. The public is generally associated with the long side of the market. Should a rumor or adverse piece of news materialize, the public might decide to liquidate. A cumulative affect results, and prices begin to tumble. Liquidation spreads. Selling caused by margin calls accelerates the movement and, for a time, the decline in futures will have no relationship to supply and demand for the cash commodity.

Volume Of Trading

Another subsidiary tool used with chart trading, one which is much easier to use than open interest figures and one which is not subject to the shortcomings of the latter, is the volume of trade. Whether or not the volume of trading in any commodity is heavy during any session is significant, when combined with the price action on that day. It helps determine whether prices can be expected to continue moving in the same direction or to reverse their trend. As with open interest figures, the *total for all delivery months combined* is significant. The volume of trading, like the open interest, is an indication of whether or not traders are willing to follow the existing price trend.

The rule for using volume of trade figures is: *Prices will tend to move in the direction in which the volume of trade increases.* Thus, if the total volume of trade increases while prices are rising, we can expect that the upward price trend will remain intact and that any price reaction which may occur will prove to be moderate in extent and short-lived. Conversely, if the total volume of trading increases as prices are declining, we can expect the price trend to continue downward and rallies to be limited in extent and short-lived.

Figure (13) indicates how open interest and volume figures are used in conjunction with price charts. They are rarely used with point and figure charts, because of the difficulty involved in separating daily action on that type of chart. They are most frequently used with bar charts (daily or weekly), and occasionally with moving averages. The volume of trade is usually plotted as a vertical bar. The open interest is plotted as a line connecting the daily totals. The scale for the volume is on the left, the scale for the open interest is on the right. The open interest will always be several times as large as the volume of trading. This is a logical expectation since most people do not get into and out of a market in one day. The scales used for measuring volume and open interest changes will reflect this difference.

As prices moved higher, in our hypothetical example, the volume and open interest increased, indicating a technically strong market and belief that reactions will be short-lived and limited. As expected, when prices reacted from peak #1, the decline lasted only two days and was not sharp. The volume and open interest declined with the price level, still indicating technical strength. The same pattern of volume and open interest is displayed before and after peaks #2 and #3.

As the market begins rallying again toward peak #4, however, we find a change in the action of the open interest and volume. Instead of increasing with the price level, as before, we find that volume remains low and even declines somewhat. The open interest continues to decline. This activity is indicated by bracket "A" on figure 13. From the previous

FIG.13 VOLUME, OPEN INTEREST & PRICE

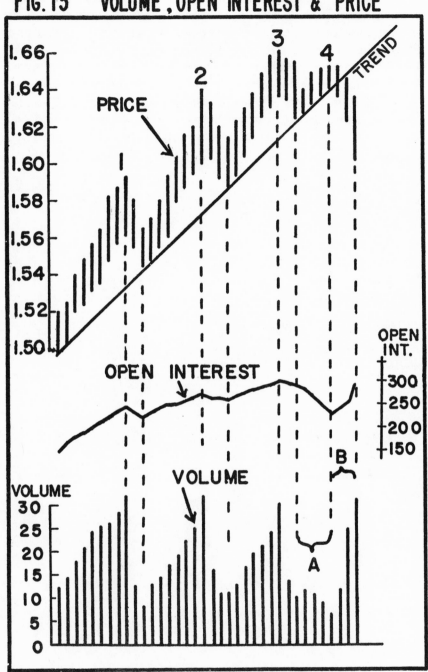

discussion, you will remember that prices going up while open interest is going down is an indication of technical market weakness and the unwillingness of new buyers to enter the market at these higher price levels. Although prices are still advancing and remain above the trend line, the open interest and volume figures give us our first danger signal.

As the market begins to react from peak #4, the volume and open interest increase sharply. These increases (bracketed as area "B" on the volume chart) appear to confirm the fact that a downtrend has developed, and that the breaking of the upward trend line is not merely a chance occurrence.

CHAPTER 20.

THE ROLE OF THE SPECULATOR

Since the commodity futures markets are designed primarily to meet the hedging needs of the business community, many people fail to understand the necessity of permitting and, in fact, encouraging speculative trading. On the contrary, speculative activity in commodity futures has been attacked as an unnecessary evil which developed as a by-product of a useful and desirable activity.

Nothing could be further from the truth. Extensive speculative activity is a necessary adjunct to the smooth flow of commodity futures transactions. Without speculative participation it would be virtually impossible for firms in the commodity trades to follow a consistent hedging policy, and for futures exchanges to perform their basic economic functions.

Speculators: a) supply needed risk capital, b) increase the volume of trade to allow easy market entry and egress, and, c) keep the various markets in alignment through arbitrage operations.

Trade firms use the futures market to hedge; this is, to limit or offset price risks. For this to occur there must be some group willing to absorb these risks. It is the speculator who supplies the risk capital necessary to offset hedging operations. He does so, of course, with the hope that the market will move as he anticipates thus affording him a profit in exchange for his capital risk.

The statistics which have been compiled over the years by the Commodity Exchange Authority, an agency of the U. S. Government, indicate that trade hedging is overwhelmingly on the short side of the market. That is, hedging is primarily done by selling futures contracts to protect inventories against price declines. Most agricultural commodities are harvested, or become available for consumption, in a concentrated period of a few weeks. However, they are consumed over a full calendar year period. Someone must own and store these commodities between their production and consumption. The person who does this is subject to the risks of the heavy financial losses which could occur from falling prices. Protection against this eventually is obtained by selling in the futures market as a hedge. The CEA figures also point out that the trade use of the buying hedge is, as yet, relatively small. Buying hedges, therefore, would not be sufficiently plentiful to offset the selling hedges. If speculative trading were prohibited, hedge selling would, of necessity, have to be sharply curtailed, thereby also curtailing the price protection futures trading affords.

In addition to supplying the risk capital necessary to offset hedges, the increase in the volume of trading resulting from speculative participation allows hedges to be placed and lifted by the trade without affecting the price level. If a firm wishes to hedge by selling say 50 contracts, and the daily volume is 1,000 contracts, the price effect of that one order would probably be negligible. However, if the daily volume of trade were only 100 contracts, a marked price-depressing influence could well result. In fact, the hedge order probably would not even be given. Thus, the liquidity provided by speculative activity is also of great importance to the achievement of the beneficial effects of futures trading.

Finally, the flexibility of speculative transactions allows the development of arbitrage operations which would not legally be possible if trading were limited only to hedging. Commodity markets are highly interrelated. For example, oats and corn, both competitive feed grains, should sell within a relatively restricted price ratio. The same is true for wheat selling on the Chicago, Kansas City and Minneapolis Exchanges. Of course, varying economic and market conditions prevent the establishment of rigid relationships. However, a relationship does exist, and by a careful study of existing conditions arbitrageurs hope to discover when one market or commodity is out of phase with another. That is, when a speculator feels that Chicago wheat is selling "too high" relative to Kansas City, he would purchase Kansas City wheat and sell Chicago wheat. The combined, persistent activity of speculators selling in the high-priced market and buying the low-priced market tends to bring about the readjustment in values at all markets, even those on another continent.

While the purpose of commodity exchanges is primarily to serve the hedging needs of the various industries, speculative participation is necessary to its fulfillment.

CHAPTER 21.

"SPREADS AND STRADDLES" —
A METHOD OF COMMODITY SPECULATION

Many opportunities for speculative profits arise out of the ever-changing price differences that develop between different commodity futures contracts.

The words, "spread" and "straddle" have come to be used interchangeably in commodity futures trading. They designate the purchase of one commodity future against the sale of another. Both the purchase and sale are usually, although not necessarily, made simultaneously. The idea behind this kind of transaction is that the *price difference* between the two contracts will change in such a manner as to result in a profit.

A popular form of spread involves the simultaneous purchase and sale of two different futures delivery months in the same market, when the spreader thinks they are temporarily "out of line."

Example Of A Typical Spreading Operation

For example, as shown below, one contract may be purchased at a 10¢ discount to another contract which is simultaneously sold. Later, when the price difference between the two contracts has, let us say, narrowed to 4¢, both contracts are simultaneously liquidated—resulting in a 6¢ profit.

To illustrate:

October 15th	
Buy 5,000 bus. Jan. Soybeans at $2.36	and Sell 5,000 bus. May Soybeans at $2.46
December 10th	
Sell 5,000 bus. Jan. Soybeans at 2.49	and Buy 5,000 bus. May Soybeans at 2.53
PROFIT $ .13	LOSS $ .07
Net Profit $.06/bu. == $300.00 (less commission)	

To initiate the spread, the order "buy 5,000 January Soybeans—sell 5,000 May Soybeans when May is 10¢ premium" is given by the trader to his broker. (Remember that 5,000 bushels of grain is one contract.) The initial position is established several months before first notice day on the closest contract (January). This allows sufficient time for the price spread to change before the trader is forced to liquidate his position to avoid receiving delivery of the actual commodity.

After a period of time the price spread has narrowed. Both contracts have advanced in price, but the January has advanced faster than the May. When the spread between the two contracts has narrowed to 4¢, the trader decides to take his profit. He places an order to "Sell 5,000 bus. January Soybeans—Buy 5,000 May Soybeans at May 4¢ over." When this order is executed, his entire position is liquidated, resulting in a profit shown by the illustration.

There are several important things to be noted in this kind of operation. In placing both the initial order to establish the spread and the one to liquidate, no exact fixed prices at which to buy and sell the two contracts are specified. Only the price difference between the two contracts is established. That is, the order is *not* stated to buy the January at $2.36 and sell the May at $2.46. If that were done, possibly only the January would be bought, but the May could not be sold, or vice versa. The exact prices at which the two contracts are obtained are not important, only the price difference is. When the order is placed specifying only the price difference, the broker has greater latitude in fulfilling the order. This increases the certainty that both contracts will be acquired. Because of the constant state of flux in the market, the two contracts might be obtained at ½¢ lower than the figures shown in the illustration or 1¢ higher. It does not matter to the trader. As long as the specified price difference is achieved, the position that he wants is properly established.

The same is true when the position is liquidated. Look back at the illustration. Suppose both contracts were liquidated on December 10 at prices 1¢ higher than shown, or 3¢ lower, or 10¢ lower. It would not change the net profit whatsoever. As long as January was sold at a 4¢ discount to the price paid for May, the results are the same.

This illustrates another important point. Establishing a spread avoids the necessity of having to pick the direction in which the entire market will move. Since, in a spread, one contract is bought and one is sold, there will be a profit on one of the contracts and a loss on the other, no matter which way the entire price structure goes, up or down. Whether the entire market goes up or down is not important. What is important is that the price difference between the two contracts in our example should narrow. This could happen either in a general price advance, or in a downtrend. The type of commodity spread we have illustrated will usually, although not necessarily, be most profitable if an uptrend is established after the spread has been instituted. We have purchased the near month and sold a more distant delivery month. As pointed out in the section on hedging, when prices are rising the nearer months tend to advance more rapidly than the more distant futures. However, notice that we do not have to catch the bottom of the price trend, or even pick the exact time that the trend will turn upward. This can occur weeks later and begin at much lower price levels.

Suppose, however, that an upward trend does not develop. It is possible for this spread to narrow, even in a downtrend market, although probably not as much as it would otherwise. But, suppose it does not narrow at all. Suppose instead the differences widen and the January goes to more of a discount under the May. How much can be lost?

The answer to this question will indicate why we have taken up so much time with this particular spread. The worst that could happen would be a loss of only one cent per bushel or $50 for the spread, plus commission. This type of spread represents a limited risk.

The Limited Risk Spread

In an earlier chapter, it was pointed out that for grains and other non-perishable commodities, there was, in most cases, a limit to the premium of distant months over near months. This limit is the carrying charge, which we estimated to be 2¾¢ per bushel per month. The four month period from January to May, multiplied by a carrying charge of 2¾¢ per month, is 11¢ per bushel. The maximum premium of May over January would, therefore, be 11¢. Since we bought January and sold May when May was at a 10¢ premium, then the worst that could happen would be for the spread to widen out by an additional cent, to full carrying charges. The risk, involved, therefore, is very small.

On the other hand, the profit potential is not limited. Also, as previously pointed out, there is *no* limit to the premium of a nearer month over a more distant position. Thus, the January contract could not only narrow its premium from 10¢ to 4¢ as shown in our illustration, but could go to a premium over May. While the possible loss is limited to 1¢, the possible gain is theoretically unlimited. If January lost its discount and traded even with the May, the profit would be 10¢—or ten times as great as the possible loss. If January went to a premium, the profit would be even greater.

The final thing to notice about this spread is that the nearer month was purchased at the discount and the distant month sold at a premium. This is the only way that the limited risk situation could be obtained. The difference between the spread and the full carrying charge is the calculated risk. If the reverse were done (occasionally it may be desirable), then the risk could not be calculated in advance but the profit potential would be limited to the full carrying charge. If the nearer month was sold at a discount and the distant month bought at a premium, the profit on the spread would depend on the price difference widening still further; that is, on the distant month going to a still larger premium over the nearer month. As previously pointed out, the most that this can widen is to full carrying charges.

IN SUMMARY, the limited risk spread involves buying the nearer month at a discount and selling a more distant month at a premium. The larger the premium of the distant month, the smaller the risk of loss. This type of spread makes unnecessary the attempt to forecast the timing of trend reversals. While it would most likely be profitable only if an uptrend develops, that trend could develop a week, two weeks, or a month after the initial position is established. In the meantime, even if the entire market breaks 20¢ a bushel, the worst that could happen would be for the spread to widen out to full carrying charges. The short position on the distant month protects the trader against any major loss. When the market does reverse, however, the profitability could far outweigh any possible loss.

Example Of When Near Month Should Be Sold Against A Distant Month

In many of the post-war years, however, inverted markets have been the rule. That is, the nearer months sold at premiums to the more distant positions. Under these circumstances, spreads can be established designed to profit by a further widening of the premium of the near month over the distant month (purchase the near and sell the distant month) or a spread could be established to profit by a narrowing of the price difference (sell the near month and buy the distant month). Ordinarily, selling the near month and buying the distant month is not to be recommended because the profit potential is limited while the potential loss is not. You will recall that the near month can go only to a full carrying charge discount under the more distant contract. Nevertheless, there are times when the price difference and surrounding circumstances make such a spread desirable. One such example was the May-July wheat spread early in 1958.

At one point, May sold more than 30¢ over July. July wheat is the

— 230 —

first of the new crop months. The excellent weather and large planted acreage had indicated a bumper crop was in prospect. In addition, many of the farmers had over-planted their acreage allotments and would be ineligible for government loans. Finally, and most important, the loan level for new crop wheat had tentatively been set at $1.78 per bushel, which was 22¢ below the previous year. All of these factors had combined to force July wheat prices down to a level that represented a small discount to the potential lower loan.

However, agitation began to develop to raise the wheat loan back to the 1957 level. As this drive gained momentum in the Senate, many traders began to establish long positions in July. Others were more cautious and preferred to institute a spread. They sold May and bought July with the idea that if the new crop loan was eventually actually raised the difference between these two months must narrow considerably. The spread did narrow considerably while the debate raged. Congress finally passed the bill, but the President vetoed it. When it became obvious that there were insufficient votes to override the veto, the spread once again began to widen.

In dealing with a spread of this sort, where price differences can widen indefinitely, some method must be established to determine the right time to enter into, and liquidate, positions. The May-July spread appeared too wide to many traders at 20¢ or 25¢. Suppose someone had established the spread at 22¢. Where could he logically limit his loss and decide he was wrong? There was no logical place. If he felt the spread was worthwhile at 22¢, it must have appeared even better at 23¢, 24¢, etc. The size of the trader's purse would have to determine how far against him he could permit the market to go. This, however, is not a particularly logical way to trade.

Trading on news events, or on charts, are two of the more acceptable methods of determining when to establish these spreads.

The example cited above is a good illustration of the first method—establishing a spread when some particularly important piece of news develops (such as the Senate drive to increase wheat price supports). If a trader's analysis of the importance of the news is accurate, the spread should begin to show a profit within a day or two. If the market fails to respond, the spread should be liquidated. It rarely pays to continue to hold a losing spread. The change in price differences between delivery months is a relatively slow process, but once a pattern is started, it tends to continue for a prolonged period of time. That is, once a spread begins to narrow, it will continue doing so for quite a while. Those who have established a wrong position will rarely gain by holding it in the hope that something unforeseen will occur to enable them to break even. Instead, the market will probably continue to work against them, little by little.

Line Charts As An Aid In Spreading

Spreading operations lend themselves rather well to line chart analysis. The chart is simply a record of the daily price differences connected by a straight line. On the vertical axis is the scale of price differences; let us say from 1¢ to 30¢. On the horizontal axis are the calendar dates. Thus, if on three successive days the price difference of a spread was 13¢, 13½¢, and 14¢, then these three points would be connected by a line. The extension of this line creates the price patterns which all chartists look for—the trend line, double top, etc. The charts are utilized in the same manner as the others discussed earlier in the text, indicating probable points at which to enter the market, liquidate, or use stop-losses.

For example, suppose May wheat had widened its premium over July from 13¢ to 30¢, over a period of several months. The chart then begins to show the possibility of a reversal in trend. A trader, there-

FIG. 14

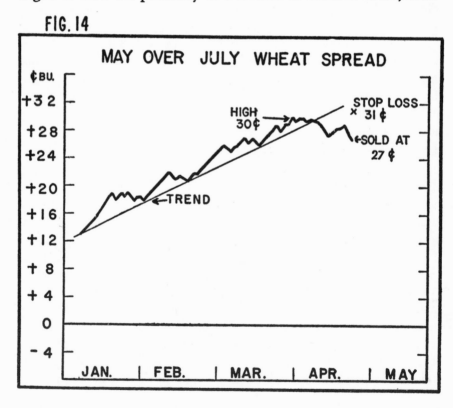

MAY OVER JULY WHEAT SPREAD

fore, sells May and buys July in the expectation that the price difference will narrow. Let us say the spread is established at May 27¢ over July. (See Figure 14.) If he is correct, then the spread should continue to narrow, or at least should not widen out further than it has been previously. If it does, the trader must assume he was wrong and should liquidate his spread. Since the widest price at which our hypothetical spread had previously sold was 30¢, a stop-loss at 31¢ might have been used.

Margin Requirements Smaller

Because spreads generally involve smaller risks than outright long or short positions, the margin requirements generally are smaller. Ordinarily, a trader would put up margins for a contract on the long side, and equal margin for a contract on the short side. In most spreads, however, margin is required for only one side of the transaction. That is, while a spread consists of dealing in two contracts (one long and one short), margin is usually required for only one contract and many times even less. The fact that there will be some profit on one contract which would largely offset the loss on the other, no matter which way the market price goes, allows this reduced requirement to be made.

In addition to reduced margins, many commodity exchanges also reduce commission charges on a spread. Although two contracts are bought and sold, the commission charged, in many cases, is less than twice that of a single contract. The reduction in commissions varies.

Straddles Involving Two Different Commodities

The spread we have illustrated is one involving two different delivery months of the same commodity, on the same exchange. There are other types of spreads. One involves buying and selling different, although related, commodities such as corn vs. oats. Others involve the purchase and sale of the same commodity in two different markets such as wheat at Chicago vs. wheat at Kansas City.

Neither of these nor similar type spreads can be considered the "limited risk" variety. While there is a historical relationship between the prices of various related commodities and various markets, there is no practical "limit" to their possible price spreads. Even the cost of shipping commodities from one market to another is not necessarily always a limiting factor. Certainly, many profit possibilities arise when spreads widen to levels which are abnormally wide, as compared to historical precedent. However, before entering into these spreads, it is important to investigate the current reasons for the wide price difference and to determine whether or not the situation will change.

Let us take, as an example, the corn-oats spread. A bushel of oats weighs a little more than half a bushel of corn. On a pound for pound basis, the feeding value of oats is a little better than that of corn. Both feed grains are good substitutes for each other and the relative prices of the two grains will help determine their demand. That is, if corn is cheap relative to oats, more corn will be used in feeding operations. What then should be a "normal" price difference? As previously stated, a bushel of oats weighs a little more than half the weight of corn, and has a better feed value. Therefore, a bushel of oats should sell for a little more than half the price of a bushel of corn. At recent price levels, this "little more" could be considered about 3¢ per bushel. When the entire grain price structure is low, as in years such as the early 1930's, the difference should be smaller. When the entire grain price structure is high-priced, such as the early 1950's, the difference would be somewhat higher.

There is one major difference between these two grains. Oats are harvested in July-August while corn is harvested in October-November. This means that seasonally each year we can ordinarily expect price pressure to develop in cash oats and oats futures just prior to, during, and just after, the bulk of the harvest—namely June through August. During this period, corn prices need not decline. In fact, since there may well be an end-of-season tightness, or a weather scare, during these months, corn prices might actually advance. Oats, therefore, will tend to become cheap relative to corn during this period. In fact, many times oats prices sell at less than half the price of corn during the summer.

On the other hand, conditions are reversed during October and November. This is the period of the corn harvest, and of the subsequent price pressure exerted on the market by the large volume of new crop corn normally being offered. Also, by this time, the major pressure on oats prices should have passed and oats prices should be rallying relative to corn. The process of oats prices readjusting to the "normal" level of a little more than half the price of corn, should be underway.

This then is the background to the spread. Sometime during the summer, oats can be at a price that is less than half the price of corn— an abnormal price relationship, considering feed value. Sometime during the autumn, the normal relationship should be established, therefore: 1) buy oats and sell corn in mid or late summer, and, 2) liquidate the spread in late autumn: for example:

```
                         August 15th
Buy 5,000 bus.                    —   Sell 5,000 bus.
    Dec. Oats at .................. 55¢           Dec. Corn ..............$1.15
                    Oats less than ½ the price of corn

                         November 15th
Sell 5,000 bus.                   —   Buy 5,000 bus.
    Dec. Oats at .................. 58¢           Dec. Corn ..............$1.10
                    Oats more than ½ the price of corn
                    _____                      _____
    Profit ..................... 3¢        Profit ................ 5¢

    Total Profit 8¢/bu., or $400. for the spread, less commission.
```

There are several things to be noted about this spread.

1) The December contracts were used. This was done for two reasons. First, the spread would be held from August through November and, therefore, a contract maturing later than November was necessary. Second, the spread depends in part on new crop harvest pressure on corn prices. The December corn contract is the first delivery month to reflect new crop prices.

2) In the illustration, oats prices advanced and corn prices declined after the spread was initiated. This need not have been the case. Both prices could have advanced, or both could have declined and the spread could still have proven profitable. Remember it is the price difference between the two contracts that is important, not the price trend.

3) As the spread worked out, the return would have been close to 100% on the margin deposit necessary. Smaller margins on spreads mean a larger number of contracts can be traded, as well as the possibility of a larger percentage return on the investment.

4) This is not a limited risk situation. While this spread usually works very well, there are factors that could set it awry. Therefore, it is necessary to check the surrounding circumstances each year before initiating the position. For example, a drought could develop in August which could seriously hurt new crop corn production prospects. Thus, the price of December corn could well advance to 10¢ or more, above twice the price of oats. In our example, oats were purchased and corn sold when corn was twice the price of oats plus 5¢. If the drought became serious, the price difference could widen continuously. There is no theoretical limit at which it would stop, as there was in the first type

of spread discussed earlier in this chapter. Eventually, the realignment to a more normal price relationship would probably take place, but in the interim a serious loss could occur. Investigate before you act.

5) Because a bushel of oats weighs so much less than a bushel of corn, and because the amplitude of oats price fluctuations are usually only half those of corn, this spread is oftentimes established by purchasing two contracts of oats against the sale of one contract of corn. This compensates for both the smaller weight of a bushel of oats and its narrower price movement, and, therefore, makes the success of the spread less dependent on the reduction of corn prices.

Tax Straddles

Straddle and spread operations are also useful, under certain circumstances, to obtain tax advantages. Situations can be developed which:

1) transfer short-term capital gains from one year to the next,

2) convert short-term capital gains into long-term capital gains,

These tax spreading operations are not generally suited to the ordinary trader. Usually it will be necessary for the trader to have substantial short-term net capital gains, and to be in the upper income tax brackets. Once these conditions are met, it is then necessary, of course, to check the particular spreads involved for possible price risks, the direction of the trend, and commission charges.

To properly detail all of the possible situations in which specific straddles can be used for any of the three above listed purposes, as well as the possible pitfalls that could be encountered would take the equivalent of a small book.

Suffice it to say that spreads can be used advantageously in many instances, for one or more of these purposes. However, before a trader establishes a tax straddle, it is highly recommended that a tax accountant or other tax expert be consulted to see whether or not such a transaction will suit his particular needs. Furthermore, the position should be established through a commodity specialist who is familiar with this type of transaction and, hence, can avoid some of the pitfalls into which the unitiated can wander.

CHAPTER 22.

SOME SPECULATORS MAKE MONEY — RULES FOR SPECULATIVE TRADING

No discussion of commodity futures trading would be complete without attempting to develop some guides to be followed by speculative traders. Those which are given are not unique or original, but have been developed by many people out of past experience.

Many of the trading cues outlined below have been discussed or implied in the foregoing text. Nevertheless, grouping them should prove valuable, both for clarification and for increasing the resolve of the trader to utilize them.

Spreading operations are one phase of commodity trading, but most of the positions to be established by a commodity speculator will be outright long or short. That is, one or more contracts will be purchased in the expectation that the price will rise and that at a subsequent time, the futures can be sold at a profit; or futures will be sold first, in the expectation that prices will decline and that they can be purchased later at a lower price for a profit. The latter is the short sale.

Don't Be Afraid To Sell Short

As indicated early in this text, a short position is just as simple to initiate as a long position. Most speculative traders shy away from this, failing to understand how one can sell something which he does not own. The sole difference between taking a short or a long position is the sequence of the purchase and sale. Virtually no speculators expect to take delivery of the actual commodity when they buy futures, and virtually no speculators should expect to make delivery of the actual commodity when they sell short. Both will liquidate their positions before this becomes necessary. Whether or not one owns the commodity, does not enter into the picture at all.

By being prejudiced against the short sale the average speculator is not only apt to miss some very profitable trading opportunities, but is also left with a dangerous innate bias towards the long side of the market. He is always looking only for "buying spots", and, therefore, is likely to enter the market on the long side too soon.

Limit Losses And Let Profits Accumulate

This is by far the most difficult of the rules to follow, but may also be the most important. There is a natural preference for taking profits quickly for fear that they will evaporate. There is also a natural reluctance to take quick losses, with too much reliance on the hope that the market will reverse itself and turn a loss into a profit. This is just the reverse of what must be done. These natural prejudices must be overcome. You cannot trade on hope alone, and be successful. There are countless examples of speculators sticking doggedly with a losing situation until all or most of their funds are gone. Just one such bad mistake is enough to wipe out all the profits of previous trades. Furthermore, the taking of quick profits means that when a major price trend occurs, the trader will miss it. His profits, even when he is right, will be small. By following these natural prejudices the trader is, in effect, limiting his profits and letting his losses accumulate. By doing just the reverse, by getting out of a position when it looks wrong and holding on while the trend is still going with the position, the net result is added profit. Nobody will be 100% correct in his market forecasting, nor is this necessary for profitable trading. Even if only 50% of the trades entered into are profitable, the net result at the end of the year should be on the profit side, providing losses have been quickly cut short and profitable positions allowed to work out.

Enter The Market Only When The Potential Profit Is Several Times The Potential Loss

This rule seems like common sense, yet it too seems to be just the reverse of the natural tendencies of many traders. It cannot be followed unless the previous rule is followed. Before entering the market, try to obtain some idea of a price objective. This can be done by any of the methods discussed in the chart theory chapters, or by a study of supply and demand of the commodity involved. Once a reasonable price objective seems to have been found, decide how far against your position the price would have to move before you would be willing to say you were wrong and you would liquidate. In other words, what would be a logical stop-loss? Compare the profit potential with the possible stop-loss. Only if the profit objective is several times the stop-loss, should the position be established. This is the only way that the average profit on each trade can work out to be above the average loss. Determining a logical profit objective before establishing a position is helpful in encouraging a trader to hold on and resist the temptation to take a quick, but small, profit. If, after thought and consideration, a logical profit objective appears to be 9¢, then taking a quick 3¢ profit will not seem too desirable. Of course, one cannot be inflexible about these things. If a change in the news, or a change in either the action of the market or the chart pattern, indicates that the original profit objective has become dubious, then by all means change it. However, do not do so impulsively. Remember that you gave considerable thought to this before entering the market. Once a position has been established, the viewpoint of many traders tends to change. Many become a little nervous, their views become a little clouded, and they tend to over-emphasize the importance of small price fluctuations. This leads us to another rule.

Don't Overtrade

By overtrading is meant trading in more contract units than you can afford, either financially or emotionally. If the market is going against you by a few points and, as a result, you can't sleep at night, your food tastes unpalatable, your kids get on your nerves and you are sure the boss is "picking" on you, you are definitely overtrading. In addition to making you a cross, irritable and disagreeable person, overtrading will warp your judgment and result in your making foolish trading errors which will probably mean unnecessary losses. Remember that there is no "sure thing" in speculative trading. You are assuming a price risk. Be sure that the risk is one you can afford to take. The old adage about "nothing ventured, nothing gained" certainly has applicability in commodity speculation, but be sure the risk is one which does not cause you excessive concern, nor reduce your objectivity about the market. Your life should not depend on the market moving a few points one way or another.

When In Doubt — Stay Out

This rule is self-explanatory, but needs emphasis. You are speculating to make money. You are taking a risk. Don't increase that risk by entering into positions you are not more or less convinced should prove profitable. It is better to let your money remain idle than lose it. There are many commodities and many commodity markets, each of which is open five days a week. There is no need to press for a position. If there does not seem to be an opportunity one day, wait for the next. Something is bound to come up which looks interesting and profitable.

Trade With The Trend — Not Against It

Commodity prices generally follow a trend which is basically either up or down. However, there are always fluctuations about this trend, sometimes wide, sometimes narrow. Many speculators are often tempted to trade against the trend, trying to catch these small "technical corrections". It rarely proves profitable. First, there is the commission charge which can loom large if you are only trying to obtain a quick "few points". Second, the reaction (or the rally) is often not as large as it is expected to be. The basic trend reasserts itself before the speculator expects it, with the result that the trade may have to be liquidated with a loss. Third, it will be rare that the market will be sold just as the technical reaction gets underway, or bought just as the technical rally develops. It will usually be done too late, or too soon. That is (assume the basic trend is up) a trader will wait for the anticipated dip to begin before he will sell. Thus, the market may be down 1¢ or more from the high before the sale is made. If a dip of 3¢ is expected (normal, let us say, for wheat), then the combination of this plus the commission means that half the anticipated move is over before any profits can begin. Suppose the dip doesn't extend a full 3¢, but only goes down 2⅞¢. The trader does not cover, and in fifteen minutes the market can have recovered and eliminated any chance for a profit.

Some traders anticipating a technical correction will not wait for the dip to begin, but will sell at a price they think will be the high, or very close to it. Just how great do you think the chances are of any individual trader selling just at the top of a move, or of buying at the exact bottom? Obviously, they are infinitesmally small. The market, in all likelihood, will keep on going up and the trader will be in the position of having to hope for a technical correction, merely to break even.

Some traders go a step further. If they sold, and the market keeps advancing, they sell some more to try to "average" their selling prices. They hope for a dip which will allow them to come out even. Why should their chances of picking the top of the move be any better on the second try than the first?

Some traders try to pick the top of a move not just in the hope of a technical reaction, but still worse, in anticipation of a complete reversal of trend. They feel the market is "high enough". Again, it is very rare that such action will prove to be correct. Commodity prices are quite volatile, and there is an oft-noted tendency for prices to move in excessive swings; that is, to over-discount market factors. Short covering by those who thought the market was "high enough" at a lower price may alone be sufficient to cause this strength to continue for a time. Also, as a major trend gets underway (for simplicity let us again assume it is an upward trend), news items which favor the trend are given greater publicity, adding to the strength of the market. Traders become more responsive to bullish news. Thus again, after the trend is underway, new factors reinforcing the move can (and often do) develop.

A good example of the above is the action of the cocoa market in 1957/1958. Early in the year, the market began to rally from close to the 20¢ level. Many traders felt, as the market approached 30¢, that prices had gone "high enough", and accordingly proceeded to sell short. After all, prices had advanced almost 50% in ten weeks. Yet, it was not until the market had advanced above 30¢, that aggressive trade buying began to enter the market. Nor was it until the market approached 35¢ that apparent confirmation developed of a low crop outturn. As the market approached 40¢, speculative selling based on the "high enough" concept was again aggressive. This was again proved wrong. Why not wait for the market to display some resistance to the advance before selling short? Why not wait for a point where one can sell with a logical stop, to limit the loss if one is wrong? In cocoa, a 1¢ move is equal to $300 per contract. There are very few traders who can afford to sell at 28¢ because the market is "high enough", and stay with the loss or sell more at 30¢, 32¢, 35¢, 40¢, etc., letting losses accumulate.

Would it not be more logical to trade with the trend? The cocoa market was advancing. The downward trend appeared to have been decisively broken and an upward trend established in the first half of the year. It would have been much more profitable to seek points at which to buy cocoa, with a logical stop-loss, and ride with the trend.

Money is made in speculation by trading with the trend, not fighting it. Waiting for an obvious reversal in trend before establishing a position could still result in taking advantage of a major part of the move, and a substantial profit. It should also mean a smaller number of trades, and a smaller number of losses.

"Selling on strength" (that is selling short when the market is advancing) and "buying on weakness" can still be justified, but only under the condition that it be used to obtain a better price while still trading with the trend. In this way, the minor fluctuations which generally occur as part of a trend can be used to advantage. For example, assume that the trend has turned upward. A long position is, therefore, desirable. The question then becomes where to establish it. If the price pattern has indicated that periodic fluctuations occur, then it might be desirable to await such a price dip before going long. You are still trading with the trend, not against it, yet still profitably utilizing the fact that fluctuations occur. This is quite different than trying to profit from these fluctuations by selling against the trend or trying to pick the top or bottom of a move.

Another example of advantageously using the fluctuations which occur as part of a major trend was shown back in figure 9, the head and shoulders formation. The "return movement" often occurs after a chart formation breakout, and can be used to add to a position, in the direction of the major trend.

Get Information On The Current Market Picture — Use Charts As An Additional Tool

There is no full substitute for knowing something about the market in which you expect to establish positions. It does not take too much time to obtain the necessary information. Most, if not all, of it can be obtained directly from the broker through whom you trade. What information to seek, and other sources for obtaining it, are listed elsewhere in this book. On the basis of this information, determine whether or not you can expect prices to move higher or lower. Once this is done, look over the chart picture. If nothing else, it will indicate at a glance where prices have been and what the current trend appears to be. It will be helpful in determining points at which to enter the market and where to place a stop-loss.

If the chart picture indicates a trend which is contrary to the position you wish to establish, it is a "when in doubt—stay out" situation. By all means keep watching the market for a trend reversal signal before you establish a position. Don't fight the market.

As was previously pointed out, chart reading is subjective. What one trader will take to be an indication of a trend reversal, another will interpret as merely a minor fluctuation in an existing trend. Most of us approach the particular charts with some innate bias towards either the long or short side. This bias should at least be based on some knowledge. Then the use of a price chart can be a valuable subsidiary tool. (For the argument that the chart picture should be given dominance in trading, refer back to the appropriate chapter.)

Never Meet A Margin Call — Liquidate Instead

This may sound rather irregular at first glance, but a little thought will indicate that this is just an extension of our rule to limit losses. Margin is required as a safeguard to all traders, and as a guarantee that a trader has sufficient capital to offset any possible loss. In commodity trading, a request for additional money is usually sent to a trader when 25% of his original margin has been impaired. For example, suppose a trader has a long position in a market and he has deposited $1,000 as margin. The price continues to decline until he has lost $250 on paper. He is still in the market, and is asked to deposit an additional $250 to bring his equity back up $1,000. If the trader deposits the additional money he will maintain his position in the market. If he does not put up additional margin within a proper time, then his position in the market will be liquidated at the discretion of the brokerage firm. The authority to do this is included in the margin agreement the trader signs when he first opens an account with the firm.

It is, of course, unnecessary for this to happen. If a trader does not wish to meet the margin call by depositing additional funds, he can simply inform the brokerage firm that he will liquidate his position. The firm will usually allow him some leeway in determining at which point to liquidate—say an extra day's time. The end result is the same, the client has liquidated his position. However, the trader's reputation and credit standing is not impaired.

The position entered into was on the wrong side of the market. Depositing additional margin funds will not alter the trend. It is often an indication of the inability of the trader to admit he was wrong. While watching prices move against him, the trader has become inflexible and reverts to the hope that "something will happen" which will reverse the trend. This may occur but, until it does, the trader may have to meet a second margin call, or even a third.

Many successful operators feel that margin calls should act as a stop-loss order. Had an actual stop-loss order been used, the position probably would have been liquidated before the margin call developed. Some people, however, prefer for various reasons not to use stop-loss orders. If you have not done so, then a margin call is a fair substitute. It usually means that at least 25% of your trading capital has been lost on that particular position. This should be enough of a loss to take on any trade. By liquidating, the remainder of your trading funds is conserved. It is available for use at a later time to help you recoup your losses. Remember that it is very possible to be correct only 50% of the time and still make money over the year.

Don't Straddle To Avoid Taking A Loss — Liquidate

Many traders refusing to take a loss frequently compound their error by entering into an opposite position in another future. For example, if a trader has bought March wheat and the market declines 3¢, he will not liquidate and take the loss. Instead, he will sell May wheat (or any other month) against it. The trader is now straddled by being long March and short May. This is done presumably on the theory that, if the market continues down, he will take a profit on the short May future or if the market rallies he will break even or take a profit on his long March position.

This is nothing but an act of desperation, indicating the thorough confusion of the trader. It has simply postponed the day of reckoning and has given him two diametrically opposed positions to worry about. The straddle that results was put on at two different times, the second half being established only after a 3¢ loss existed on the first half. By putting on the straddle, the *existing 3¢ loss is locked in*. It is not avoided. The straddle that results is not at the price difference that exists in the market between the March and May delivery. It is 3¢ worse, as shown below:

January 1 — Buys 5,000 bus. March
Wheat at 1.50

January 23 — When the March Wheat is   Sells 5,000 bus.
down to 1.47, he   May Wheat at 1.45

The trader is straddled: long March at 1.50 and short May at 1.45 or 5¢ March over May. The actual market price difference, however, on January 23 when the second half of the straddle is instituted is: March at 1.47 and May at 1.45 or March 2¢ over May.

The trader is straddled with a locked-in loss of 3¢. If the entire wheat price structure continues to decline, he will make some money on his short position in May, but lose it in March. If the market rallies, he will make back his loss in March but probably lose an equivalent quantity in May.

What does he do now? Within a few days, the trader will probably take a stand by liquidating one side of the straddle. This is called "lifting a leg." Whichever side he liquidates will leave him with a loss, because the straddle started with a loss. By going into a straddle instead of taking his initial loss, the trader merely delayed its realization. He did not avoid it. Now he has the problem of trying to get out of the other half of the straddle.

By straddling, the trader indicated that he was confused as to the direction of the trend. Now he hopes that he knows the direction. After he has liquidated half of the straddle, he is once again in an outright long or short position and in an entirely new market situation. What has he gained by straddling? Nothing. If anything, chances are that his confusion was actually increased by being on both the long and short side, and he has probably lifted a leg at the wrong time. He may well have to suffer a loss on the second leg of the straddle too.

It would have been simpler to have taken his initial 3¢ loss, stepping aside to reappraise the situation before entering into another position.

His thinking would not have been clouded or biased by having an existing position in the market. Chances are his second outright trade would have been more profitable than the position he was forced into taking by the fact that he did not want to absorb his initial loss.

There is one other alternative. The trader could have kept the straddle over an extended period of time, hoping that the straddle itself would eventually work to his advantage and overcome the initial 3¢ loss. While this is possible, it usually does not work out in practice. The straddle which results is usually a bad one.

We will use the example above to illustrate this. The initial action by the trader was to establish a long position in the expectation that prices would move higher. Since March was selling at a premium to May, an upward trend had probably been in effect for some time. (This is illustrated in the explanation on why premiums and discounts develop, and in the chapter on hedging in practice.) However, the trend could have been changing since the long March position works into a loss. Thus, the sale of May against the long March is made at a time when the trend appears to be turning downward. May is sold at a discount to March. In a downward trend, the near month will tend to lose its premium and go to a carrying charge discount. Thus the straddle would probably be wrong. The March (which the trader has bought) would very likely go to a discount to May. Thus the trader, in an effort to prevent taking his initial loss, would probably end up with a poor straddle and a greater loss.

Straddle operations are a separate and distinct type of trading and should be approached with that in mind. They too entail risk, although in some cases the risk is limited. To enter a straddle in an effort to avoid taking a loss will certainly lead to new problems and, more often than not, to the wrong kind of straddle and to large losses.

A Final Word

A logical trading procedure must be developed by each trader. Trading in the market on hunches and hopes can't lead to anything but losses and regrets. Some speculators make money. It can't be done without a little study, time and effort. These could prove very rewarding.

GLOSSARY

The following are a selected list of terms used in commodity futures trading and their usual meaning.

ACREAGE ALLOTMENT—The limitation on planted acreage established by the Government for each farmer, for some basic crops.

ACREAGE RESERVE—A part of the Soil Bank which applied solely to Basic Commodities under which the farmer received payment from the Government for not planting part or all of his acreage allotment.

ACTUALS—The physical commodities.

ARBITRAGE—The usually simultaneous purchase of futures in one market against the sale of futures in a different market to profit from a difference in price.

BASIS—1) The difference between the spot price and the price of futures.

2) The grade of a commodity used as the standard for the contract, i.e. the BASIS grade.

BEAR—1) One who believes prices will move lower—a BEAR

2) A market in which prices are declining—a BEAR market.

BID—An offer to purchase at a specified price.

BREAK—A rapid and deep price decline.

BROKER—One who executes the buy and sell orders of a customer for a commission.

BULL—1) One who expects prices to rise

2) A market in which prices are rising—a BULL market.

CALL—1) A period in which trading is conducted to establish the price for each futures month at a particular time, i.e.—a noon time CALL

2) BUYER'S CALL—a purchase of a specified quantity of a specific grade of a commodity at a fixed number of points above or below a specified delivery month in futures with the buyer being allowed a certain period of time within which to fix the price by either purchasing a future for the account of the seller or indicating to the seller he wishes to price fix.

3) SELLER'S CALL—The same as BUYER'S CALL with the difference that the seller has the right of determining the time to price fix.

CARGO—In grains, usually 350,000 bushels.

CARLOAD—For grains approximately 1,800 bushels.

CARRYING CHARGE—1) The costs involved in owning commodities over a period of time, such as storage, insurance and interest charges on borrowed working capital.

2) In futures, the cost, including all charges, of taking actual delivery in a given month, storing the commodity, and redelivering against the next delivery month.

CASH COMMODITY—The actual physical commodity.

C.C.C.—The Commodity Credit Corporation.

C.E.A.—The Commodity Exchange Authority.

CERTIFICATED STOCK—Stocks of a commodity that have been graded, have passed various tests and found to be of deliverable quality against futures contracts; which are stored at the delivery points and in warehouses designated for delivery by the exchange. More simply—stocks of a commodity available for delivery.

C.I.F.—Cost, insurance, and freight paid at point of destination included in the price quoted.

CLEARING HOUSE—The separate agency associated with a futures exchange through which futures contracts are offset or fulfilled and through which financial settlement is made (also CLEARING ASSOCIATION).

CLEARING MEMBER—A member of the Clearing House or Association. Each clearing member must also be a member of the Exchange. Each member of the exchange, however, need not be a member of the clearing association. If he is not, all of his trades must be registered and eventually settled through a clearing member.

CLEARING PRICE—See SETTLEMENT PRICE

COMMISSION HOUSE—A firm that specializes in executing buying and selling orders for customers in spot and/or futures markets for a commission and does not itself deal in futures or actuals.

CONTRACT GRADES—The grades of a commodity listed in the Rules of an Exchange as those that can be used to deliver against a futures contarct.

CONSERVATION RESERVE—The section of the Soil Bank Program calling for long term contracts for the conversion of crop land into grasses, trees and water conservation uses.

CONTROLLED COMMODITY—Commodities subject to Commodity Exchange Authority Regulation, which are those listed in the Commodity Exchange Act. They are domestically produced agricultural products.

COUNTRY ELEVATOR—A grain elevator located in the immediate farming community to whom the farmers bring their grain for sale or storage, as distinct from a terminal elevator which is located at a major marketing center.

COVER—The purchase of futures to offset a previously established short position.

DAY ORDER—Orders that are placed for execution, if possible, during only one trading session. If the order cannot be executed that day, it is automatically cancelled.

DELIVERY—The tender of the actual commodity in fulfillment of a short position in futures during the period specified by the futures contract.

DELIVERY MONTH—The month in which the futures contract natures and within which delivery of the physical commodity can be made.

DELIVERY POINTS—The areas specified in the Rules of an Exchange in which delivery of the physical commodity can be made.

DIFFERENTIALS—The price differences between grades of a commodity.

DISCRETIONARY ACCOUNT—An account for which buying and selling orders can be placed by a broker or other person, without the prior consent of the account owner for each such individual order; a blanket agreement having been initially granted by the account owner for such action.

EVENING UP—Offsetting previously established positions by either liquidating them or straddling.

EXCHANGE FOR PHYSICALS (E.F.P.)—The transfer of a long futures position by the buyer of a cash commodity to the seller of the cash commodity. The transaction usually also involves a cash settlement depending upon the basis.

EX-PIT TRANSACTION—A trade made outside the exchange trading ring or pit which is legal in a few instances. It is primarily used in price fixing transactions involving the purchase of cash commodities at a specified basis.

FIRST NOTICE DAY—The first day on which notices of intentions to deliver actual commodities against futures market positions can be made or received. First notice day will vary with each commodity and exchange. It will usually be several days before the beginning of the delivery month.

FIXING THE PRICE—The determination of the exact price at which a cash commodity will be invoiced after a "call sale" has previously been made based on a specific number of points "on or off" a specified futures month.

FLOOR BROKER—One who executes orders for others (as well as himself) in the trading ring or pit of an exchange.

F. O. B.—Free on board—the transportation cost to the point of destination is not included in the quoted price of the commodity.

FREE SUPPLY—The quantity of a commodity available for commercial sale. The supply excluding Government held stocks.

FUTURES—Contracts for the purchase and sale of commodities for delivery some time in the future on an organized exchange and subject to all terms and conditions included in the Rules of that Exchange.

GIVE UP—At the request of the customer, a brokerage house which has not performed the service is credited with the execution of an order.

GOOD-TIL-CANCELLED (G.T.C.)—An order which will remain open for execution at any time in the future until the customer decides to cancel it. For example: Sell one May Cotton at 36.00 G.T.C.

HEDGE—The establishment of an opposite position in the futures market from that held in the spot market.

INCENTIVE PAYMENT PLAN—The type of support program used for domestic clip wool in which a cash subsidy is paid to the wool grower based upon his selling price.

INVERTED MARKET—A futures market in which the nearer months are selling at premiums to the more distant months.

JOB LOT—A unit of trading smaller than a full contract in which transactions are permitted by some futures exchanges.

LAST TRADING DAY—The day on which trading ceases for a particular delivery month. All contracts that have not been offset by the end of trading on that day must thereafter be settled by delivery of the actual physical commodity.

LIFE OF CONTRACT—The duration of the period in which trading can take place. In some cases this phrase is used to denote only the period already passed in which trading has already occurred. Example: "The life-of-contract high so far is 2.50."

LIMIT (UP OR DOWN—1) The maximum price advance or decline permitted in one trading session by the rules of the exchange.
2) The maximum number of contracts one can hold under the rules of the C.E.A.

LIMIT ORDER—An order which is restricted in some way, usually as to price. For example, an order to buy one May Cotton at 36.00 stop, limit 36.02.

LIQUIDATION—The closing out of a long position. It is also sometimes used to denote closing out a short position, but this is more often referred to as "covering."

LOAN PROGRAM—The primary means of Government price support in which the Government lends money to the farmer at a pre-announced price schedule with the farmer's crop as collateral.

LONG—1) One who has bought futures; 2) One who owns actual commodities that are not hedged.

LONG PULL—An indefinite period of time but usually implying several months over which some specific price action is expected to occur.

MARGIN—The funds put up as security or a guarantee of contract fulfillment.

MARGIN CALL—A request for funds, usually for money in addition to that originally deposited as collateral against the initiation of a trade.

MARKET ORDER—An order to buy or sell a futures contract at whatever price it is obtainable at the time it is entered in the ring.

MARKETING QUOTA—The Government restriction on the amount of a commodity that a producer is permitted to sell. It is usually the quantity of wheat or cotton the farmer can grow on his acreage allotment.

MATURITY—The time at which the futures contract can be settled by delivery of the actual commodity; the period between first notice day and last trading day.

MEMBERS' RATE—The commission charge for the execution of an order for a person who is a member of and thereby has a seat on the exchange. It is less than the commission charged to a customer who does not have a seat on the exchange. A member who also belongs to the Clearing Association pays no commission for his trades. He just pays clearance and other fees.

NOMINAL PRICE—An estimate of the price for a futures month. Used at times to designate a closing price when no trading has taken place in that particular month during the final few minutes of the trading session. It is usually the average between the bid and asked prices.

NOTICE DAY—A trading day during which notices of intention to deliver actual commodities against short positions in the spot month are made.

OFF—In quoting the basis, the number of points the cash price will be under a specified futures price. Example: 20 points off December.

OFFSET—1) The liquidation of a long or short position.

2) The balancing of a net long or short position by establishing an opposite position in another futures month (thus ending up with a straddle).

3) The completion of both sides of a transaction by a broker, the buying side being done for one account and the selling side for a different customer.

ON—In quoting the basis, the number of points the cash commodity is above a specified futures month. Example: 20 points on December.

OPEN INTEREST—The number of contracts which remain to be settled. It is equal to either the number of long positions in a market or the number of short positions. Since it takes both a long and a short to make one contract, the number of longs and shorts in a market are always equal.

OPEN ORDER—See "Good-Till-Cancelled."

OPTION—Commonly but incorrectly used to indicate a specific futures delivery month.

ORIGINAL MARGIN—The margin needed to cover a specific new position.

OVERBOUGHT—A technical market situation in which prices are believed to have advanced too far, too fast.

OVERSOLD—A technical market situation in which prices are believed to have declined too far, too fast.

PARITY—An equal relationship between commodity prices and all other prices.

PIT—The place on an Exchange trading floor designated for the execution of orders.

POINT—The minimum price fluctuation in futures. It is equal to 1/100 of one cent in most futures traded in decimal units. In grains it is 1/8 of one cent. In wool and wool tops it is 1/10 of one cent.

POSITION—To be either long or short in the market.

PREMIUM—The amount that one future sells above another or that one grade of a commodity sells above another.

PRICE FIX—See "Fixing the Price."

PRIMARY MARKET—The centers to which the farmers bring their crops for sale, such as country grain elevators.

PUBLIC ELEVATORS—Grain storage facilities in which space is rented out to whoever wishes to pay for it; where grain is stored in bulk.

PURCHASE AGREEMENT—A form of Government price support in which the Government agrees to buy commodities from a farmer at a specified time at the loan price.

PURCHASE & SALE STATEMENT—(P & S) The statement sent by a brokerage house to a customer after the liquidation of a position, showing the amounts and prices bought and sold, the gross profit or loss, the commission charged and the net profit or loss.

PYRAMIDING—Using the profits on previously established positions as margin for adding to that position.

RANGE—The high and low prices recorded during a specified time.

REACTION—A downward price movement.

REALIZING—Taking profits.

RESTING ORDER—Open orders or Good-Till-Cancelled orders which have previously been given and are still valid.

RING—See "Pit"

ROUND LOT—A full contract as opposed to the smaller job lot.

ROUND TURN—The completion of both a purchase and an offsetting sale.

RULES—The regulations governing trading established by each exchange.

SCALP—Trading for small gains, many times for less than a full cent profit. It usually involves establishing and liquidating a position quickly, possibly within the same day.

SELLER'S OPTION—The right of the seller to determine the grade, place and day of delivery of actuals within the delivery period specified by the Rules.

SETTLEMENT PRICE—The daily price established by the clearing house, usually the closing price, which is used to adjust variation margin payments between clearing house and its members.

SHORT—Initiating a transaction by the sale of futures, i.e. selling futures first without having previously purchased. The opposite of long.

SHORT SQUEEZE—The shorts are forced to repurchase their futures due to an inability to obtain deliverable supplies. This makes prices advance rapidly.

SOIL BANK—A Government program designed to take farmland out of productive use. The Government pays the farmer not to plant crops and/or to plant grasses or trees.

SOLD OUT MARKET—See "Oversold."

SPECULATOR—A trader who is not hedging.

SPOT COMMODITY—See "Actuals."

SPOT PRICE—The price at which the physical commodity is selling.

SPREAD—See "Straddle."

SQUEEZE—See "Short Squeeze."

STOP LOSS ORDER (Also A STOP)—An order which becomes a market order to *buy* only if the market *advances* to a specified level, or to *sell* if the market *declines* to a specified level. It is generally used to limit losses but can also be used to initiate new positions.

STRADDLE—The usually simultaneous purchase of one futures month and the sale of another either in the same or different commodity, or Exchange.

SWITCH—The simultaneous liquidation of one futures commitment and establishment of another such as switching a long position from the March delivery to the May.

TECHNICAL RALLY (OR DECLINE)—A price movement resulting from conditions developing within the futures market itself and not dependent on outside supply and demand factors. These conditions would include changes in the open interest, volume, degree of recent price movement and approach of first notice day.

TENDER—Delivery against futures.

TERMINAL ELEVATOR—A grain storage facility at one of the major centers of agricultural product marketing such as Kansas City and Chicago.

TRADING LIMIT—1) The maximum price movement permitted in one trading session under the Rules of an Exchange.

2) The maximum futures market position anyone is permitted to own or control under the law.

TRANSFERABLE NOTICE (T.N.)—The document issued by the seller indicating the time, place and quality of the commodity which he intends to deliver in fulfillment of his futures market position.

TREND—The general direction of the price movement, either higher or lower.

VARIATION MARGIN—The additional funds required if a market has moved against an established position.

VISIBLE SUPPLY—The quantity of a commodity that can be counted. Its precise coverage varies with individual commodities. It may include port stocks, stocks afloat, licensed warehouse stocks, farm stocks, etc.

VOLUME OF TRADE—The number of transactions occurring during a specified period of time. It may be quoted as the number of contracts traded or in the total of physical units, such as bales or bushels.

WAREHOUSE RECEIPT—The document signifying ownership of a specified quantity of a commodity of specific grade located at a specific storage site.

FUTURES TRADING FACTS

Following is a compilation of the commodity exchanges of North America, together with pertinent contract and commission data for the commodities traded. The table is up-to-date as of early 1974 but is subject to change. (In the past, at infrequent intervals, some of the exchanges have announced minor changes in trading hours, commission rates, etc.)

COMMODITY	NAME OF EXCHANGE Trading Hours—N.Y. Time Mon. thru Fri.	CONTRACT	MINIMUM FLUCTUATION Per Lb., etc.	Per Contract	ROUND TURN COMMISSION Domestic Non-Member
BROILERS, ICED**	Chicago Board of Trade 10:15 A.M. - 2:05 P.M.	28,000 Lbs.	2½/100¢	$7.00	$30.00
CATTLE, LIVE BEEF (Midwestern)	Chicago Mercantile Exchange 10:05 A.M. - 1:40 P.M.	40,000 Lbs.	2½/100¢	$10.00	$40.00
COCOA*	New York Cocoa Exchange 10:00 A.M. - 3:00 P.M.	30,000 Lbs.	1/100¢	$3.00	$60.00
COCONUT OIL*	Pacific Commodities Exch. 10:30 A.M. - 2:15 P.M.	60,000 Lbs.	1/100¢	$6.00	$33.00
COFFEE "C"*	N.Y. Coffee & Sugar Exch. 10:30 A.M. - 2:45 P.M.	37,500 Lbs.	1/100¢	$3.75	40¢ — 49.99¢ $60.00 50¢ — 74.99¢ $70.00
COPPER*	Commodity Exch., Inc., N.Y. 9:45 A.M. - 2:10 P.M.	25,000 Lbs.	10/100¢	$25.00	$36.00 + 50¢ Exchange Fee
COTTON* #2	New York Cotton Exchange 10:30 A.M. - 3:00 P.M.	100 Bales (50,000 Lbs.)	1/100¢	$5.00	$45.00 when price is under 40¢ Add $5.00 for every 5¢ rise thereafter
EGGS, SHELL (FRESH)*	Chicago Mercantile Exchange 10:15 A.M. - 1:45 P.M.	22,500 Doz.	5/100¢	$11.25	$40.00
Grains—Chicago* WHEAT, CORN OATS, SOYBEANS	Chicago Board of Trade 10:30 A.M. - 2:15 P.M.	5,000 Bus.	1/4¢	$12.50	$25.00 $30.00

* Special rates for Straddles and Day Trades.   ** Special rates for Straddles.

COMMODITY	NAME OF EXCHANGE Trading Hours—N.Y. Time Mon. thru Fri.	CONTRACT	MINIMUM FLUCTUATION Per Lb., etc.	Per Contract	ROUND TURN COMMISSION Domestic Non-Member
WHEAT —Minneapolis	Minneapolis Grain Exchange 10:30 A.M. - 2:15 P.M.	5,000 Bus.	1/8¢	$6.25	$30.00
WHEAT —Kansas City	Kansas City Board of Trade 10:30 A.M. - 2:15 P.M.	5,000 Bus.	1/4¢	$12.50	$22.00
Grains—Winnipeg OATS, RYE, RAPESEED, BARLEY, FLAXSEED	Winnipeg Commodity Exch. 10:30 A.M. - 2:15 P.M.	5,000 Bus. 1,000 Bus.	1/8¢	$6.25 $1.25	5,000 Bus. $25.00-Rapeseed, Flaxseed 1,000 Bus. $5.50 5,000 Bus. $20.00 - Oats, Barley, Rye 1,000 Bus. $4.50 [Canadian Prices]
HOGS, LIVE*	Chicago Mercantile Exchange 10:20 A.M. - 1:50 P.M.	30,000 Lbs.	2½/100¢	$7.50	$35.00
LUMBER	Chicago Mercantile Exchange 10:00 A.M. - 2:05 P.M.	100,000 Bd. Ft.	10¢/1000 Board Ft.	$10.00	$40.00
MERCURY*	Commodity Exch., Inc., N.Y. 9:50 A.M. - 2:30 P.M.	10 Flasks (76 Lbs.)	$1.00	$10.00	$40.00 + 50¢ Exchange Fee
MILO*	Chicago Mercantile Exchange 10:30 A.M. - 2:15 P.M.	400,000 Lbs.	2½/100¢	$10.00	$40.00
ORANGE JUICE** (Frozen Concentrated)	New York Cotton Exchange 10:15 A.M. - 2:45 P.M.	15,000 Lbs.	5/100¢	$7.50	$45.00
PLATINUM	N.Y. Mercantile Exchange 9:45 A.M. - 1:40 P.M.	50 Ozs.	10¢	$5.00	$45.00 + $2.00 Clearance Fee
PLYWOOD	Chicago Board of Trade 11:00 A.M. - 2:00 P.M.	69,120 Sq. Ft.	10¢/1000 Sq. Ft.	$6.91	$30.00

* Special rates for Straddles and Day Trades.   ** Special rates for Straddles.

(CONTINUED)

FUTURES TRADING FACTS (continued)

COMMODITY	NAME OF EXCHANGE Trading Hours—N.Y. Time Mon. thru Fri.	CONTRACT	MINIMUM FLUCTUATION Per Lb., etc.	MINIMUM FLUCTUATION Per Contract	ROUND TURN COMMISSION Domestic Non-Member
PORK BELLIES	Chicago Mercantile Exchange 10:30 A.M. - 2:00 P.M.	36,000 Lbs.	2½/100¢	$9.00	$45.00
POTATOES*	Maine-N.Y. Merc. Exch. 10:00 A.M. - 1:30 P.M.	50,000 Lbs.	1¢	$5.00	$30.00
	Idaho Russet-Chicago Mercantile Exchange 10:00 A.M. - 1:50 P.M.	50,000 Lbs.	1¢	$5.00	$30.00
PROPANE GAS (LPG)	N.Y. Cotton Exchange 9:45 A.M. - 3:10 P.M.	100,000 Gals.	1/100¢	$10.00	$40.00
SILVER	Commodity Exch., Inc., N.Y.* 10:00 A.M. - 2:15 P.M.	10,000 Troy Oz.	10/100¢	$10.00	$45.00 + 50¢ Exchange Fee
	Chicago Board of Trade** 10:00 A.M. - 2:25 P.M.	5,000 Troy Oz.	10/100¢	$5.00	$30.00
SILVER COINS	N.Y. Mercantile Exchange 9:35 A.M. - 2:15 P.M.	$10,000 face amt. (dimes, quarters and half dollars)	$1.00 bag	$10.00	$35.00
SOYBEAN MEAL**	Chicago Board of Trade 10:30 A.M. - 2:15 P.M.	100 Tons	10¢	$10.00	$33.00
SOYBEAN OIL**	Chicago Board of Trade 10:30 A.M. - 2:15 P.M.	60,000 Lbs.	1/100¢	$6.00	$33.00
SUGAR #10 (RAW)* (domestic)	N.Y. Coffee & Sugar Exch. 10:00 A.M. - 2:50 P.M.	50 Tons (112,000 Lbs.)	1/100¢	$11.20	$42.00
SUGAR (RAW)* (world) #11	N.Y. Coffee & Sugar Exch. 10:00 A.M. - 3:00 P.M.	50 Tons (112,000 Lbs.)	1/100¢	$11.20	$42.00 - 5.49¢ or under $62.00 - 5.50¢ or over
WOOL* Grease/Crossbred	Wool Associates of the New York Cotton Exchange 10:00 A.M. - 2:30 P.M.	6,000 Lbs.	1/10¢	$6.00	$50.00

* Special rates for Straddles and Day Trades.   ** Special rates for Straddles.

DAILY TRADING LIMITS
(Following table subject to change)

Commodity	Limit Above or Below Previous Close (or Settlement Price)	Permitted Range Between Day's High and Low
Barley	10¢ per bushel	20¢ per bushel
°Broilers, Iced	2¢ per lb.*	4¢ per lb.*
Cattle (Feeder)	1¢ per lb.	2¢ per lb.
Cattle, (Live Beef)	1¢ per lb.	2¢ per lb.
Cocoa	2¢ per lb.*	4¢ per lb.*
Coffee	2¢ per lb.*	4¢ per lb.*
Copper	5¢ per lb*	10¢ per lb.*
°Corn	10¢ per bushel	20¢ per bushel
Cotton #2	2¢ per lb.*	4¢ per lb.*
Eggs, Shell (Fresh)	2¢ per doz.	4¢ per doz.
Flaxseed (Winnipeg)	30¢ per bushel	60¢ per bushel
Hogs (Live)	1½¢ per lb.	3¢ per lb.
°Lumber	$5 per 1,000 bd. ft.	$10 per 1,000 bd. ft.
Mercury	$50 per flask*	$100 per flask*
°Oats, (U. S.)	6¢ per bushel	12¢ per bushel
Oats, (Winnipeg)	8¢ per bushel	16¢ per bushel
Orange Juice, Frozen Concentrated	3¢ per lb.***	3¢ per lb.***
Palladium	$4 per 100 oz.†	$8 per 100 oz.†
Platinum	$10 per 50 oz.†	$20 per 50 oz.†
°Plywood, (Chicago)	$7 per 1,000 sq. ft.*	$14 per 1,000 sq. ft.*
Pork Bellies, (frozen)	1½¢ per lb.	3¢ per lb.
Potatoes, (Maine) New York	50¢ per cwt.†	100¢ per cwt.†
Potatoes, (Idaho) Chicago	50¢ per cwt.	100¢ per cwt.
Propane	1¢ per gallon†	2¢ per gallon†
Rapeseed (Winnipeg)	20¢ per bushel	40¢ per bushel
Rye, (Winnipeg)	15¢ per bushel	30¢ per bushel
°Silver, (Chicago)	20¢ per ounce*	40¢ per ounce*
Silver, (N. Y.)	20¢ per ounce*	40¢ per ounce*
Silver Coins	$150 per bag†	$300 per bag†
°Soybeans	20¢ per bushel	40¢ per bushel
°Soybean Meal	$10 per ton*	$20 per ton*
°Soybean Oil	1¢ per lb.*	2¢ per lb.*
Sugar (Domestic & World)	1¢ per lb.†#	2¢ per lb.†#
°Wheat (Chicago, Minn., K.C.)	20¢ per bushel###	40¢ per bushel
Wool, Grease	10¢ per lb.***	10¢ per lb.***

* Limit is removed from spot month on first notice day.
** Limit is removed from spot month on first day of delivery month.
*** Limit is removed from spot month on eighth day of delivery month.
† Limit is removed from spot month on last trading day.
†† Limit is removed from spot month after the 10th day of delivery month.
# Sugar#11—No limit during month prior to month of delivery.
Kansas City—25¢ and 50¢.
° On the Chicago Board of Trade, after 3 successive limit days, the limits are widened 50% for 3 days.

INDEX